Uzi Eilam

Producer & International Distributor
eBookPro Publishing
www.ebook-pro.com

Night Raiders
Uzi Eilam

Copyright © 2021 Uzi Eilam

All rights reserved; No parts of this book may be reproduced or transmitted in any form or by any means, electronic or mechanical, including photocopying, recording, taping, or by any information retrieval system, without the permission, in writing, of the author.

Translation: Eyal Michaeli
Edit: David Olesker

Contact: eilamuzi@gmail.com
ISBN 9798501996199

NIGHT RAIDERS

THE STORY OF THE LEGENDARY UNIT 101
DURING THE IDF RETRIBUTION OPERATIONS

UZI EILAM

CONTENTS

Foreword 7
1. Preface 9
2. Introduction 13
3. Wingate's Night Squads 29
4. The Reprisal Operations, 1953–1956 44
5. The Story of Unit 101 50
6. Operation "Silk Gloves," December 21, 1953 76
7. Ariel Sharon and Meir Har-Zion 91
8. Operation Shoshana: The Qibiya Action, October 14, 1953 ...97
9. The Diplomatic Consequences of the Qibiya Action 103
10. Israeli Media Following the Qibiya Action 110
11. Whiplash Operations, February 1954 120
12. Azun Action on June 29, 1954 – "Operation Baruch" 131
13. Operation "Eye for an Eye," July 10–11, 1954 136
14. Beit Likiya Action, Operation "Benjamin B," September 1954 142
15. Motta Gur Establishes Company D 147
16. The Egyptian Front Comes into Focus 159
17. Operation "Black Arrow" – Gaza Action, 1955 166
18. Outcomes of the Gaza Action 184
19. Operation "Elkayam," August 31, 1955 191
20. Customs House Action, "Operation Sa'ir," October 22, 1955 199
21. Kuntilla Action, "Operation Egged," October 27, 1955 202
22. The Sabcha Action, "Operation Volcano," November 2, 1955 105

23. Operation "Olive Leaves," Kinneret Action, December 11, 1955 215
24. Ar-Rahawa Action, "Operation Jonathan," September 11, 1956........ 222
25. Gharandal Action, "Operation Gulliver," September 13, 1956.......... 228
26. Hussan Action, "Operation Lulav," September 25–26, 1956 232
27. Qalqilya Action, "Operation Samaria," October 10, 1956 237
28. Moshe Dayan, Battalion 890 and Adopting the Raid Concept 251
29. An Inside Look into Battalion 890 and the Development of
Its Special Character 255
30. The Reprisal Actions and Their Part in the Development of the
Arab-Israel Conflict 270
31. The Impact of the Reprisal Actions on Israel's International
Status and Political Strategy 282
32. Meir Har-Zion's Personal Reprisal Action 288
33. Arik Says Farewell 298
34. Conclusions and Transitions in Forming IDF's Power 329
35. Epilogue and Looking Forward 334
Appendix A: (Partial) List of Attacks, 1953–1956 338
Appendix B: "The Reprisal Actions – the Way We Were and the
Actions We Performed" 343
Appendix C: An Article by Uzi Eilam in Haaretz Following the
Passing of Meir Har-Zion 363
Sources 367
Acknowledgments... 368

FOREWORD

During its long years of fighting, the IDF impressed upon its officers and troops a series of values. Foremost among these were fidelity to the mission (meaning one does not return until the mission is completed), leading by personal example, leaving no one behind, and primarily, striving to take the initiative and the offense. These values were developed over the years, from such units as *Hayedid* ("The Friend")[1] Orde Wingate's Night Squads, Yitzhak Sadeh's Mobile Unit "Hanodedet," and Ariel Sharon's Unit 101. These have also built the ethos and the IDF spirit that has lasted for many generations.

As I see it, it is not by chance that when I first came to visit the IDF's newly established Commando Brigade 89 in 2016, the brigade commander asked to start the visit in the ethos and legacy room established in memory of "The Friend" before I began my review. These personalities have served as beacons of light throughout the years, for reprisal actions and special operations.

This book by Brigadier General (Ret.) Uzi Eilam describes the background for reprisal actions and provides a detailed description of them while analyzing their contribution to the security of the State of Israel.

The book has much historic value, but further it is of great importance to current and future generations of commanders, who can learn about the spirit, initiative and professionalism of past commanders and soldiers.

Respectfully,
Lieutenant General
Gadi Eizenkot

---

[1] This non-Jewish British army officer was so highly regarded in Israel that he became known by the title of *Hayedid*, "The Friend."

1. PREFACE

The Israel Defense Forces (IDF) has an international reputation for both daring and competence. How were those qualities developed and institutionalized? You might assume that they were the natural outgrowth of the struggle for survival against overwhelming odds experienced in Israel's War of Independence in 1947–1949. In fact, this is not the case. Audacious proficiency did not start to develop for several years, and sprang out of the unique qualities of a small group of officers and men. In this book, I will introduce you to them and demonstrate their far-reaching influence.

The subject matter of this book is wide, potentially covering many issues. I am approaching it with care, knowing that I will only be able to address a small part of it. Although many books and articles have been written about the subject, there are still areas that are crucial to describe and analyze. Before I go into detail about the various reprisal actions themselves, it seems right to me to first look back to 1936–1939, the period of the Arab Revolt. It is important to briefly describe this rebellion and its operations, which were mostly directed against the increasing immigration and settlement of Jews from Europe. The resistance of the Arabs to the immigration of Jewish people to Palestine had begun many years before, and the effort to damage Jewish settlement did not begin at the end of the Israel's War of Independence in 1949. In addition, the Arab Revolt of 1936–1939 was also aimed at the British rule and included damaging its facilities in Palestine, including repeated sabotage of the oil pipeline. This was the backdrop for the impressive rise to fame of one young British officer named Charles Orde Wingate, who came up with the concept of the Night Squads. I will present this topic later and show the weight it carried in forming the fighting spirit and knowledge of combat that Wingate bequeathed to the people of Israel.

Israel's security after the War of Independence was both difficult and complex. The IDF was left with very few commanders who had combat experience. The country's economy was just taking its first steps while facing the nearly impossible task of integrating waves of Jewish immigration from post-World War II Europe and the Arab nations. In addition, there was a need to deal with threats to the borders Israel shared with its Arab neighbors, despite the armistice agreements. The "Green Line" (the ceasefire line) as determined in the armistice discussions was breached by persistent infiltrations across all three borders. These incessant raids constantly badgered new immigrants as well as the government, who feared the frontier settlements would not last.

Some of the more prominent IDF actions during those years were, among others, the Golani Brigade's re-conquest of the Tel al-Mutila outpost north of the Sea of Galilee. This lasted for three days and ended with tens of Israeli casualties. The Givati Brigade required two attempts to blow up houses in the village of Falame on the Jordanian border. The shortcomings displayed in these actions showed the IDF's weakness as it was trying to rebuild itself following the War of 1948.

Between 1949 and 1956, tens of thousands of infiltrators[2] crossed the borders into Israel, some for settling, others for theft or sabotage. This infiltration reached its peak in 1952 when there were about 16,000 cases according to police records. In the following years, as the police records show, there was a gradual decline in the number of recorded infiltrations. However, many of the infiltrations were never documented. The statistics show that, while the infiltrations decreased during the period 1952–1956,

---

2   Infiltrators is the term Israel used to describe all those who illegally crossed the border, whether to engage in hostile acts or to resettle in the absence of a peace agreement.

the number of casualties among Israeli citizens told a more complex story. The number of casualties increased annually, with the exception of 1955. The number of deaths, however, decreased in 1954–1955, then doubled once more in 1956. This entire trend indicates that the phenomenon of infiltrations between 1952 and 1956 became more violent. In addition, starting in 1954, as Israel changed its retaliation policy and directed it toward military objectives rather than civilian ones, the number of casualties among IDF soldiers increased.

As for the financial damage inflicted by the infiltrations, between 1952 and 1954 there was a gradual increase in costs, but from 1954 – as the motives changed and there were more organized infiltrations for the sake of sabotage – there was a decrease in economic damage.

The creation of Unit 101 and the appointment of its first commander, Major Ariel Sharon, was the initiative of the head of the Jerusalem Military District, Colonel Mishael Shaham. The decision to authorize Shaham's proposal is regarded as one of the most important decisions made by Chief of General Staff Lieutenant General Mordechai Maklef during his brief tenure. Maklef's successor, Moshe Dayan, made another crucial decision when he determined that Unit 101 would be annexed to Paratrooper Battalion 890, a move that would have a far-reaching effect on the entire IDF.

I decided to write another book about the reprisal actions because of the need to illuminate the matter from a personal and human point of view, but mostly to expose the readers to the actual words of the combatants themselves, those who were gracious enough to be interviewed. It is also my decision as someone who was there for the lion's share of the activities as a combatant in Company A of the reconnaissance brigade of Battalion 890. For over a year (1955–1956), I served as Ariel Sharon's intelligence officer, first in Battalion 890 and then in Paratrooper Unit 202 under his command. In my opinion, the array of testimonies from the soldiers who served in Unit 101 and Battalion 890 offers an inside look at the way in which the unit conducted itself and how annexing it to the Paratroopers Battalion contributed to the shaping of the entire army's fighting spirit. To understand how that came about it was important to examine a selection of the reprisal actions that were based on Wingate's doctrine, each of them unique. The analysis of the key personalities in the post-Unit 101 annexation Paratroopers Battalion – battalion commander Ariel Sharon, deputy battalion commander Aharon Davidi and the prominent scout Meir Har-Zion – are based on my personal experience as well as the testimony of the members of Unit 101 and later Battalion 890.

A single, thread runs all the way from Yitzhak Sadeh's Mobile Unit "Hanodedet" (created to defend Jewish settlements in an active way), through Orde Wingate's Night Squads (which led the movement to come out from beyond the fence), the Palmach and all the way to Unit 101 and Paratrooper Battalion 890 to which it was annexed. That thread is "the raid." Later we will see how this seemingly simple tactic – leaving in the dead of night, attacking an objective and then coming back that same night – became the cornerstone of restoring the IDF's fighting spirit, which had been lost after the War of 1948.

I therefore thought it right to extend discussion of the raid as a vital, indeed almost exclusive, tool for the new IDF, which started building itself at the end of the War of 1948. For that purpose, I have gathered the soldiers themselves, both the veterans of Unit 101 as well as the commanders of Battalion 890, which Ariel Sharon came to command. These veterans expressed themselves candidly, without fear or reticence, adding more important information and authentic depth to the wondrous story of the combative IDF's construction through use of the raid strategy between 1953 and 1956.

2. INTRODUCTION

The "Arab Revolt" of 1936–1939 erupted spontaneously with a general strike. Only in response to pressure from the masses were Arab leaders able to find a common goal, standing at the forefront of the announced strike and taking responsibility for leading the rebellion. Some believe that April 19, 1936 marked its true beginning. That day, masses of Arabs attacked Jews who lived in Jaffa or happened to be there, murdered nine and injuring fifty-seven. Others see the opening shot as the murder of two Jewish men near Tulkarm on the night of April 15. There is also a version that claims events started with the killing of Sheik Izz ad-Din al-Qassam and a few of his men by the British Palestine Police in November 1935. In any case, the events started without any order by the Arab leadership in Jerusalem, and even against its will.

The cause of the rebellion was the mass Jewish immigration from Central and Eastern Europe that reached Palestine after the Nazis assumed power in Germany. The "immigration danger" which the people of the Arab Laborers Association and the High Muslim Council had been warning about for years now seemed more real than ever.

In the face of the Jewish immigration and settlement in the first half of the 1930s, winds of change began to blow among the Arab political class. The opposition to traditional leadership grew and in various places around the country – especially the Galilee and Gaza – radical groups formed, demanding a violent response. However, Palestinian leadership, mostly Amin al-Husseini, wanted to avoid this extreme action. One reason for that were the quarrels within the leadership itself; another was Haj Amin's hope that British policy could be changed by political means and that the Arabs should not burn the bridges they shared with the authorities.

In the two years between October 1937 and September 1939, the revolt was gangs managed by local commanders, who often quarreled among themselves and lacked allegiance to any centralized authority. The political leadership in Syria and Lebanon attempted to control activities, with only partial success. These Arab gangs took over various regions in the country, and their commanders applied much of their energies to extorting money from Arab cities and villages, causing thousands of merchants and professionals to flee abroad. Nonetheless, attacks on Jewish settlements and individuals continued. Toward the autumn of 1938, the Arabs intensified their attacks on British security forces and caused damage to police stations, trains, bridges, power lines and other facilities.

One of the most sensitive links for the British, both strategically and economically, was the oil pipeline from Iraq, which was repeatedly set afire by Arab gangs. The need to deal with these sorts of attacks during the Arab Revolt brought, as previously mentioned, the young British officer Captain Orde Charles Wingate into the arena. Thanks to his command of the Arab language, he had been posted to Palestine as an intelligence officer. Wingate, who developed an innovative and original way to fight the Arab gangs, claimed that it was vital to move the campaign to the other side's territory and to do so by using small units. While he had much opposition, the success of his strategy and the small-scale warfare he developed quickly earned him his commander's support. Wingate's Special Night Squads, which uniquely combined British army personnel and Jewish settlement members, became a success. Wingate formed the night squads to fight "beyond the fence," training them for a certain kind of commando warfare and even fighting with them. The night squads became the prototype for the future organization of day-to-day security for the State of Israel following the War of 1948. In parallel with Wingate's Special Night Squads, the Haganah was launching its own initiative to operate "beyond the fence." Yitzhak Sadeh's Mobile Unit also attacked Arab gangs but could not so as extensively as Wingate's Night Squads had, lacking the advantage of joint British and Jewish personnel.

Three years of bloody revolt ended with no real accomplishments for the Arabs. Despite the efforts of the Palestinian Arab leadership, the leaders of the Arab states, pro-Arab circles in London and even Britain's own High Commissioner, the British government did not grant their three central demands: halting immigration, forbidding land sales to Jews and the immediate creation of a national government, which would have placed the Arabs in control. The Arabs did, however, get some tangible results with Britain's publishing of the White Paper of 1939, which significantly restricted immigration and settlement in the short term, but they were unable to severely curtail it in the long run nor prevent lands from being sold to Jews. They also proved unable to paralyze trade, transportation or daily routine. Despite Jewish casualties and the damage to property – especially in the agricultural sector – Jewish settlement emerged stronger for those events.

The British had viewed the Haganah and Palmach, the independent Jewish armed forces, with suspicion. However, World War II, with the imminent threat of a German invasion of Egypt and subsequently of Palestine, forced Britain to reassess its position toward these organizations. In addition, Palestinian Jews volunteered in large numbers for the Allied war effort, leading to the formation of the Jewish Brigade that joined the battles in Europe. None of this, however, was enough to soften Britain's stance against massive immigration of Jewish Holocaust survivors. The gates of Palestine only opened for Jewish immigration following the UN's partition plan and Britain's decision to end the Mandate.

The War of 1948 ended with the nascent Israel having the upper hand. With considerable help from UN mediators, there were separate discussions with each of the neighboring enemy countries – Egypt, Lebanon, Jordan and Syria – which resulted in armistice agreements with each of them. The armistice regime that resulted from these agreements set the tone for Israel's future relationship with each of its neighbors. It should be noted that the operation and execution of the ceasefire regimes were in the hands of the armed forces, even though they concerned issues that were more political than military. This set a precedent for the relationship between the military system and the Ministry of Foreign Affairs that persists to this day. The IDF was and remains a factor that is heavily involved in the forming and execution of policies which include a combination of political and military aspects.

Israeli leadership, despite the mild diplomatic approach of its Ministry of Foreign Affairs, regarded contact with Arab countries mostly from a military-security point of view. These contacts were made in the Mixed Armistice Commissions. It eventually became clear that the armistice agreements did nothing to move the sides toward peace treaties. Some of the problems raised in the Commissions even turned into ongoing sources of friction. The issue of infiltrations, which weighed down the relationship Israel had with Egypt and Jordan, and the dispute about sovereignty in the demilitarized zones they shared with Syria, were constantly on the Commissions' agendas.

One of the issues that occupied Israel the most during its first years was that of infiltrations from its neighbors, mostly Egypt and Jordan. All the armistice agreements stated that "provisions and regulations of the Armed Forces of the Parties prohibit civilians from crossing the lines of combat or entering the territory between the lines (and these provisions) shall remain in force after the signing of this Agreement." However, before the ink on the agreements was dry, the residents of the Gaza Strip – encouraged by Egypt, those of Jordan, mostly from the West Bank, and even people from Lebanon – began crossing the Israeli border for a range of clearly unauthorized purposes.

The infiltration phenomenon was complex and multifaceted. Hostile infiltration was aimed at a range of objectives including robbery, theft, working land on the Israeli side of the border and smuggling. Even more severe acts involved espionage, sabotage, attempted murder and weapons and ammunition theft. There were even some who infiltrated for the sake of re-establishing themselves in Israel, or just to pass through it. Israeli civilians, on the other hand, hardly ever crossed the border, and this was recognized in the work of the Armistice Commissions, which discussed Israel's complaints. On the other hand, the complaints against Israel mainly focused on cross-border raids to perform reprisal actions. A large group of infiltrators – at the borders of Egypt, mostly Gaza but also Jordan – were refugees from the War of 1948, who either fled or were evacuated during the fighting. Some of them attempted to return to their homes or at least recover property they had left behind. The main motive for their actions was the harsh financial distress these refugees were in, as Israel was a tempting destination to live in or sell stolen goods.

The IDF's taking control of the Negev, all the way to Eilat, isolated Sinai from Jordan and created two more groups of infiltrators: Bedouins and smugglers. The former began looking for grazing grounds for their herds while the latter, who had always operated between Sinai and Jordan, suddenly found a new factor in the territory in the shape of IDF troops. There were also infiltrators coming in from Jordan and the Gaza Strip at the initiative of political figures such as the former Grand Mufti of Jerusalem, Haj Amin al-Husseini, as well as other Palestinian political players. These would recruit refugees to perform sabotage and shooting actions against Israeli targets, in order to have constant tension at the borders. It should be stressed, however, that political infiltrations were only a small part of the phenomenon and that most of the infiltrators acted out of economic distress.

The fight against infiltration was conducted on several levels, not just the retaliatory actions taken by the IDF. Initially the task of combating the infiltrations fell to the IDF, since it was the only armed force in the first years of the state's existence. The police service was still being organized, and it was incorporated into the fight against infiltration only at a later date. The IDF sought to divest itself of this role due to both the practical challenges involved and for fear of diluting its primary purpose – preparing for war. Among the forces that took part in the fight were the police, the Peripheral Defense System, military government, the Jewish Agency and of course the Ministry of Foreign Affairs. The attempts to form an interdepartmental body with its own authority were never realized.

The military government[3] was integrated into the war on infiltration and there were even thoughts of allocating a special force to it, but nothing came of this proposal. The authority given to the military governors to close off territories along the border, in many cases even strips of land dozens of kilometers deep, contributed to reducing the number of infiltrations but did not entirely solve the problem.

The Peripheral Defense System (PDS – *Hagamar*) was meant to solve the issue of Israel's lack of strategic depth. The frontier settlements kept in close contact with the IDF, which was supposed to arrive at the scene where enemy attacks were occurring, following the initial defense by the settlements themselves. It was only a short road from there to incorporating the settlements into the war on infiltration. However, peripheral defense did not become the main tool in managing the war on infiltration. The defense establishment and the IDF were not satisfied with merely defending the settlements themselves, although their efforts to do so were both effective and successful and significantly reduced the harm to the settlements. Rather, they strove to completely eliminate the infiltration phenomenon. In retrospect, the policy of excluding the Peripheral Defense System from an active role in the war on infiltration prevented the use of an effective and available system to fight the problem.

The Frontier Corps[4] was established with a single purpose: completely stopping the infiltrations, and Major General David Shaltiel was appointed as its commander. The goal was to form a body that resembled the French Gendarmerie with two operational branches – one positioned along the borders and the other, called the "State Guard," tasked with executing missions inside state lines. The budget for the Frontier Corps was supposed to come

---

3   Between 1949 and 1966 some areas of Israel with large Arab populations were under martial law.

4   Hebrew, *Heil Hasfar*. Founded in 1949 as a gendarmerie under the IDF, it was gradually transferred to the command of the Police and became the Border Police (*Mishmar Hagevul*).

from IDF funds, which immediately raised the question of the body's independence: Was it under the jurisdiction of the army, or the police? When arguments around the issue rose to new levels, the army cut off finances to the Frontier Corps, thus ending the entire idea, and the full responsibility for day-to-day border security returned to the hands of the IDF.

Many publications attributed the impetus for the reprisal policy as emanating from Moshe Dayan, mainly during his role as Chief of General Staff between 1953 and 1958. Although it is true that Dayan vastly contributed to the development of the policy, the stance of Ben-Gurion was less known. Already during the first years after the War of 1948, the man who was to become Israel's first prime minister considered performing reprisal actions to ease the distress of the settlers, mainly at the frontier settlements where new immigrants were repeatedly suffering infiltrations. However, the overall picture was a complicated by the fact that Israel's relationships with its neighbors were based on the armistice agreements, which placed clear restrictions on the actions of the Jewish State. This meant that there was a need to take into account the criticism of the Armistice Commissions since the reprisal actions were military in nature.

The way the reprisal mechanism was used suited the position Ben-Gurion had formed regarding the use of force to achieve the country's goals, especially in defense of the frontier settlements. Ben-Gurion was concerned about the safety of the new settlers but also wanted to avoid losing parts of Israel to its enemies.

Jordan

The relationship between Israel and Jordan holds a special place compared to the rest of Israel's neighbors. The ties between the Hashemite leaders and the pre-State Jewish leadership had formed long before the State of Israel was established. And so, the armistice discussions did not end with the signing of an agreement, but continued and dealt with extending the frameworks – even as far as reaching a peace treaty. Nevertheless, the road to that peace between Israel and Jordan was one that took many years to travel. It was not until October 26, 1994 when Jordanian King Hussein and Israeli Prime Minister Yitzhak Rabin signed their peace treaty, encouraged by US President Bill Clinton.

However, in the 1950s, infiltrations and terror attacks generated tension along their joint border, complicating the relationship between the two countries. The Israeli and Jordanian representatives on the Armistice Commission attempted to deal with the border issues together, but with very little success in restraining the infiltrations. It contrast, following the execution of many retaliatory actions by the IDF in 1951, Jordan acted to improve the situation. The Jordanian Arab Legion, under the direction of its commander, Lieutenant General Glubb, improved the guarding of the borders. In parallel, Jordanian Police forces laid ambushes to capture infiltrators, and Legion NCOs were stationed in villages to organize defense in case the Israelis attacked. In light of these developments, the IDF would usually only initiate reprisal actions when lives were lost on the Israeli side.

The difficulties endured by the Jordanian government in stopping the infiltrations were mainly due to the government's inability to incorporate the Palestinian Arabs into the Hashemite state. These problems were exacerbated by the opposition of the Palestinians to the moves of rapprochement toward Israel taken by King Abdullah as well as his orders to the Jordanian police to prevent infiltrations. The assassination of the King following Palestinian resistance to his efforts, as well as the shock to the ruling house, only made the situation worse. A succession crisis eventually led to the elevation of seventeen-year-old Hussein to the throne, although he was at first only able to rule with the backing of a Regency Council. None of this instability, however, led to any slackening of Jordanian efforts to restrain the infiltrations.

There is no doubt that the reprisal actions were meant to impress and the Israeli public and silence their criticism. The leadership sought to calm things down in the frontier settlements and give their residents, as well as the rest of the population, the feeling that the IDF was standing its ground and stubbornly fighting back against the infiltrations. The settlement endeavor of the frontier was meant to establish control in all parts of the new state, but the effort faced a number of difficulties. Most of the inhabitants of the frontier settlements were new immigrants who had been sent there straight off the boat. In addition to the economic difficulties they faced, and the barriers of language, culture and the difficulties of acquiring professional skills, they were now faced with the added burden of security, which they were unwilling or unable to deal with.

The distress of the Israeli people, both those on the frontier and in the interior, fell upon opponents to the reprisal actions, such as Prime Minister Moshe Sharett, who refused to accept retaliation as a necessary and inevitable instrument just to please Israeli public opinion. It was against this background that the IDF took on the reprisal policy as the only course of action against infiltrations, but had trouble admitting that it could not prevent the phenomenon altogether.

Another factor that aided the fight against infiltrations was the Jewish Agency's Security Department,[5] who helped provide infrastructure. The setting up of fences, lighting, secured rooms, firing positions and connecting trenches for the settlements were heavily funded by the Agency. At the same time, various ideas had been raised to attempt to resolve the manpower shortage faced in combating infiltration. In the summer of 1953, the Border Police Corps was established, meant to be the institutional and professional answer to the issue that had yet to be solved by the IDF. Although the Jewish Agency continued to fund the Border Police's activity, the new corps enjoyed operational independence.

Political contact with Jordan continued at the Armistice Commission level, but was insufficient to reach an agreement on a way to stop the infiltration phenomenon. The Jordanians claimed that the matter was not a military one and therefore should be dealt by police forces. In contrast, Israel's

---

5   The Jewish Agency is the operative branch of the World Zionist Organization and a para-governmental organization in Israel. Its responsibilities include assisting Jewish immigration to Israel and settlement on the land.

perception – influenced by pressure from the army – was that the issue was security-related, which meant it should be addressed by the Armistice Commission. The Jordanian approach was not without merit. The armistice line divided properties that had been Palestinian-owned prior to the war, and it was the Jordanian position that the areas under Israel's control continued to belong to the Palestinian Arab owners. The motive of infiltrators who sought to work or occupy their former properties was primarily economic rather than terroristic. Furthermore, the Hashemite leadership had a hard time agreeing to Israeli demands because the Kingdom had become majority Palestinian in 1950, after its annexation of the West Bank with its more than one million residents.

For its part, Israel sought to force Jordan to completely prevent infiltrations with a series of reprisal actions; the Jordanians believed that Israel's real intention was to gradually annex territories in the West Bank. These conflicting perceptions disrupted the relationship between the two countries, but not to the extent of warfare, since both sides had no interest in such a conflict. Furthermore, Israel and Jordan were never really hostile toward one another, as we know today after many years of peace between the countries.

Egypt

David Ben-Gurion perceived Egypt's monarchic regime to be fixated on revenge and a desire to wipe away the disgrace of the failure of army in the War of 1948. The armistice agreements did not end Egypt's role in the Arab financial boycott of Israel, neither did they lift the blockade they had placed on the passage of Israeli shipping through the Suez Canal. Just as on the Jordanian border, infiltrations were the main issue clouding the relationship between the two countries. The 250 thousand refugees that had fled to Gaza during the war were cut off from their fields and homes, and infiltrations were their way of gathering crops, as well as stealing or plundering any possessions they could in order to survive financially. Another issue was the behavior of the Bedouins, who refused to accept the decree that kept them away from the areas where they had lived for so many years, and were now under Israeli rule. Furthermore, the Bedouins were suspected of theft and even aiding Egyptian intelligence. It is worth mentioning that the insertion of intelligence units into Israeli territory increased after the Egyptian revolution of 1952.[6] On balance, the first three years of the armistice between Israel and Egypt was quite positive. The infiltration phenomenon did not stop; however, it was restrained, and the damage it inflicted was manageable. The low number of settlements in the south, and the fact that they were mostly kibbutzim that were well organized for self-defense, contributed to the low toll. Therefore, Israel could afford to limit her retaliatory actions.

The regime change in Egypt encouraged Israel, and mainly then Minister of Foreign Affairs Sharett and his staff, to publicly call for the new Egyptian rulers to begin talks with Israel. In parallel, they opened a secret channel through which new ideas would be raised, to perhaps forge a new relationship. Prime Minister Ben-Gurion greeted Egypt's new leaders in a speech he gave at the Knesset, and expressed his hope of improving the relationship between the two countries, however Israel did not actually present the new Egyptian leadership with a specific offer.

The new regime's position was that Egypt had no aggressive intentions toward Israel, but that they first had an obligation to solve their internal problems. The new regime was busy establishing Egypt's status and legitimacy in the Muslim world, and could not simultaneously advance toward a dialogue for peace with Israel. With that being said, one positive outcome could be seen in the renewal of participation the discussions of Armistice Commission. Maintaining the armistice mechanism allowed Egypt to discuss new agreements as long as they were presented as an expansion of the existing armistice agreements. Israel also had an interest in keeping this mechanism in place and ensuring a relatively stable status quo within her borders.

---

6   A coup d'état, led by the Free Officers Movement, that overthrew the monarchy. The revolution was led by Mohammed Naguib and Gamal Abdel Nasser.

Egypt's approach to the Palestinian refugees in the Gaza Strip was completely different from the one Jordan had adopted to those in the West Bank. The Egyptians had no intention of absorbing either Gaza or its inhabitants, and its only priority was maintaining calm at the border. The Egyptians did not hesitate to fire on infiltrators when they thought it might help keep the peace on the border. In the summer of 1953, there were riots in Ismailiyah due to the struggle to remove British forces from the bases at the Suez Canal. IDF commanders saw this as an opportunity to pressure Egypt to restrain the infiltration phenomenon. The attack on the al-Bureij refugee camp in August 1953, which we will discuss at length later on, was a manifestation of this decision. Another chapter of the Israeli-Egyptian relationship was the issue of control over the demilitarized zone at Auja al-Hafir. When the Armistice Commission assembled in Auja, as the agreements stipulated, Israel claimed the predations of the Bedouin tribes were being encouraged by the Egyptian authorities in order to use the nomads as proxies to conquer parts of the demilitarized zone.

The infiltration phenomenon at the Egyptian border was, as previously mentioned, different from the one at the Jordanian border. The kibbutzim's ability to defend themselves and the low number of casualties made it easier on Israel to manage the situation without escalation. Egyptian President Nasser, who positioned himself as the leader of the Arab world, could not be seen to being open to peace with Israel. This, as well as Israel's unequivocal stand against infiltrations, caused relations between the two countries to worsen. Another key element, strategic in nature, had to do with Britain's withdrawal from Egypt in general and especially its bases along the Suez Canal. Israel saw Britain's exit as a significant strategic threat to its security, since Britain had served as a buffer between the Jewish state and Nasser's ambition to make Egypt the leader of the entire Arab and Muslim.

Syria

Israel–Syria relations between 1949 and 1953 revolved mainly around conflict over control of the demilitarized zones on the northern border. In contrast to the Jordanian and Egyptian borders, the armistice lines with the Syrians did not take farmers away from their lands and there was no large concentration of refugees formed across the border. The approximately one hundred thousand Palestinian refugees who had fled to Syria had been quickly absorbed and presented no source of conflict. Meanwhile, three demilitarized zones were established: one in the northern corner of Israel, a central one from the north of Hula Lake all the way to its south, and the southern zone that surrounded almost the entire eastern shore of the Sea of Galilee. Israel's struggle to claim ownership of the demilitarized zones was complex and convoluted. Israel could take advantage of the fact that many parts of the zones – mainly in the central and southern areas – were owned by Jews. Internal crises of regime changes in Syria also played out in Israel's favor.

In the middle of the 1950s, the Israeli government decided to dry out the Hula Lake and the swamps south of it. The project was civilian in nature, and was thus entrusted to civilian hands. The IDF supposedly had no role in this project, but the heads of the defense establishment and the IDF command quickly learned that the project had become a security issue. IDF representatives at the Armistice Commission made sure to notify the Syrians of their lake-drying project. In the beginning, the Syrians had no objection – but they protested vigorously when heavy equipment was deployed. In Israel's opinion, responding to the Syrians' demands might lead to Israel effectively relinquishing ownership of the demilitarized zones, which she emphatically did not intend to do. When work in the demilitarized zone resumed, the workers were fired upon. Syrian representatives at the committee claimed that the shooting was done by Arab landowners in the demilitarized zone. The Israeli prime minister concluded a high-level political discussion in his office with a decision to continue carrying out the works, even if this would lead to an armed conflict.

During April and May of 1951, there were two serious incidents on the Syrian border which had nothing to do with what happened in the demilitarized zone, but were exacerbated by the tensions surrounding the area. On April 4, Syrian forces attacked an Israeli patrol headed to Hamat Gader and killed seven soldiers. The IDF retaliated with an aerial attack on the outpost from which the patrol had been fired upon (in many ways, this is the operational method used by Israel to this very day).

At the start of May, a Syrian force crossed the border and took over Tel al-Mutila, a hill on the Israeli side of the border, around Corazim, and was driven away only after a three-day battle. The Syrians did not try to escalate the incident, while Israel marked it as a resounding failure with an astonishing forty-one IDF casualties, exposing a critical weakness in the army at that time.

Over the following months, there were negotiations between the UN and senior members of the Israeli defense establishment on the nature of the police force that would be stationed at the demilitarized zones, with Israel willing to compromise on its structure. Israel also agreed to provide the Chairman of the Armistice Commission limited jurisdiction regarding the recruiting and operating of the police force. Although Israel's military activity to establish sovereignty over the demilitarized zones had been completed, its ongoing security activity needed to continue. Incidents of shooting from the Syrian side persisted until 1953, but they were local and were limited in number.

All this took place within the context of Syria's ongoing aspiration to annex Jordan, as well as Lebanon, in order to create "Greater Syria." Although seldom discussed, this is an aspect of the history of the region that is vital for an understanding of many Syrian policies. The outspoken Syrian support for the PLO in September 1970, which was intended to threaten King Hussein's reign, is only one instance of many of the tension between the two countries.

The mechanism of the committees for coordinating and maintaining the ceasefire did nothing to prevent the infiltrations, which took place mainly from the borders with Jordan and Egypt. The IDF, which had just started organizing itself after the War of 1948, attempted to stop the waves of infiltrations, along with the resulting theft and casualties, which mostly targeted frontier settlements and the new immigrants sent there. The various efforts by the security forces to stop infiltrations during the early 1950s proved unsuccessful, making it essential to develop new and effective methods. This was the backdrop to the authorization given by the chief of general staff to form a unit that would operate differently than any other IDF unit had before – Unit 101.

The complete story of Unit 101, which was active for only five months – from August 1953 to January 1954 – is a very important chapter in the history of the IDF, and it will help us evaluate the process of creating the IDF fighting spirit. Later, I will review the unique way in which the unit was established, and will examine how the use of the raiding tactic led to the unit's success and made its fighting style a model for the entire IDF.

I will also later review the importance of the patrols carried out across the border and the part played by the scout Meir Har-Zion in making these the key to taking the initiative in combat. On a cold snowy night in Hebron on December 21, 1953, Meir Har-Zion, Shimon (Katcha) Kahaner, Eitan "Hanabat" Bentov, and Guy Kochva initiated operation "Silk Gloves." Ariel Sharon came to see this action as a model that everyone must learn from.

The Qibiya village reprisal action, called "Operation Shoshana," was a turning point for the IDF in shaping its later strategy. Attacks would henceforth be focused on military and security facilities in order to convince the neighboring countries to act on their own initiative to restrain the infiltrations and attacks. This new focus was also required due to the enemy's change of operational methods. As the years passed, "economic" infiltrations by the Arab refugees in the War of 1948 decreased, and there was a gradual transition to state-sponsored terrorism.

The disbanding of Unit 101 as an independent force and its incorporation into Paratroop Battalion 890 was another turning point, one that which would not have been completed if Major Ariel Sharon had not been appointed the paratrooper battalion's commander. It was later claimed that it was Moshe Dayan and David Ben-Gurion's decision that brought about the transformation of the entire IDF fighting spirit, taking on the use of raids as a central component in future actions – according to the legacy of Wingate's Night Squads, Yitzhak Sadeh and the Palmach.

3. WINGATE'S NIGHT SQUADS

Orde Charles Wingate was born in India to upper-middle class parents who belonged to a puritanical and ascetic religious Christian sect. His choice of a military career was a continuation of family traditions on both his parents' sides. Wingate graduated from the Royal Military Academy at Woolwich and was appointed as an officer in the Royal Regiment of Artillery. With the encouragement of his relative, General Reginald Wingate – Governor-General of the Sudan and the Sirdar (Commander-in-Chief) of the Anglo-Egyptian army in the 1920s – Wingate set his sights on the Middle East and completed a crash course in Arabic before joining the Sudan Defense Force in 1927.

At that time, service in the Sudan was considered adventurous and demanding, and Wingate was given command of 275 Sudanese soldiers. Though his years in Sudan did not involve actual military encounters, he did gain much experience, which proved to be useful in the future as he commanded heterogeneous squads. The British Chief of the General Staff was very impressed by him, and in September 1936, he received the coveted appointment as an intelligence officer in Mandatory Palestine, first at the regimental headquarters in Haifa, and later at the Jerusalem headquarters.

In September 1937, Major General Wavell was appointed general officer commanding of the British Forces in Palestine and Transjordan. Wavell was favorably impressed by the young intelligence officer, and the curiosity Wingate aroused in him led the General to approve the activation of a special Night Squad for use against the Arab rebels, under Wingate's command.

The Arab gangs' raids on settlements and traffic began in 1936. British-owned and -operated facilities were attacked, and Jewish settlements were harassed all over Palestine. The oil pipeline that led from Iraq to the Haifa refineries and the Mediterranean ports was not deep underground and made a tempting target for Arab attackers; it was repeatedly cut and set afire. The British could not find a reliable way to defend it. The Jewish settlements, the moshavim and kibbutzim, adopted a defense strategy based on fortified positions, establishing observation posts and firing points as needed. By the time Captain Wingate arrived to serve as intelligence officer at the British Forces headquarters, the Arab Revolt had already gained momentum and continued to take its toll on both Jewish communities as well as British forces, with a series of murderous attacks.

Wingate quickly realized the magnitude and impact of the gang attacks, which caused him to formulate a new tactic. He believed that fighting the attacks required leaving behind the passive mindset and going on the offensive. He proposed that the core of the new strategy should be nighttime attacks by small forces, deep inside enemy territory. Four principles characterized his approach: boldness, surprise, mobility and deception. To these Wingate added the meticulous planning and physical fitness that he was determined to instill in the Night Squad fighters.

Yitzhak Sadeh, Red Army veteran and one of the leaders of the Haganah, implemented the Haganah Command decision to establish a Jewish underground Hanodedet ("The Mobile Unit," literally, "The Wanderer"). This commando unit, although numbering only a few troops, aimed to actively fight the Arab gangs. Sadeh, much like Wingate with whom he was in contact, thought that the Jewish settlements could not simply be defended from within, but defenders had to emerge and bring the battle to the enemy. Sadeh determined that it would not be effective to address every settlement individually, but that a regional defense system needed to be created between the different settlements. The Mobile Unit therefore adopted a mobile and offensive style of combat, based on patrols and nighttime ambushes. Yitzhak Sadeh saw the importance of deep reconnaissance into hostile territory in order to assess their numbers, deployment and the terrain.

At the core of Wingate's proposal to his commanders in Palestine was fighting the Arab rebel gangs by incorporating armed members of the settlements of the Jezreel Valley into a British unit. In fact, that paved the way for British authorities to accept the idea of Hanodedet. Wingate believed that because the Jewish Haganah members knew the terrain like the backs of their hands, and because some of them were Ghaffirim (members of the Jewish Settlement Police),[7] they would serve as a good basis for a new combat unit. And yet the idea of incorporating British policemen and soldiers with Jewish fighters was not well received by the Mandate authorities. Another objection by the bureaucrats was that the British police did not have enough Ghaffirim for this purpose. The British police also rejected the idea that military officers could command policemen. Among pro-Arab figures in the British civil and military authorities – of which there were many – a suspicion also arose that the combination of British military and Jewish units would provoke the Arabs to claim that the British were raising a Jewish army against them.

When Wingate began advancing the idea of establishing the Night Squads, he demanded a dozen British soldiers from the army base at Nazareth. He followed this up with an agreement with the commanders of the Jewish Settlement Police. He was promised one Ghaffir per day from each of the bases in the area. These men would have to be skilled with weapons and know the roads and surrounding area. As soon as his personnel were organized, Wingate began taking mixed squads into the field in order to collect intelligence and ambush gang members. It was during those first skirmishes that Wingate's original and innovative thinking bore fruit in the form of novel strategies and tactics.

The importance of establishing the Night Squads, according to Yitzhak

---

[7] The British set up a number of police forces in Palestine. In addition to the Palestine Police Force (staffed by British, Jewish and Arab personnel) there was the Notrim (an exclusively Jewish gendarmerie) that was divided into the Jewish Settlement Police and the Jewish Supernumerary Police.

Sadeh, was that they gave legitimacy and legality to the armed resistance of the Jewish settlements, which had become active and effective. It was important to turn a handful of sporadic actions around the region into an organized campaign, on such a scale as would defeat the Arab rebellion. The special Night Squads were a catalyst to institutionalize the Jewish resistance in those years and implement the knowledge and professional equipment the British provided. Sadeh described Wingate emphasizing to the men of the Night Squads the need for psychological warfare against the civilian population in the Arab villages, and how to differentiate between those who were not involved and the enemy, the active gang members who were to be dealt with decisively. Yitzhak Sadeh claimed that the Night Squads proved to the British the military potential of the Jewish settlements, as well as its human quality and strength, which had been unrecognized until then.

Initially the Squads' activities consisted of patrols and ambushes – around the oil pipeline at first, then throughout the Galilee. The mobility of the Night Squads astounded everyone – Arabs, British and Jews alike. Wingate and his men would march dozens of kilometers in one night; they were often seen in one place at the beginning of the evening, somewhere else in the middle of the night and at a third place early in the morning, as far as fifty kilometers away from their starting point. The unit began operation in June 1938, and the attacks on the oil pipeline quickly stopped. Its men showed exceptional professionalism in dealing with the Arab outlaws, while using unconventional combat techniques such as approaching the target and launching the attack under cover of darkness. In addition, Orde Wingate was the first to teach small unit tactics to the young men of the Haganah. In the framework of the unit he had established, the young Jewish men would conduct active defense actions for the first time, under military discipline, resulting in an operational level never before seen by the Haganah.

Yitzhak Sadeh greatly appreciated the cooperation between himself, a leading commander of the Haganah, and Wingate. Sadeh agreed that, when needed, Wingate would temporarily take men from the Haganah's Field

Companies,[8] whom he would dress in the uniforms of Notrim, allowing him to suddenly field a sizable force for a single action. At first, Wingate's activities were, at least officially, limited to guarding the oil pipeline from Iraq to Haifa, but they quickly expanded into actions against the Arab gangs in a range of locations. Sadeh claimed that, although there was no principal or tactical difference between Wingate's methods and those of the Field Companies of the Haganah, Wingate's character left its mark on each and every action. They were bold, well-planned and tailored to their place and situation. At the base of it all, Wingate's subordinates learned the need for thought and the importance of the commander's independence, as well as adjusting the action to the situation, location and enemy rather than merely adhering to theory and the "academic form."

The units of the Night Squads searched for the enemy and moved around the field constantly, with each unit acting independently. During the month of June 1938, the Night Squads carried out approximately ten operations. In five of them, they encountered large gangs and killed over sixty of the bandits. Wingate went on to develop his tactical perception in light of the lessons learned from the patrols and operations and committed it to writing. He was convinced of the ability of a military force to overcome the gangs, if they were trained well enough in anti-guerrilla warfare, and particularly if they were used to maneuvering and fighting at night.

After several successful operations, the British military authorities realized that Wingate's use of guerilla tactics was a new and effective form of countering the guerilla warfare of the gangs. And indeed, the successes of Wingate and his men in preventing attacks reduced the British authorities' objections to his approach. There were some who claimed that by using the Jewish Settlement Police in his operations, Wingate was diminishing their effectiveness in their day-to-day duties. Pro-Arab members of the British Civil administrations even claimed that he entered Arab villages to kill and wreak destruction. Wingate replied that he was only attacking the gangs

---

8   The Field Companies (*Plugot Sadeh* in Hebrew, abbreviated to POSH) were the elite commando arm of the Haganah.

who were targeting the oil pipeline. The British Military Headquarters, who understood the military and economic importance of those preventative actions, authorized Wingate to continue developing the project, even allowing him to recruit Haganah people to establish more Night Squads.

In May, Wingate was joined by a British officer called Bardin, who became his right-hand man, along with three other British officers and thirty-six soldiers who had volunteered to serve with him. Wingate saw it was necessary to take British soldiers out of their regular bases, free them of the rigid strictures of the army, and get them to adopt his new warfare doctrine. Eighty Haganah volunteers were added to the British force, along with members of the Jezreel Valley settlements. The number of recruits grew, and activity spread over more and more areas. At first, Wingate formed sub-unit posts at Tel Amal, Geva, Afikim and Kinneret. Each post had two units of the Night Squads and, later on, they created two more extensions to the north, at Hanita and Ayelet HaShahar.

Wingate's headquarters was established in a building called "the Common Stage," between the kibbutzim of Tel Yosef and Ein Harod. The activity around the headquarters fired the imagination of children from Ein Harod and Tel Yosef. The rumors of a unit operating at nighttime against the Arabs added to the mystique of Wingate's activity in the Common Stage's basement, which often also served as a venue for music performances, puppet shows and even operas. The children quickly discovered the stores of combat rations kept there, the highlight of which were the dry biscuits they liked so much...

Right after the Night Squads were formed, a short training course was held for the volunteers, after which Wingate began deploying nine patrols to the field daily. Training was simple and concise, and included time on the shooting range, learning to read topographic maps and familiarization with a range of weapons. As part of this training, nighttime maneuvers were also practiced, with emphasis on navigation and keeping silent while moving. There was also training toward engaging the enemy as well as ways to disengage quickly, once an operation was complete. Wingate was strict and demanded nothing less than perfect execution of each of component of his tactical doctrine. He did not hesitate to use strong language for any mistake made by the troops.

One night, while Wingate was leading a Night Squad on a training exercise, they passed by the Tel Yosef kibbutz. Sarah Bluemenkrantz, a member of the kibbutz who was guarding the north fence, heard the force approaching. She did not hesitate to open fire, thinking they were Arabs about to attack. Wingate thundered in Hebrew, with an unmistakable British accent, "Don't shoot, you donkey!" employing the Hebrew vernacular for a fool. "Tel Yosef is a donkey farm," Wingate declared, which became a description that the members of the Tel Yosef kibbutz suffered for many years to come.

Wingate had selected gear for the men that included a rifle, webbing full of ammunition, and hand grenades. The Squad members learned the worth of the grenades in particular while charging into battle with the gangs. Members of the patrols were on duty for two weeks, followed by a week off to rest.

The wide-brimmed, Australian-style slouch hat was chosen by Wingate as a unique element for the Night Squads. He ordered them himself from a workshop in England, another testament to the improvisational and persuasive abilities of this extraordinary officer. He himself wore a colonial pith helmet, which became his trademark. The way in which the patrol was organized when traveling was standardized. Two patrolmen took the point position, armed with grenades, a few patrolmen following behind, after which the main column advanced in ranks, always with an officer heading it.

The brigade's first operation was on a patrol along the oil pipeline, where they discovered an Arab gang preparing to blow up a section of pipe. When Wingate surprised them and injured two of them, the members of the gang fled without a fight, and thus the British officer gained his first victory. The second expedition to defend the pipeline took place a week later with a reinforced patrol. While still on their way, a section of the pipe exploded a few meters in front of them. The unit charged forward and chased the Arab saboteurs all the way to the nearest village. Once the village was surrounded, the Night Squad members, led by Wingate, charged in. In the ensuing battle against the gang, the Squad managed to kill two members, injure three and capture six, along with their weapons. The area was calmer for days following that operation.

There was a difference in Wingate's demeanor when there was calm, and his behavior when an operation was taking place. In action Wingate would not only deliver insults for mistakes, such as navigation errors or making noise while walking in enemy territory, but he would also strike people who were wrong or failed to follow his methods. Nighttime discipline was his top priority and therefore sacred in the Night Squads. All soldiers were equal in the eyes of Wingate, which is why, when having arrived at a water source, he punished a British sergeant for drinking before his soldiers did. After a battle, Wingate joined his troops, behaving as their equal and listening to them in order to learn the lessons of the operation.

One of the early activities carried out was sending a Squad patrol to the west bank of the Jordan River, where the members of the Shata tribe resided, to warn them not to interfere with the oil pipeline. They found no men at the first encampment, but as the force approached the second encampment, they were surrounded by dozens of Arabs who opened fire on them. The patrol took cover, returned fire and killed two of the attackers. The truck drivers who had transported the force there drove back to Ein Harod to bring reinforcements. The Arabs ambushed the forces that came back with the trucks, but were met with fire that killed ten more of the gang's members.

One example (of many) of incorporating real-time intelligence, deception, night and day action and sticking to the target could be seen in the operation against a gang residing within a Bedouin tribe located at the ruins near El-Awadin. We can describe the area within which the tribe resided as a triangle with vertexes at Moshav HaYogev, Kibbutz Mishmar HaEmek (as it is now known), and Kibbutz Megido. Verified intelligence revealed to Wingate that there was a large gang at the El-Awadin ruins. There were a few stone houses in the area, with hundreds of Bedouin tents around them.

When planning the operation, Wingate grappled with several questions: Deception – what could be done to mislead them into believing that the

Night Squads were operating in a completely different area? Concealment – how could they get close enough without being discovered? Identifying the target – as mentioned, the gang members were at the heart of a large Bedouin encampment, in which there were men, women, children and the elderly. The question arose as to how the gang members could be identified so that only they would be targeted, and not innocent civilians. This time, contrary to his standard practice, Wingate decided to attack during the day. According to the Night Squads' tactical doctrine, any daytime patrols would rely on deception. In this case Wingate's order was to reconnoiter the area "with great noise," in order to make everyone think that they knew exactly where the force was operating. At a late hour, the forces converged on Kibbutz Sarid. After dinner, Wingate briefed them while accentuating one order in particular: "The goal is to hit the gang members, not civilians. Therefore, every measure must be taken to ensure the execution is precise and mistake-free."

Force A left for its mission from kibbutz Sarid at 2 a.m. The force consisted of Squad members and Field Company volunteers from the Afula and Nahalal areas, marching under Wingate's command, in a silent flanking movement around the encampment.

Force B left from Afula, turned east and took up position southeast of the encampment, blocking the escape route to Jenin.

Force C, under the command of Yonatan Abrahamson, split off from force B at some point. Its role was to be used as bait. The force consisted of seven Squad members dressed in railroad workers' dungarees; they took a civilian truck onto the dirt road along the Jezreel Valley railway ("the Valley Train"), whose tracks went close to the encampment to its north.

As dawn broke, all the units were in position and well hidden. The "train workers," close to the encampment, began mending the railway, while deliberately making noise which woke a few of the gang members up. Angry at the government employees who dared disturb them, six armed gang members came out and started marching toward the workers. To get to the workers, the gang members had to pass the rear end of the truck. As they approached, the doors of the truck were thrown open and long burst of fire from a Lewis machine gun broke the silence, killing the Arab gang members on the spot and signaling the beginning of the fight. The Arab bandits emerged from their tents to see what had happened and were faced with fire from the forces surrounding the encampment. Realizing they had been taken by surprise, the gang members attempted to escape east, toward Jenin, where they encountered the members of Force B. Some tried escaping northeast by crossing the rails, only to run into the "rail workers" awaiting them there, firing with their machine gun. Many gang members mounted their horses and tried to flee. Although fifteen of them did manage to escape (ten of whom were wounded), of the remainder, fourteen were killed and three were captured. The subsequent search by the Night Squads at the encampment discovered about thirty rifles. Not a single Night Squad member was injured.

The operation was regarded as one of the best operations carried out by the Night Squads. In the clothes of Sheik Taba al-Hawrani, the commander of the gang who died as he was trying to break through the siege, they found a seal and two letters from Yusef Abu Dor of Silat el-Harthiya village, who was one of the leaders of the Arab Revolt. Based on these letters, they later forged a letter to the Arab village of Tantura and signed it with the Arab seal. The next night, Wingate left for Tantura and hit the gang that resided there. To his great disappointment, one of the Jewish fighters shot and killed the headman of the Arab village before they had a chance to interrogate him. Operations such as the one executed at El-Awadin lasted for a few months, non-stop, and spread over dozens of kilometers, from Kohav HaYarden (Kawkab al-Hawa) in the east all the way to the coast (Tantura) in the west.

After the experience gained by the Night Squads, British intelligence and its staff began providing Wingate with field information, in order for him to plan out his next major operations. One occurred in July 1937 with a patrol under the leadership of Bardin, Wingate's second-in-command. The lieutenant, accompanied by nine soldiers, both British and Jewish, patrolled along the Kohav HaYarden axis, leading up to the Crusaders' fortress. He noticed about a hundred gang members who were assembling. The Arabs opened fire on the patrol and injured two of its men. Bardin split the force and surrounded the hill; as a result, the gang members retreated, even though they had the upper hand.

One of the Night Squads' most famous operations was at the village of Daburiyya: the goal of this operation was to "find and destroy a gang responsible for the occupation of Nazareth a few nights before, as well as attacks on the local police." On July 11, 1938, Wingate gathered his men and divided them into four units. Unit A was driven to Nazareth where, on foot, they would seal off the village's exit route to the west. Unit B would secure the route to Kfar Tavor to the northeast of the village. Unit C came from the south, from near the current location of Kibbutz Dorat. The main force, under Wingate's command, consisting of forty-five soldiers and Notrim, was driven on a circuitous route (from Ein Harod through Beit She'an and Tiberias all the way to Nazareth), with the vehicles' lights off. On the way, near Ilaniya, the men got out of the vehicles, which kept moving, and went north toward Tur'an in order to deceive any Arab scouts or spies; after a few moments, they turned south through the mountain paths and toward Daburiyya. Unit C arriving from the south encountered an ambush near the village, in which Avraham Yaffe suffered a head injury. Wingate and his men, who were about ten kilometers north of Daburiyya at that point, rushed to the unit's aid, bypassing the village and joining them as they positioned themselves around the village's granary. The Arabs, who had the higher ground, dominated the area with their firepower. Wingate commanded Israel Carmi to advance his force toward the village and he accompanied them. A few of the soldiers in the unit found abayas and white blankets to warm themselves. Their comrades, mistaking them for gang members, penetrated their ranks and shot them. There was great chaos, and by the time the mistake was made clear, the Noter, Yosef Ben Moshe, had already been killed and Wingate and two of his soldiers had been injured. Wingate relinquished command to Carmi. An order was immediately given to enter the other granary, next to the village, where the gang members were situated.

Nine of them were killed, among them the son of the village's head man, who was a known gang leader. Since the element of surprise had been lost and the unit from Kfar Tavor was nowhere in sight, Carmi decided the stop the operation. They began gathering the men and sending the injured ones to the hospital. Though wounded, Wingate refused to leave and went back to Ein Harod with his unit. Only after Bardin telephoned the commander of the northern military region, Brigadier Oates in Haifa, did Wingate accept his order and went to the hospital at Sarafand (modern-day Tzrifin).

Wingate performed military maneuvers with his men which seem simple, structured and entirely logical nowadays. The methods of warfare the Night Squads applied are known to any squad commander in the army, but back then they were considered groundbreaking. The British officer's astounding success gained him attention of all sorts, for better and for worse. Later on, in an attempt to strengthen the forces at the northern border, the British Command decided to reinforce the area with a battalion of British troops. This unit took up position at the northern border resulting in the Night Squads' folding up their positions in Ayelet HaShachar and Hanita, after two months of successful operations on the Lebanon-Syria border.

Wingate was no administrator but was known as a person who could procure whatever he wanted. Most of his efforts went into getting weapons, ammunition and transportation for his Night Squads. That is why there was always a shortage of food and clothing at the Squads' camps. That shortfall was made up by the kibbutzim, the Haganah and the logistics system of the British army in Palestine.

Wingate would arise early and exercise. After a patrol, when all the men were fatigued, Wingate would make sure the weapons had been cleaned and the administrative affairs were all taken care of, down to the last item. He would leave for his meeting at Headquarters afterwards and then plan the next operation. Wingate's doctrine stated that the way to deal with the Arab rebel gangs was to convince them that their brutal raids would have a great probability of encountering "a government gang" determined to destroy them. They would know this was not to be an exchange of fire at long distance, but face-to-face combat, with grenades and knives. To achieve this, Wingate stated that a force must be established and trained in precisely such methods. Wingate had no intention of giving up what the regular army had to contribute: discipline and knowledge of basic warfare principles, advanced weapons, and superb communication and control abilities, which allowed for joint intelligence and coordination between all forces in the field. However, this officer's doctrine also made considerable room for mobile ambush methods as opposed to stationary ones. The nighttime actions, accompanied by field awareness and a high level of navigation skills, completed the principle of mobile ambushes, forming a constant element of surprise and keeping the initiative and control over the unique battlefield in which the Night Squads operated.

In October 1938, Wingate went on leave back to England, and it is possible he followed Haim Weitzman's request to meet important people in the British political system, among them the Secretary of State for the Colonies, Malcolm McDonald, as well as Member of Parliament Winston Churchill. Wingate sent out his memos, which clearly and authoritatively defined the perspective he recommended – fighting wars against an enemy using unorthodox methods – to the journalist and historian of security matters, Basil Liddell Hart, who forwarded them to Winston Churchill along with the following letter:

> A few days ago I met with Captain Orde Wingate, at the Palestine Intelligence Headquarters, where he has been serving a role similar to that of Lawrence (but the other way around) in battling the Arab terror gangs. It is possible that you have already noticed hints of his activity, as he was awarded a decoration for his achievements. He is currently on leave in London and I believe you will find great interest in meeting him, if you are able to do so. The methods he has been establishing so successfully are hereby detailed in the attached memo. Wingate has received a mandate to attempt these methods in establishing and training the SNS in this manner. It is unfortunate to learn that the

option of expanding this activity has encountered hesitation from politicians in increasing the force to the extent required. Apart from the memo's contribution to the solution of the immediate difficulties in Palestine, I believe it will arouse the curiosity of your military mind.

In his London meetings, Wingate attempted to convince leading British political figures of the importance of a pro-Zionist policy. He passionately argued that Arab demands should not be accepted. The wrath of his military commanders in response to such inappropriate meddling in political matters by a serving officer was understandable. That was probably the reason for his removal from command of the Night Squads. As is well known, that was not the end of Wingate's military career. WWII gave him a chance to apply his unique approach, both in Ethiopia against the Italians, and later on in Burma, heading a guerrilla squad which fought using his unique methods, where he rose to the rank of colonel.

Yitzhak Sadeh, Yigal Alon and their men freed themselves from conventional forms of maneuvers and chose an extraordinary method, originating in Palestine. That method of action, the raid, thoroughly reflected what they learned from Wingate. The conceptual framework Wingate left behind for future commanders of the Palmach offered original ways of dealing with issues which constantly arose during military operations. And so Yitzhak Sadeh and Wingate's students (and admirers) included Special Forces, based on the model of the Night Squads, into the Palmach, who functioned in unconventional frameworks.

To summarize, it can be said that Orde Charles Wingate, justly dubbed in Israel as "The Friend," brought about a change in the perception of combat among the Jewish defense forces in pre-state Palestine. The change, as we have learned from Yitzhak Sadeh, was the result of Wingate's character and personality. In the following chapters we will see how the combat principles devised by Wingate influenced the next generations of defense forces in Israel. Exiting the fences and initiating strikes, skill at navigation, nighttime action, the element of surprise and tenacity in reaching the objective, all were adopted by the Palmach during the 1947–1949 War of Independence, as well as later on by Unit 101 and Battalion 890, into which 101 was annexed. Thinking outside the box and creativity in planning operations were key components of Wingate's doctrine. Ariel Sharon and Meir Har-Zion of Unit 101 adopted these principles in practice and ingrained them into Battalion 890, after the appointment of Sharon as its commander. Thus, Wingate's doctrine became that of the entire IDF, to this very day.

4. THE REPRISAL OPERATIONS, 1953–1956

The following list does not include all the reprisal operations, but only those executed in reaction to murderous attacks that resulted in heavy losses. These attacks mostly originated from across the border with Jordan but some also took place on the Egyptian and Gaza Strip borders, and in a few cases, even on the Syrian border.

1. OPERATION "OFRA"
A raid by Battalion 890 paratroopers on the village of Idna (near Moshav Amatzia). January 25, 1953.

2. OPERATION "ASHES AND DUST"
Battalion 890 paratrooper operation to blow up a house in village of Rantis. January 28, 1953.

3. OPERATION "A VIPER ON THE ROAD"
Battalion 890 paratrooper operation consisting of a number of raids, on Beit Sira, Husan, Beit Nuba and Beit Likiya. May 18–20, 1953.

4. THE NABI SAMUEL ACTION
Paratrooper operation, prior to the establishment of Unit 101, to blow up the house of terrorist Mustafa Samweli in retaliation for the murder of two soldiers at Moshav Even Sapir. July 12, 1953.

5. OPERATION "AVENGED AND PAID FOR"
A combined operation of paratrooper forces and the Givati, 16th and 7th Brigades. The parachutists attacked the village of Idna and block the road against reinforcements from Turkimeih. The Givati troops raided other villages at the same time in response to the grenade attack on the orphanage at Kiryat Ye'arim, near Jerusalem. August 12, 1953.

6. THE BATAN ABU-LAHIYA ACTION
Unit 101 operation at the village of Batan Abu-Lahiya, near Kibbutz Ma'ale HaHamisha, in retaliation for the terror attack on the orphanage at Kiryat Ye'arim. August 1953.

7. THE AL BUREIJ ACTION
Unit 101 raid on an Egyptian post by the Al Bureij refugee camp, Gaza Strip. August 31, 1953.

8. THE BEIT MIRSIM ACTION
Unit 101 raid on the Beit Mirsim Jordanian military facility near the village of Burj al-Bira in the mountains southwest of Hebron. September 1, 1953.

9. THE AZAZAMA BEDOUINS ACTION
Unit 101 action to deport the Bedouin tribes from the Nitzana area. September 1953.

10. THE BEIT SIRA ACTION
Unit 101 raid on the village of Beit Sira, east of Modi'in, in response to the murder of Israelis near Moshav Ahiezer. September 10, 1953.

11. THE QIBIYA ACTION, "OPERATION SHOSHANA"
Unit 101 raid on the village of Qibiya and surrounding villages, in response to the murder of a mother and her children. October 14, 1953.

12. OPERATION "SILK GLOVES"
Unit 101 special force operation to destroy a wanted man's house in Hebron, considered one of the most difficult operations in the history of the IDF. December 12, 1953.

13. "OPERATION LION"
A raid by combined paratrooper forces on the village of Nahlin, in response to the massacre at Ma'ale Akrabim and the murder of a guard at Moshav Kisalon. March 28, 1954.

14. "OPERATION CIGARETTE"
An operation by Battalion 890 officers to capture Egyptian prisoners in order to exchange them for an abducted Israeli soldier. April 2, 1954.

15. THE "BARUCH OPERATIONS"
Paratrooper force raid on Azun village on the Qalqilya-Nablus road, in retaliation to the murder by infiltrators of a farmer in Ra'anana. June 29, 1954.

16. "OPERATION EYE FOR AN EYE"
Paratrooper operation to conquer a fortified Egyptian post in the Kissufim area. July 10, 1954.

17. "OPERATION WATER"
Paratrooper operation to blow up the Gaza water supply system, in retaliation for the blowing up of the water supply line to the Negev at Kibbutz Nir Am. August 14, 1954.

18. "GIL OPERATIONS"
A series of commando raids by paratroopers to capture Jordanian soldiers in order to reclaim the prisoner Yitzhak Jibli. August 30, 1954.

19. "OPERATION BINYAMIN B"
Battalion 890 paratrooper raid on the villages of Beit Ur a-Tahta and Beit Likiya, in response to the murder of two Jews in Moshav Mata, Jerusalem corridor. September 2, 1954.

20. OPERATION "BLACK ARROW"
Battalion 890 operation in the Gaza Strip, in response to a series of murders and violence committed by infiltrators. February 28 to March 1, 1955.

21. "OPERATION PLESHET"
Paratrooper raid on Egyptian army posts and camps around Rafah, in response to an infiltration into the city of Ashkelon and the death of soldiers who stepped on a land mine near Kibbutz Be'eri. August 29, 1955.

22. "OPERATION ELKAYAM"
Paratrooper Battalion force operation to occupy and blow up the Khan Yunes Police building. August 31, 1955.

23. "OPERATION GEFEN"
Paratrooper operation to seize control of the UN Observers' headquarters in Auja al-Hafir. September 22, 1955.

24. "OPERATION EGGED"
Paratrooper Battalion raid on the Kuntilla Police station, Sinai. October 27, 1955.

25. "OPERATION VOLCANO"
Operation by Golani Brigade and paratrooper forces to re-occupy the Sabcha posts, following infiltration of Egyptian forces to the Nitzana area. November 2, 1955.

26. "OPERATION SEYIR"

Unit 101 raid on the Upper Customs House, Golan Heights, which was used as a Syrian army post, in order to capture Syrian soldiers to trade for Israeli prisoners. December 22, 1955.

27. "OPERATION OLIVE LEAVES"

Raid on Syrian army posts on the outskirts of the Golan Heights, near the shore of the Sea of Galilee. Carried out by Paratrooper Battalion forces together with reserves soldiers and Givati forces. December 11–12, 1955

28. "OPERATION MALLET"

88th Nahal[9] Paratroopers Battalion force raid on an Egyptian military camp; retaliation for a murder carried out by a terror squad in the South of Israel (Shafir Center). August 30, 1956.

29. "OPERATION YEHONATAN"

Paratrooper Battalion force operation to blow up Ar-Rahawa Police station near the city of Dahariya, Hebron area; retaliation for the murder of Israeli reserve soldiers by the Arab Legion near Beit Guvrin. September 10, 1956.

30. "OPERATION GULLIVER"

Paratroopers' Battalion 890 and 88th Nahal Battalion raid on Gharandal Police station on the Jordanian border; retaliation for the murder of three Druze guards at the Ein Ofarim oil drilling camp, Arava region. September 13, 1956.

31. "OPERATION LULAV"

Raid by paratroopers and Nahal battalions on the Hussan Police station in the Bethlehem area; retaliation for the murder of five Israeli scientists by Jordanian soldiers in Ramat Rachel. September 23, 1956.

---

9   Nahal (acronym for *Noar Halutzi Lohem*, "Fighting Pioneer Youth") was established as a special program within the IDF that combined military service with the establishment of agricultural settlements, often in border areas.

32. "OPERATION SAMARIA"
Raid by Paratroopers' Battalion 890, 88th Nahal Battalion, a unit from Givati Brigade, Armored Corps and Artillery Corps forces on Qalqilya Police station; retaliation for two murders inside Israel by infiltrators from Jordan. October 10, 1956.

This list of sabotage actions stretches from January 1953 to October 1956. Most of the reprisals were carried out, as mentioned, in response to civilian and military lives lost in Israel.

I have chosen to recount a selected number of these reprisals in detail, letting them serve as examples of all the actions taken at each of the locations in Egypt, Jordan and Syria. As I will show below, each of the actions had a different background to it, yet there is a link which connects almost all of them.

5. THE STORY OF UNIT 101

Following the War of Independence, Israel found itself taking waves of immigration, both Jews from North Africa and other Arab countries as well as Holocaust survivors from Europe. The state was near bankruptcy and threatened not only by infiltration but also by terror attacks by the neighboring Arab countries. The constant infiltrations and murders brought about a decline in the sense of security among Israeli residents, mostly the new immigrants who were sent to live near the borders. Following the war of independence there was also a decline in the IDF's ability to perform combat missions. The IDF therefore did not have the ability to effectively deal with the threat of infiltration and terror attacks. The IDF's diminished combat ability in transitioning from quasi-militia of the pre-state era to an orderly and organized national army was both obvious and disturbing. I shall now highlight the reasons for that: a massive release of battle-experienced command – both senior and junior; the dismantling of old frameworks and building new ones; and a massive recruitment of non-elite soldiers, most being new immigrants with no military experience.

The obvious fact that the fighting spirit which characterized the IDF during the War of Independence had dissolved was the catalyst that led the army to search for an "out of the box" solution. During the first years of the state, the Chief of General Staff Lieutenant General Mordechai Maklef rightly focused on building and organizing the worn-out, post–War of Independence IDF, focusing on building manpower rather than issues of leadership and the warrior spirt. The quality of soldiers and commanders severely diminished during the post-war period, especially among the lower ranks. This was due, among other reasons, to the deaths of many combat-experienced soldiers and commanders in battle during the war. There was also a great influence on the departure (willing or not) of many soldiers who returned to their civilian lives. In addition, a large portion of the new recruits were immigrants who suffered during the process of settling into the new country. These recruits, who came from different countries, ethnicities and sections of the populations, had trouble adjusting to their new roles. The main obstacles were a lack of Hebrew, a low level of education, and mental, social, economic and cultural gaps. The low levels of competence of the units severely damaged the IDF's operational capacity. This happened precisely when Israel had to deal with the weakening of the Armistice regime and the non-stop penetration of thousands of infiltrators across the borders.

One of the events which best demonstrated to IDF commanders the poor state of the fighting force was the incident at Tel Mutila, which took place in May of 1951 in the Israeli demilitarized zone where the Jordan River meets the Sea of Galilee, and served as a significant case study for the IDF. According to the Armistice Agreement, two small Syrian villages had been left in that area along with their residents, who had not been evacuated during the War of Independence. There was no steady IDF presence in that area except for random patrols, and there were no Israeli settlements nearby. On May 2, a Syrian military unit crossed the Jordan and settled at Tel Mutila (now Almagor). Their goal was to support the Syrian villagers who possessed the land west of the Jordan River. The Syrians controlled the surrounding area by virtue of Tel Mutila's commanding position and their superior firepower. A routine IDF patrol that was sent to the area uncovered the Syrian presence and reported it to Headquarters. A reinforced patrol was sent to follow up on the report encountered heavy Syrian fire and had to retreat. At night, a Golani force stormed the mound and conquered it. However, as dawn broke, it became clear that the Syrian force was still in control of the two hills south of the mound.

Heavy fighting persisted over the following four days, May 2–6. The IDF deployed forces from three different infantry brigades – one of which was a reserve unit – as well as a force from the Golani Brigade's section commanders' course. The infantry was backed up by artillery and air force units. Serious failures were found in the Israeli troops' performance, which lead to the deaths of forty soldiers with a further seventy-two wounded. The participating forces, most of whom were on active duty, demonstrated poor combat ability. The company sent to the battle from the nearby reserve brigade was one that was failing their training. There were fierce critiques of the forces' operation from throughout the IDF. Some of these were factual and to the point, while others were no more than gossip. The Chief of General Staff, Yigal Yadin, sent a letter of condolence to Meir Amit, the brigade commander, as well as the battalion commander, Rehavam Ze'evi (Gandi). Yadin simply "forgot" to mention that Ze'evi had directed the battle from Villa Melchet on the shore of the Sea of Galilee, more than sixteen kilometers away. With the headquarters located so far from the battlefield, the battalion medic could not even reach the battlefield to attend to the wounded on all of the three days of fighting. The letter Yadin sent praised both the battalion and the brigade's performance, but did not overlook "the errors which we are obligated to exhaustively study in order to improve our forces and learn from experience – a thing we are all at work on now." The letter was distributed to all the highest-ranking officers of the IDF, from Colonel and up.

The battle of Tel al-Mutila was forever etched in the collective memory of the IDF as a resounding failure. However, this is not to say that the Golani battalions and brigade headquarters were less able than other active duty brigades and units. The chief of general staff's letter regarding this affair referenced many instances during the War of Independence which had also ended in failure and high casualties. With that said, the context, conditions, level of training, military knowledge and fighting norms in 1948 were those of an army in formation. Yet almost three years after that war, in a localized and isolated battle, with the entire IDF free to engage, the outcome was devastating. The chief of general staff's attitude to this affair was still that of the 1948 era, i.e. "let's move on to the next battle, since there will be another tomorrow, and we must therefore be forgiving."

Even though the goal of finally driving the Syrians away from the demilitarized zone was achieved, the battle of Tel al-Mutila is still considered one of the IDF's harshest and deadliest failures. A large number of those who fought and died there were immigrants who had arrived in the post–War of Independence immigration wave. Some of them hardly spoke Hebrew and had not received sufficient military training. One of the lessons learned from the battle was that there should be more veteran Israeli recruits allocated to the infantry units. The Syrians, for their part, admitted to two hundred casualties, from both their active and reserve forces.

One might have thought that these disastrous battles would be a tipping point, but that was not the case, as many further failures followed. On the night of December 13, 1951, a group of soldiers moved, under cover of darkness, from West Jerusalem to Mount Scopus, where the inactive Hebrew University was located. This was an Israeli enclave, with the entire surrounding area under Jordanian control. The IDF troops carried munitions on their backs to resupply the Israeli presence there; these were not the kind of munitions that were permitted in the official UN and the Jordanian army sanctioned biweekly convoys that made their way up the mountain. The "National Guard"– a Jordanian militia which operated in the West Bank and was mostly comprised of Palestinian residents – detected the movement and fired on the soldiers. The force fled and left their backpacks behind, along with other identifying material.

On the night of January 25–26, 1953, an active duty squad from the 5th Givati Brigade, headed by a battalion commander, left for the village of Falame, near Qalqilya. The village lay only a short distance from the Armistice line. The IDF archives testify as to what happened during Operation "Ofra," the first attack on the village.

1. The mission: Attack the village of Falame, blow up the three houses and kill their inhabitants.
2. Operating force: An infantry company headed by the commander 54 Battalion.
3. Enemy force: Local National Guard militia.
4. Execution: Our forces were unable to penetrate the village.
5. Losses: Enemy – none. Our forces – one killed, six wounded.

The force, tasked with destroying a few houses in the village, was discovered and some riflemen from the "National Guard" opened fire at them. The company retreated without completing the mission, with one killed and six men wounded.

The General Staff ordered the Givati Battalion to re-execute the operation. And so, on the night of February 28–29, a unit of that same battalion left for the field, headed by the 54th Regiment commander.

The description of the second attack on Falame village, named Operation "Sheaf and Ashes" on the night of January 28–29, 1953, is in the IDF archives. The essence of the events unfolds thus:

1. The mission: Attack the village of Falame, blow up the houses and attack their inhabitants.
2. Operating force: A battalion from the Givati Brigade, headed by the 54th Battalion's commander.
3. Enemy force: Local National Guard militia.
4. Execution: Three houses were blown up.
5. Losses: Enemy – one killed and seven wounded.
6. Our forces – one killed and seventeen wounded.
7. Notes: A lot of equipment was left in the field.

Once again, just as with the first attack, the battalion came under rifle fire by the soldiers of the National Guard in the village. As mentioned, they did manage to blow up the three houses on the outskirts of the village before retreating. Despite the encouraging words from the chief of general staff to the Givati commanders, it was a clear and disturbing failure.

Former Etzel[10] veteran, Brigadier General (Ret.) Mordechai Tzipori relates:

> I commanded a company in the 52nd Battalion of the Givati Brigade. On January 23, 1953, the commander of the 54th Battalion, Baruch Gilboa, who was a veteran Palmach member, was ordered to carry out a reprisal action at the village of Falame, in the western mountains of Samaria, six kilometers northeast of Qalqilya. I was assigned the task of preparing a company to be held in reserve. We gathered at Beit Nabala then boarded a train and got off beyond Qalqilya, from which we left for the location on foot. I positioned myself in the rear, with my subordinates. I heard fire and then the retreat of Gilboa and his men, which seemed more like a rout. It turned out that they were fired upon, they lost one soldier and Gilboa decided not to continue with the mission but retreat. The head of Operations Directorate, Moshe Dayan, ordered that the operation should be repeated immediately – with the same forces. And there we were again, on the night of 28–29 January, and once again Gilboa and his men fled. My men and I rushed ahead of them, cut the village's fences, blew up a few houses and came back to our territory. There was a debriefing with Moshe Dayan the following morning. Gilboa presented himself as if he was Napoleon, his deputy presented himself as if he was an international hero and the other commanders told stories that never were and never could be.

Tzipori's statement clarifies the truth about the two reprisal attempts by the Givati Brigade against Falame village. These actions, which were a

---

10 Etzel (the National Military Organization in the Land of Israel) was the pre-state militia of the rightwing Revisionist Zionists. Before its incorporation into the IDF it had been commanded by future Prime Minister Menachem Begin.

resounding failure, stand as an object lesson on how not to act and how not to stick to a mission until its completion. Tzipori and his men did, however, manage to blow up a house or two at the village's outskirts, and suffered a few casualties, but there was once again a hasty retreat of the battalion from the battlefield, leaving behind weapons and ammunition. The failure of the retaliation against the village of Falame added weight to the decision to establish a fighting unit which would operate differently.

In light of these events, the following reprisal missions were entrusted to the active duty paratroopers battalion (890) which was considered an elite unit. And indeed, the battalion executed three reprisal missions later in 1953. The first was at the village of Rantis, east of Kibbutz Nachshonim; the second at the village of Hussan, west of Bethlehem; and the third at the village of Idna, west of Hebron. And yet, despite the fact that those villages were close to the Armistice line, these missions were not even partially completed. In the village of Idna, a paratrooper was also killed and left behind in enemy territory.

The issue of the combat capability of both active duty and reserve units was raised repeatedly in General Staff meetings. These discussions took place against the backdrop of Ben-Gurion's instruction to cut down on military spending, since there were still constraints on the national budget and the general financial situation had not improved. Thus, the Planning Department of the General Staff Coordination Unit was ordered to cut down on reserve service and lower the maximum age for reserve duty.

There were attempts to establish special units on an ethnic basis after 1951. That is how the units of Druze[11] and Circassians[12] minorities were established, which also took part in the fight against the infiltrators. In August 1951, Moshe Dayan, then the head of Southern Command, initiated the

---

11 An Arabic-speaking ethnoreligious group, it forms minoirites in Lebanon, Syria, Israel and Jordan.

12 A minority group in Israel descended from Muslims expelled from the Caucasus by the Czarist Russian government in the nineteenth century and resettled by the Ottomans in various parts of their empire.

establishment of another special unit, called Commando 30 or the Desert Raid Unit, with the sole purpose of acting against infiltrators. The unit, which would also map their operational area and gather intelligence, operated until the end of 1952. Commando 30 had no chance to accomplish any significant achievements in its short lifetime, and it was disbanded when Moshe Dayan left Southern Command. The appointments of Maklef as chief of general staff and Dayan as his deputy brought on a change in the thinking and methods of the IDF's operational units. Maklef and Dayan were particularly experienced in operating with Special Forces. They had both been members of Wingate's Night Squads and were favorably impressed with the operation of small elite units. Dayan had noticed the comparative incompetence of regular British army units, which operated according to a hidebound doctrine that did not suit conditions in the field. In contrast, the gang members knew the terrain and the population well, and were thus able to pick an appropriate time and place to suit their action.

The idea of establishing a special raid unit did not originate with the General Staff, but was a personal initiative by the commander of the Jerusalem district, Colonel Mishael Shacham, who was also the commander of the Jerusalem Brigade. Shacham decided to initiate a reprisal mission against one of the leading terrorists in his area, Mustafa Samweli, resident of the Nabi Samwil village. Ariel Sharon was at that time a student at the Hebrew University in Jerusalem. During the War of Independence, he had fought as platoon commander in the Alexandroni Brigade and was injured during the operation to conquer the Latrun police station. Sharon was also a reserve battalion commander in the Jerusalem Brigade.

While Ariel Sharon was serving with Northern Command, he had come to the attention of the then head of the Northern Command, Moshe Dayan. Dayan had asked him to look into the option of capturing Jordanian soldiers for prisoner exchanges. Sharon reported in the very next day with two Jordanian soldiers whom he had kidnapped himself…

Colonel Shacham, upon hearing of Sharon's role as an intelligence officer in Northern Command and his operational past, summoned him to his office, where he informed him there was a green light for the mission at Nabi Samuel village to assassinate Samweli, who had initiated many attacks on Israeli settlements and civilians. Shacham asked Ariel Sharon to take on the mission. Sharon assembled a team of seven men that he knew from his War of Independence and subsequent service. On July 11, 1951, after a short briefing, Sharon and his seven men left for Nabi Samuel village. Among them were Shlomo Baum of Kefar Yehezkel and Yitzhak "Gulliver" Ben Menachem, who had served with Sharon in the Givati Brigade during the War of Independence. After three hours on foot, the force arrived at the village and blew up a house which seemed to belong to Samweli. During the mission, the force was spotted and fired upon. The unit retreated to Jerusalem and later discovered that the house they had blown up did not belong to Samweli at all. Sharon's disappointment at not hitting Samweli was expressed in the report he submitted to Colonel Shacham. He emphasized the need for thorough training to improve the soldiers' physical fitness, as well as the need for purchasing adequate equipment for the force taking part in the raiding missions. Shacham wrote a detailed report on the matter, which was relayed to the chief of general staff, as well as to David Ben-Gurion who served as both prime minister and minister of defense. In his proposal, which was sent that very night, Shacham wrote that to carry out the reprisal missions effectively, what was needed was a company of highly motivated volunteers.

The failures at Tel al-Mutila and Falame served as a reference point for Unit 101 from the moment it was established. They also later served as a lesson and a source of insight for Battalion 890, which absorbed Unit 101. It was a great example of how *not* to fight and what should *not* be done while executing a military mission.

The battle of Tel al-Mutila was one of a series of engagements concerning Israel's right to use the demilitarized zones on the Syria-Israel border. As mentioned, in accordance with the Armistice Agreement signed July 20, 1949, the Syrians retreated from the Israeli areas conquered in May and June of 1948; in exchange, these areas were declared "demilitarized," the term used in the English version of the agreement, which was the definitive version. The Syrians claimed it meant no Israelis should be allowed in the demilitarized zones, while Israel declared the prohibition only applied to military personnel and not civilians.

The IDF's Intelligence Department, which later became a branch of the General Staff, was also quick to learn the lessons of the failed battles of Tel al-Mutila and the reprisal mission in Falame village. The intelligence officers joined the voices within the IDF in support of the need to establish a special unit to deal with infiltration. The Intelligence Department believed that such a unit, the size of a company, highly mobile and with knowledge of the border area, would give the army an effective tool to use for reprisal missions immediately after any incident. Such a unit, they claimed, would also serve as an excellent resource for intelligence gathering. It had become clear that that the IDF's operational methods must be changed from deployment of large forces supported with heavy weapon, to small unit commando actions, and that it was vital to raise the IDF's operational level. These realizations led to the establishment of Unit 101.

The chief of general staff approved the establishment of such a unit and Moshe Dayan, who was already Deputy Chief of the General Staff, became an avid supporter of the idea, pushing Chief of General Staff Maklef to establish the unit at once. The message was also relayed to the Prime Minister and Minister of Defense, David Ben-Gurion. On July 30, 1953, Unit 101 was officially given the role of executing special, cross-border reprisal missions. It was also determined that the unit would consist of fifty men and would be equipped with non-standard weaponry.

Sharon began recruiting his men from active duty and reserve units, among them a few of the fighters who had raided Nabi Samuel village with him to try to assassinate Mustafa Samweli. Shlomo Baum became Sharon's deputy, and soldiers from kibbutzim and moshavim were added, who in turn brought some of their friends. Many of them were kibbutz and moshav members from the Jezreel Valley. The unit was initially headquartered at the Schneller Camp in Jerusalem (Jerusalem Brigade headquarters), then it was transferred to Abu Gosh police station and eventually settled itself at the abandoned Arab village of Sataf. The General Staff defined the purpose of the units in the following way: "In order to perform cross border actions in those non-standard missions that require special training and an advanced skill level and which cannot be carried out effectively by all IDF units." The unit's troops were to undergo special training and professional studies of radio, interpretation of aerial photography, sabotage and parachuting. The unit was directly subject to and operated by the General Staff, with the emphasis that it was to be used exclusively for executing missions across the border.

By the beginning of September, Sharon had twenty soldiers at his disposal, and by October he had forty-five. One of his first recruits was Meir Har-Zion, from Moshav Rishpon, who moved to Kibbutz Ein Harod to live with his father.

As a boy, Har-Zion had toured the country on foot and even crossed the borders on more than one occasion. In 1951, when he was almost seventeen, Har-Zion was walking with his sister Shoshana along the Israeli-Syrian border when they were captured by Arab sheepherders and put in Damascus Prison, where he and his sister spent three weeks. Har-Zion never told his classmates and friends what the Syrians had done to them, but wrote it down in his journal, which he secretly kept all those years, including a chilling description of what the two endured in Syrian captivity. You can read about it in his book and lack of control over their men *Pirkei Yoman* ("Journal Chapters") published in 1969.

In his first year with the IDF, before joining Unit 101, Har-Zion found the time to go to Petra with Rachel Savorai, a former Palmach fighter from Ein Harod, forty kilometers inside Jordan. Har-Zion's fascinating description of this hair-raising adventure with Rachel Savorai can also be found in his book.

While he was on leave from the army, Har-Zion and his classmate Uri Oppenheimer (now Ofir) departed Jerusalem on foot for the Dead Sea, through Jordanian territory. The two returned safely, but Har-Zion's sister and her boyfriend, Oded Wegmeister – of Kibbutz Afikim – who attempted to "repeat" Har-Zion's and Oppenheimer's trip, paid with their lives as they were captured by Bedouins in the Judea Desert and murdered.

The risky trip by Meir Har-Zion and Uri Oppenheimer, from Jerusalem to Ein Gedi, was indirectly a milestone in the history of Unit 101. That was the reason their names came up when Shlomo Baum and Ariel (Arik) Sharon were looking for volunteers for their new unit.

Uri Oppenheimer, one of the first people to join Unit 101, describes what had happened:

> Meir and I were in the same class at school. Meir was at a Nahal reconnaissance course in Beit Daras and I had already completed my combat sergeants' course. During Passover vacation, we decided to go from Jerusalem to Ein Gedi. We knew it was illegal. We took a look at a map we had, but eventually forgot it somewhere, so we went on our way without any map.
>
> Meir memorized the way and he was hardly ever wrong. We walked through Herodion, and from there, straight down to Ein Gedi. During the day, we hid out in a cave and at night, we kept going toward Ein Gedi.
>
> One day, while we were still on holiday, Shlomo Baum appeared in my house and told me: we are establishing a unit, you and Meir are coming with me. It was a Saturday night. I told him, wait, I am serving in a unit, I have gear, I even have a rifle from the course here, I can't just leave. He told me everything was taken care of and I shouldn't worry about it. As usual, Arik had taken care of everything! After a few days they said: Wait, we need to do something, we need to train. We did very little combat activities. Mostly we hiked, generally in the Jerusalem mountains.
>
> One day, Arik came to us and said: That's it, we have to start hiking beyond the border. He took us to the border. There were

no fences there, nothing, there was really no problem crossing it. We crossed it at nightfall, when it was already dark. We were two groups, one led by Shlomo Baum and one led by Arik. We were a total of nine people.

At Sataf we learned how to operate the weapons we did not know. We trained here and there, but not much. Nobody cared about your military rank in Unit 101. We were divided into groups: Meir was in the Scouts group and I was in the Sapper group.

Shimon (Katcha) Kahaner, a childhood friend of Meir Har-Zion from Rishpon, who came to the 101 from the Nahal, recounts:

Meir and I were very close as kids, we would do our homework together, cut grass for the cows together, and play together a lot. Meir got drafted in July and I in September. We were both in the Nahal. One day, Meir came to me and said: come, they're establishing a special unit, right up your alley and right up mine. There would be an interview with Arik – which was not an official acceptance interview, but was more of a conversation – from there you would go to training and they would see how you behaved there. There was a kind of oversight on you.

After I got to the 101, Meir told me: Come on, let's go train. We took webbing and went out. The Sataf village we were at was partially abandoned. We shot, we threw grenades, we snuck up on each other, those kinds of exercises and navigation; just Meir and I. We each knew which group we belonged to. Meir Har-Zion's group was the "flagship." We knew that Meir was the most determined and mission-oriented person there.

Arik had a central role in the training. He never used flowery words or fiery speeches, but we still knew how important our role was and how much responsibility we had. Arik was very talented and a great tactician. That gave us enormous confidence; if Arik planned something, it was always doable.

Yishai Zimmerman, also of Ein Harod, arrived at Unit 101 from the Armored Corps. Ariel Sharon made sure to come all the way to his base to convince his company commander, Shmuel Gorodish – who would later become head of Southern Command during the Yom Kippur War – to release tank commander Zimmerman so he could join the unit; and so it was.

The Yishai Zimmerman story sheds a different light on the way the unit was running and the varied attitudes towards killing within the unit:

> All in all, it was pretty sloppy at the Sataf camp. However, what they did right there, and it was very important, was to learn how to navigate across the border. They gave a sense that the border was nothing. While you do have to watch out for the Legion at first, once you passed two kilometers, you could run on the roads as much as you wanted.
>
> With that said, it would take us a few hours to cross the border at first, mostly by crawling. We decided not to take the wadis. We crossed the border, and if there was a hill, we would walk up it, never along the ravines. We attained such a level [of skill] that we were comfortable enough in the area to travel longer distances, even all the way to Hebron.
>
> Meir had amazing senses. He would roam around all over those places.
>
> One day he passed by Haras village and a dog barked at him, so the owners came out and fired in the air. Meir marked the house and told us we would deal with it.
>
> There were five of us and we considered canceling the mission. Of course, Meir would not cancel it… We advanced to the house

and the dog didn't bark. We went to move the dog, but it was asleep... Meir sent me to the door and said that when the man opened up, I should kill him. I'm standing by the door, it opens and a girl comes out. She sees me and immediately jumps back. I went back to Meir and said, listen, there was a girl there, what am I supposed to do...? Meir did not give up, obviously. He took an explosive brick, put it on the door and blew it up. You walk into a house filled with dust and darkness. I walk with my back against the wall, along it. I reach a corner. Suddenly, someone grabs me and my "Uzi" with a trembling hand; it was the Arab. I told Meir, I got him, but I can't kill him. The whole thing at Haras took us about ten, fifteen minutes. By noon we were already at the bar at Tel Nof.

Elisha Shalem of Kibbutz Ramat Yohanan, who served in the Nahal, preferred to go to the officers' course, as he put it, "like everybody else," rather than join Unit 101. His story sheds light on the process in which the special unit was put together:

I came back to Beit Daras to be an instructor in the 6th section commanders' course, where I met the guys from Ein Harod, Uri Oppenheimer, Yoram Nahari and Meir Har-Zion. Meir had just finished the section commanders' course and joined us as an instructor. Our role was to instruct the recruits on Topography and Navigation. There were five of us instructors there together for six months, after which Meir and I were supposed to go to the officers' course. A few days before the course began, Meir came to me and said he had met with some Major who was establishing a special unit. I told him I was going to the officers' course and that he shouldn't bother me with all those blowhards.

Meanwhile, Ariel Sharon arrived at Beit Daras and saw the head of the section commanders' course. He had authorization to take volunteers from the course to that new unit. I still insisted on going to the officers' course.

Meanwhile, the 101 was starting to make waves. Arik was authorized to take four cadets out of our officers' course, Moishe Stampel, Levi Hofesh, myself and Haim Malda. Arik arrived and told us: I want you to stay here, finish the course and then come join the unit.

While this was happening, the 101 kept going on missions. How did it seem? In today's terms it is like "price tag policy"[13] but authorized. They went on the Qibiya operation even before the course was over, killing many civilians in this operation further escalated things both in Israel, but also internationally. I came as an officer, straight from the course to Battalion 890.

The Unit 101 recruits went into a rather loose training regime aimed at physical fitness and familiarization with their weapons, which were intentionally different from the ones used in the rest of the IDF. Field navigation and reconnaissance skills were a key component, especially cross-border patrols. Encounters with the enemy patrols or village guards across the border were considered the best training for future missions.

Unit 101 operated for only five months, from August 1953 to January 1954. The missions it carried out were characterized by boldness, adherence to mission and the meticulous selection of its members, who had been tested to the highest standards with clear proof of their navigational skills. The men were divided into small groups, each of them had a commander. The troops disguised themselves as civilians.

---

13   Actions of vandalism and violent attacks carried out by right wing Jewish extremists against Arabs, the security forces and political opponents, in reprisal for perceived wrongs.

One of the first ones to join the unit, Shmuel Merhav, tells the story of his recruitment:

> I was a platoon commander in the 13th Battalion of the Golani Brigade, and I was sent to an intelligence officers' course. The course commander was Yoram Lavi, who Ariel Sharon asked to recruit people for him. He was the one who recommended me to the 101. I came to meet Arik at Sataf. We spoke and I knew how things were in the country and that the solution to the infiltrations and attacks was not at the battalion level. I didn't return to the battalion from the intelligence officers' course; I went straight to the 101, in August, I was one of the first ones there. There were four of us from Kibbutz Mizra, five from Kibbutz Ein Harod and five from Moshav Nahalal. The unit slowly grew, little by little. I commanded a group which consisted of Yoram Nahari, Yair Tel Tzur, Ehud Gavrieli and Yohanan from Kfar Malal.
>
> This was a typical mission: a reconnaissance patrol in the Jerusalem area, a new bridge that needed inspecting, east of Ramat Rachel. We had to arrive from the north, from Tzur-Bahar village; of course we couldn't be discovered on the way. We were a squad of five and made our way very quietly. We had to be back at Ramat Rachel by 1 a.m. We left the Ramat Rachel orchards and entered the village from the main road. We were dressed in civilian clothes, kaffiyahs, and the roads were empty. All of a sudden, a call: "*Min Hada?*" ["Who's there?"] I spoke Arabic and answered them: "*Jesh al-Arab*" (an Arab army). I took the chance; we were Unit 101 after all...we reached Ramat Rachel on time and met with Ariel Sharon.

The unit members often contemplated the moral questions, especially in light of the criticism directed toward them, mostly by the Palmach people, concerning matters of Purity of Arms.[14] The argument was not about trifles, but rather principles.

The term "Purity of Arms" was controversial in the unit, as mentioned, with one side – for instance, Shlomo Baum – claiming that "the arms should not pure but rather clean…," and on the other hand – for instance, Shmuel Nisim, Hafalach ("The Farmer") – stuck to the term verbatim. In one case which occurred in August 1953, the former Palmach fighter Shmuel Nisim refused to take part in a mission against the al-Bureij refugee camp at the Gaza Strip, claiming that it went against his principles. However, many in the unit acted mostly from a professional approach, their concerns reduced solely to performing the task at hand – as efficiently as possible.

Shmuel Nisim tells about the way in which he joined Unit 101 and what went on there, from its early days:

> Motke Ben Porat, commander of the Armored Brigade, was a good friend of mine. He was the commander of reconnaissance in Jerusalem. He invited me to his wedding and made sure I had a ride with Ariel Sharon, who was his acquaintance. Arik took me to the wedding and we also talked on the way back. We obviously talked about the state of security and how we, who defeated seven Arab nations, could not overcome the actions of Arabs who were infiltrating, stealing and killing. Would you join a unit who would act against these infiltrators now? Arik asked. I immediately replied "yes." I joined the regular army a few days later and was there ever since, until the 101 was disbanded and transferred to the 890 Paratroopers' battalion.
>
> In the beginning, it was Shlomo Baum, me and two other friends – Barbut from Misgav Am and Yair Skyler, a relatively young officer from Jerusalem. There were four of us, we went to Jaffa, enlisted and served as the nucleus of the unit.

---

14   The Hebrew term *Tohar HaNeshek* is the official term for military ethics in combat.

We did some physical fitness training and some hikes, blew up some huts that were left at Sataf from the Mandate days. There was no structured course plan. We repeated a little of what we knew, to fill up the days. In the meantime, there were new recruits coming in every day; within a few weeks, with one friend bringing another, we were already at the unit's full strength, between thirty and forty people. These were people who were more adventurous, who'd prefer the activity in such a unit rather than the grind of military routine.

There was also no clear plan on how to recruit more people. We didn't go and make a campaign; we also didn't publish in any media or anything. The unit, in the beginning, kept things very secret, we didn't even talk about where we were. We were mostly members of kibbutzim and some moshavim.

Meir was a scout and an excellent field man. He was extraordinarily fit, a real strong man. But the ability to learn from him, or be inspired by his ability and valor, was available mostly in his team. The teams didn't mingle, and in this way, I think Meir's influence was more in the stories told about him at the unit's meetings.

We had very lively social lives. At the end of each mission, we would gather, eat and sing. It was like a youth movement activity, with a joy of life and a sense of adventure. But as far as implementing the whole navigation issue, most of Meir's influence was on his team, as I've said. For all that, he was a great inspiration in the discussions, how and where we were going. His voice was always heard, and he was influential in that way.

Whenever we finished a mission, if Arik would take part in it, he would gather everyone and we would each say what we did, what we saw or what we thought was wrong, and so on. When

Arik wasn't there, everyone wanted to be together all the time, a kind of social gossip which was easy to explain in the youth movements but might have been a bit more complicated in the context of a military unit.

Purity of Arms? In that sense, Shlomo Baum was a nihilist. He did not think that values were needed, or that values should be preached. We needed to be efficient, practical – get results. In that sense, Shlomo really was not guided by any values. He showed that side of him in various ways, like in the several encounters we had with Bedouins, in which Baum did not hesitate to fire at them in order to 'encourage' them to leave the area.

In the summer of 1953, the Arab infiltrators provided Israel with an abundance of reasons to react. The first violent military operation of Unit 101 was the attack on the al-Bureij refugee camp at the Gaza Strip, on August 29, 1953.

The mission was carried out following the murder of Yeshayahu Frenkelman, a fifty-eight-year-old Ashkelon resident, and the injury of his twenty-five-year-old daughter Zipora. The murder was carried out by infiltrators from Gaza Strip on August 16, 1953.

It was unclear whether the initial goal of the mission was to attack houses that were suspected to be bases for infiltrators or a preparatory reconnaissance patrol toward future action. It seems likely, knowing Ariel Sharon's methods, that the green light was given only to the patrol, and when the two forces, that of Arik and that of Baum, were in the field they decided to attack the refugee camp.

As mentioned, two five men teams of Unit 101, one headed by Sharon and one headed by his deputy Shlomo Baum, took part in the mission. As Sharon's team approached the camp from the northwest, according to Sharon's report after the fact, they were fired upon by some riflemen. Arik decided it would be best to go through the camp and slip through the other side rather to try and get back via the area from which they came. He claimed, in his post-mission briefing, that he decided it was better to attack rather than leave the impression of a retreat. He broke into the camp at the head of the team, and they were quickly surrounded by many Arabs. The team took cover inside one of the houses and fired in every direction. That was when Sharon ordered the other team to break into the camp and join them. Once the teams were joined, they both cleared a path toward the Israeli border by shooting their way out.

A total of forty-three Palestinians were killed in that attack, including seven women and five children, and about twenty-two were injured. The attacking force had two injured men.

Foreign observers defined the raid on the al-Bureij refugee camp as "an appalling case of deliberate mass murder." And indeed, after the fact, there were also arguments within Unit 101 regarding the matter. "Is a crying and screaming mass considered an enemy? What did those farmers do wrong?" the objectors within the unit claimed. "War is cruel," claimed the supporters. Either way, it seems that this time there were no heroic stories told about the operation. In addition, at least one minister, Welfare Minister Moshe Shapira, criticized the raid from within the government.

"The incident at the refugee camp created anxiety and restlessness around the Strip," reported Leslie Crower, acting director of UNRWA in Gaza. He demanded that the UN submit a stern objection to Israel for attacking innocent and unarmed refugees without just cause.

Israel denied responsibility for the act and led diplomats and senior officials to understand that "Israeli settlers" or "local kibbutz members" were the ones who performed the raid, of their own initiative.

It seemed that Lavon, then the minister of defense, was deceived by the IDF's senior command both before and after the act when it came to the affair of the al-Bureij raid. Dayan asked Defense Minister Lavon for authorization to perform a "small" operation, ambushing cars. However, after the raid, Lavon was told that the raiding party had encountered an Egyptian patrol and had no choice but retreat to the al-Bureij refugee camp, where they were forced to kill civilians.

On the same night of the al-Bureij operation, a third team from the unit, headed by Shmuel Merhav, attempted to locate the house of Major Mustafa Hafez, the head of Egypt's Military Intelligence in the Gaza Strip, and assassinate him. Major Hafez was not home, as the description by team commander Shmuel Merhav shows, which also included Shmuel Nisim and the sapper Micki.

Shmuel Merhav tells:

> There was a suspicion that terrorists were coming out of the al-Bureij refugee camp, and it was decided to attack it. But there were also women and children in that refugee camp. I didn't like it and neither did Shmuel Nisim (Hafalach). He argued with Ariel Sharon; he was not intimidated by him or ashamed. Hafalach told him that he thought it was unjust, that it was not the objective. That this way we would not be taking down attackers but women and children, and that he did not want to take part in that. In my own quiet way, I also expressed my dissatisfaction with that operation. Instead of taking part in the al-Bureij operation, Arik gave me a mission: get Hafalach and Micki the sapper, and take down Mustafa Hafez, the head of the Egyptian intelligence in the Gaza Strip. Arik said I would lead the operation. The 101 did not pay much attention to ranks, and I didn't feel anyone minded it either. Arik's instruction was to go there and come back through the same ravine. We left near Kissufim and I had to find a large house at the entrance to Gaza. We used maps and aerial photos, we reached the house and surrounded it. The plan was for Hafalach and me to break in while Micki was left behind to cover us. We were only three, no reserves, no radio, no IDF uniforms. We got close to the house, there was a large, locked gate, I got there, placed an explosives brick and detonated it. I flew back from the shockwave, and Hafalach, who was a bit further back, went into the house; I immediately recovered and followed him. We checked, but our "friend'" Hafez was not home.

For me it was an operation with huge personal responsibility, with a team of only three people. This operation was the kind of activity Unit 101 did throughout the entire five months of its existence.

As mentioned, Shmuel Nisim, nicknamed "Hafalach" by everybody, was assigned to Merhav's force after refusing to join the attack on the al-Bureij refugee camp. Hafalach impressed everyone at the 101 with his candor and bravery and was the benchmark in the unit for maintaining Purity of Arms. Hafalach tells of his refusal to take part in the al-Bureij operation:

> As for the al-Bureij refugee camp operation, there were others who thought the same as I did but refused to speak up, since Sholmo Baum would have made fun of them – he was capable of being very assertive and aggressive. The only one who would argue with him was me. I was "the barrister," which was a derogatory term coming from a farmer such as Shlomo Baum.
>
> I thought if we opened the door to killing innocent people at the refugee camp, they would do the same to us in retaliation. To go into a place, for no reason – I mean it is not an infiltration base – to kill women and children, what kind of a heroic act was that? You shouldn't do those kinds of things.
>
> Arik did not see it as a reason to spark a war of opinions or to open a debating club. He sent me to a place more dangerous and difficult that night than the al-Bureij refugee camp. Nearly our entire unit's force was at the refugee camp, while I was sent with Shmulik Merhav and our explosives officer, Micki, to take down Mustafa Hafez. We found the house that night, went in, but he was not there.

Another early operation by Unit 101, in September 1953, involved the banishment of Azazama tribe Bedouin families from the demilitarized zone of

Nitzana (Auja) to Egypt. The Azazama tribe was used by Egyptian intelligence for information gathering, sabotage and to lay mines in Israel. Ariel Sharon, Shlomo Baum and fourteen members of Unit 101, along with a few Nahal soldiers from the Givat Rachel settlement in the demilitarized zone – which would later on become Ktziot – raided a few of the Azazama encampments on two jeeps and two command cars, aided by a surveillance plane. They set some of them on fire and destroyed Bedouin property. In the shootout during the raid, a few Bedouins were probably injured.

Sergeant Guy Kochva, commander of the Nahal platoon at Givat Rachel in the Nitzana area, joined a backup force to Unit 101's operation. At the end of the operation, Guy turned to Arik and was convinced to join Unit 101 – and so he did.

Here is the story of Kochva joining the 101, as told by him:

> I was a sergeant in the Nahal as a "Farms Platoon Commander" (Nahal units sent to stay at kibbutzim for working and training), with a unit staying at Ma'agan Michael. We were taken down to 404 Southern Battalion and placed under the command of (captain at that time) Danny Matt. I commanded a 130-person platoon there – today it is considered more than a platoon – which included both men and women.
>
> One day, Danny Matt told me: Take two command cars in the morning, go north to Wadi Abyad where you will meet a group of people. That will be Unit 101. You are assigned to them for a week. I arrived at Wadi Abyad. I met a group of eleven people, none of whom I knew. They seemed like a very strange unit, hardly military at all.
>
> The mission was to banish the Azazama tribe, who had taken over the entire demilitarized area. There were many tents and livestock there; we were more of an auxiliary and supporting force. It took us a week to clear out the entire grounds. At the

end of the operation, I went to Arik and told him I wanted to transfer to his unit. He told me, "So, come over." And I replied, "What do you mean come over? I'm a soldier." He replied, "Come to the Sataf, I'll make sure everything is taken care of." I arrived at the Sataf, Shlomo Baum greeted me warmly and gladly; he knew me from the time of the Bedouin banishment. He told me, "Go to Meir Har-Zion's squad." I did so, and he also accepted me kindly, and that is how I joined Unit 101.

Zeev Solel, who joined the unit later on, was placed in a new squad of people who came from special non-combat units. He tells about his first steps in the unit:

They put together a squad consisting of people who came from non-combat units, our commander was Avraham Meiri, he was from the Nahal, and they took us on a patrol that same evening. It was pouring with rain, very cold, late October. They took us for a night patrol in the Jerusalem mountains. As a matter of fact, they did it only to see if we were able to pass the first stage; it was not easy. That was actually Arik's way: the test was to walk in the rain, at night, to go up and down the hills and see who survived the physical test and who didn't. It was a simple screening, but an effective one. A week later, I was already in action across the border. There was no attempt to build unit cohesion or regular training there. Training was done while in action, patrols and actual operations.

My first action, a week after I had arrived, was not a patrol. We went to Driya, we had to blow up a house there and kill someone inside. Meaning it was an actual operation. We learned everything from scratch at the 101. At first, we didn't even know what it meant to go across the border.

Davidi told me, years ago, that all he and Arik knew about guerilla warfare came from "Har," which was everyone's nickname for Meir Har-Zion. I never saw him study military books. He would only look at maps and learn everything he needed from them; that was his hobby. But he was the one who planned the raids, the way we marched to our destinations and whether we would go this way or that."

The personal stories of the people of Unit 101 reveal a very unorganized and unplanned recruitment to the unit. "Bring a friend" was the common way and there was probably a lot of weight put on the recommendations of people within the unit. The real test was the patrols, and those who did not complete them were eliminated. Arik was the one who made the decisions, but Meir Har-Zion was the one who set the bar – which was very high and challenging – for what was a successful patrol. The decision to hide the identity of Unit 101 as a military unit, with civilian clothing and weapons not commonly used by the IDF, contributed to the loose and free atmosphere in the unit. In fact, according to Arik's own testimony, the insistence on discipline in the unit was only when it came to the operational area of patrols and actions, which were relatively minor back then.

6. OPERATION "SILK GLOVES," DECEMBER 21, 1953

The operational order from the Operations Directorate to the head of Unit 101 bears the signature of Lieutenant Colonel Rehavam Ze'evi (Gandhi), head of the Operations Department. The brief order, only one page long, was given on December 18, 1953 and was marked as "Immediate – by messenger." It read:

1. On December 16, 1953, two IDF soldiers were murdered near the Beit Guvrin area.
2. The General Staff's objective: Irregular action[15] against regular Jordanian forces in the Har-Hebron area.
3. The mission: Inflicting damage to Jordanian military personnel, National Guards or police.
4. The method: The action will be carried out by three squads of up to four people, which will operate in areas outside the villages and strike the forces or individuals they encounter.
5. *Clause is deleted...*
6. Damaging vehicles is permitted, with the exception of buses.
7. Mines will not be used in carrying out the mission.
8. The activity will commence on December 18, 1953 and last no longer than ten days.

---

15 An action carried out by Unit 101 while disguised as non-military personnel.

9. Report: A plan of operations for each night will be submitted for authorization by the General Staff Operations Branch.

On December 21, at 17:15, three of Unit 101's squads left Jabel Nakar.

Squad 1 arrived at Hebron's northern suburbs at 00:00. They were discovered and many armed civilians gathered at the sound of the alarm. Shots were exchanged and two men and one woman were killed. The Israeli troops secured the gun of one of those killed and brought it back with them. They also posted a proclamation bearing the insignia of the Arab Legion, with the image of a hand making an obscene Middle Eastern gesture superimposed upon it. The squad retreated the same way it came in and returned safely to its base at 05:00.

Squad 2's mission was to lay an ambush near the Etzion camp. When the squad were a few meters from the camp, they spotted a Legion platoon scanning the area. The squad quickly retreated and arrived safely back at base at 02:00. It is likely that the Legion platoon went on patrol after hearing of the presence of the squad in the area.

Squad 3 was to lay an ambush on the road to Tarqumiya. North of the town, the squad ran into a group of armed Arab civilians who were alerted to the presence of the Israeli force by the barking of local dogs. The IDF troops opened fire on them and retreated while the enemy fired back with rifles. One of the Arabs was injured. The squad made it safely back to base at 00:00.

Ariel Sharon, the commander of Unit 101, submitted an operational report on "Silk Gloves" directly to the head of the General Staff Coordination Branch, without going through Central Command, with a copy of the report delivered to Operations/Intelligence Divisions. The report detailed the action on the outskirts of Hebron on the night of December 21–22, 1953.

HEBRON OPERATION

Executing force:

A four-man squad under the command of Sergeant Meir Har-Zion.

Operation's objective:

Causing casualties among Legion or National Guard personnel in the city of Hebron.

Course of action:

The squad left Beit Natif at 17:15 in a vehicle, through the Valley of Ella, to Jabel Nakar. From there, they moved south to the ancient Roman road, which had been discovered a day before, leading from Halhul to Beit Natif. At 23:50, the squad arrived at the outskirts to Hebron, following a strenuous five-and-a-half-hour walk along the road, which was inhabited on both sides. The squad encountered some dogs, following which an armed man came out. Once he noticed the squad – there was moonlight and a snowy surface – he started whistling and went back into the house. The squad broke in intending to kill the man. Consequently, the man was injured and his wife was killed.

During this action, some armed Arab men gathered, opened fire and shouted "*Idbachum*" (slaughter them), "*Aleyhum*" (lynch), etc. The troops had begun their withdrawal when they noticed an armed Arab man trying to fire at them from a lighted window. One of the men jumped him and killed him by firing a round into his head. Another Arab man, alarmed by the calls, ran out firing in all directions. He was also slain, and his gun, a new Parabellum pistol plus holster, was taken from him. The squad continued its retreat, chased by a few Arab men all the way to the outer houses. The squad returned to the base from which it left, Jabel Nakar, at 04:00, after walking back in only four hours.

Enemy losses:

Three dead, one injured, one gun taken. Our men were unharmed.

Shimon "Katcha" Kahaner describes the daring operation, which became a symbol of staying on mission:

> There were only four of us – Meir, Guy Kochva, Eitan "Hanabat" Bentov and I. The mission was to reach a house, or rather three houses, which had a gang in one of them. That was retaliation for the attack carried out the previous evening at Valley of Elah, near Moshav Zekharia.

The special thing about this action was the order, that if we did not arrive at these houses by midnight, we had the right to return without carrying out the mission. It was far, about twenty-five kilometers in each direction. This meant they believed we might not be able to get there and back on the same night, and that if we were still there after midnight we would get in trouble.

We arrived in Halhul at midnight, on the main road, and we had about forty-five minutes left to reach the destination. When we arrived, there was a light on in one of the houses. We saw six or seven men through the window, sitting around a big table. In other words, we had reached the exact target and did not have to waste time finding them.

We left Kochva on his own, at the entrance gate to the backyard, so that no one could come in. Then we approached the door, which was made out of thick iron, heavy and well-attached. We put two small charges there, about two kilos a piece. There was a big explosion, but the door did not break. We put two more charges, bigger ones; again, there was a major explosion and this time the door blew in. We killed six of the men who were there.

When we left, we heard children crying from a room. I opened the door; there was a woman there with two children. I calmed them down and that was that. We started vaulting fences, cutting through yards, and then we saw that "Hanabat" (Eitan Bentov) had disappeared. That was a difficult moment. Then we heard a grenade go off. We went toward the sound and found our guy lying there; he wasn't wounded, just slightly shocked. We put some snow on his face and he bounced right back.

By the time we returned, it was already morning. Arik was waiting for us and Moshe Dayan was there also, as well as some hot soup…all that after fifty kilometers back and forth.

Guy Kochva, who was in Meir's squad, tells of the action from his point of view:

> It was a harsh winter, December. We were in the hut waiting for Meir to come back from his meeting with Arik. He said five of our soldiers had been murdered near Beit Guvrin and we had permission to act freely at Mount Hebron. The mission was to go to Hebron, blow up a house and kill Arabs who were involved in the murder of the soldiers. Meir said: "I counted twenty-three kilometers one way on the map, but in actuality it will be more. We should take into account that it will be fifty kilometers, besides what we might encounter on the way, of course." We went down to Kibbutz Netiv HaLamed-Hei in the early morning by command car. We watched the road from there. Meir said we should walk in the wadi all the way to a Roman road, and from there we would go up to Halhul through the villages of Haras and Nuba. We started walking on a completely clear night. We kept on walking, there was a tough incline and a long walk; at a quarter to midnight we arrived at the outskirts of Halhul, the area was white with snow. Up in the sky there was a moon. No sound around. You could pick out a man clearly from a kilometer away as if it were daylight! It was a wintery night, and we had no more than shirts and sweaters on. It was clear to Meir that sticking to the mission meant exactly that, and he said we would continue to Hebron. Meir always knew where he was going. Suddenly we could see two- and three-story buildings, we arrived in Hebron and the dogs from all the houses started barking.
>
> Meir said, "This is the house," and ordered me to stay by the [back] entrance. Eitan was on the other side; Meir and Katcha hung a breaching charge on the door. The charge exploded but the door didn't move. They put another one on and the iron door blew inward. They came in, killed the man. There was also a woman there, they did not touch her or the kids. And outside,

Hebron was being Hebron; a rifle coming out of every window. They shot from the porches as well. We fired back and waited for Meir and Katcha to finish up inside.

We were in a pretty open space. We saw the [Jordanian] police up ahead as well as their backup squad. They advanced in line with the commander in front and did not fire. We knelt, Meir ordered us to fire and four tommy-guns thundered and barked. Those who fell there were killed, while those who didn't – managed to escape. We started to head back home. Going between the houses. In some houses, we fired straight into the window when we saw someone approaching. I walked behind and noticed that Eitan was not there. We went back and heard a grenade go off. Eitan "Hanabat" had his tommy-gun in hand and next to him was a dead Arab. He was a bit confused, but very quickly came to his senses and we started back. Meir pulled us about a kilometer west, through the slope and then right, onto the same road we came on. When we came back, there was much joy. We went on the operation without a rescue force, radio or any option of consulting anyone, with Meir making decisions on the spot as things progressed.

An eye-opening and impressive description of the operation in Hebron, which was later dubbed Operation "Silk Gloves," as mentioned, can be found in the book *Pirkei Yoman* by Meir Har-Zion. The challenging mission, the unprecedented distance of the destination and the freezing snowy winter is all there in his personal story, entitled "The Hebron Action":

A chilling, cold mountain wind whines. Streams of rain are pouring down, along with lightning and thunder. Specks of hail are occasionally mixed in with the rain, angrily pounding the tiled roofs. The night is as dark as can be, with only the cover of snow shrouding the mountain peaks, which can be seen from time to time in the pale light of the moon, breaking out of the dark skies. I run the few dozen meters between my room and the unit's office. While pinning my gaze on the whirlwind outside, I close the office door behind me to find myself in a warm, brightly lit room, as if I've entered a new world, which ignores everything going on around it.

– Sit!

I sit next to a clean table with a wide map spread on it. Arik sits in front of me. By the look on his face I can already guess what this is about.

– Well, we have authorization to move freely in Hebron.

We automatically look intently at the map. We should land a blow which will echo – they should be filled with dread, hit them right in the heart. Our eyes rest upon a dark mark in the center of the map. Is that it?

We start counting the squares: one kilometer, two, three, ten, thirty, forty, forty-two... we try again. Twenty-one kilometers are between us and the target. The initial enthusiasm wears off. The night of terrors at Nebi Daniel – the ambush two days earlier in which a Jordanian captain was hurt – surfaces and comes before me. Can we handle such a thing?

– So, Har, what do you think?

It's hard for me to decide. I turn the matter around in my mind. I have doubts, this is a difficult military operation at hand. It is hard for me to believe that I am up to the task. The sound of the bustling storm outside comes in, as if to confirm my hesitations. But maybe? What the hell, let's give it a go. I look at Arik. Doubt makes its way to the surface of his face. He does not believe.

– Well, you leave tomorrow evening.

A night near Beit Natif. The car stops by the border. Cold winds are blowing from every side. We are shaking but making ourselves ready to leave. Arik shakes my hand, "Good luck!" We're off. The boots start digging into the mud; the body warms up and the doubts melt away. We move toward the target. A big, round moon climbs above the mountains. The sky is clear, and somewhere on the mountains, the snow gleams white. We march with great vigor. A paved path rescues us from the sticky mud and safely guides us in the right direction. One hour passes, the second starts creeping in, we keep marching on, our feet pounding against the stones on the road. There are shadows stretching on both sides. A dog starts its strange, hostile bark. The mountains grow closer; the snow on their peaks is bright and intimidating. The ravines seem bleak, the cliffs shrouded in shadows. Can we overcome in the face of all of these?

Careful. We must go between two villages. A dog starts to bark a loud cheer, and an armed Arab comes out of his house. We press against the rock and wait. The Arab gives up and returns to his house. We keep going. We should skirt around the houses. We get off the road and tread through green fields and cultivated terraces. We go past the villages and a road leads us through the deep valley, slowly making its way up to the mountaintop. Fatigue began to make itself felt. We have been marching for three hours, nonstop. The vigor has diminished and we sit down for a rest.

We are marching up the ravine again. Our rhythm is now much slower. The target is still far. A sense of alienation is overcoming me; everything is so different here. We are so far away from anything safe, close, from anyone who cares for us. I look at the undersized squad, we are so small and weak. A terrible fear suddenly falls on me, a great and terrible terror. It seems to me that each tree and bush is looking at us, seeing us, plotting against us. I feel myself becoming smaller and weaker, helpless against what confronts me. I want to hide, disappear, be protected, and now – of all times – the light of the full moon seems so bright, so hostile…

I keep on marching. My hand clutches the tommy-gun. I have to get over this crisis. I know it is but a fleeting one. We'll make it!

Pure white snow covers the mountains. Our feet begin to trample it. Each step makes a horrible crunching noise which could be heard from afar. The path winds between houses scattered around the slope. The moonlight falls on the snow and shines ten times brighter. You could spot a man from at least seven hundred meters away. We leave the path and the nightmare begins. Our feet sink in the deep snow while climbing up steep terraces. Walking is labored, difficult. We advance one step at a time. Severe fatigue saps determination. We literally have no strength left. I look at the rest of the squad. Their gazes are tired, heavy. The spark has disappeared from their eyes, along with the enthusiasm. Their faces say stop, enough, we have done more than enough tonight. We cannot do anymore.

Har, the hour is late. Let it go. We will do the same thing at the nearby Halhul village…

I say nothing. I am as tired as the one who offered the plea. Every fiber of my being is shouting to stop and go back. It is obvious to me that I can no longer go on. It is obvious to me that I cannot perform the mission. Why in Hebron? What is the point of sending four people to such a place? The whole thing suddenly becomes redundant and pointless. It is so stupid. Now I am no longer afraid, I am indifferent to it all; the moonlight spreading around, the squeaking snow and the lurking dangers. I do not even care if one of the doors suddenly opens and, as we walk past, someone jumps out in front of us. I no longer care if we succeed.

Actually, why not do it at Halhul?

Come on, Har, are we going to Halhul?

Once again, that senseless insistence. We are not going to Halhul, we will perform the mission. Perform the mission despite the temptations, the feelings and crises. We perform the mission and that's that, without thinking to ourselves why or how we do so.

We march forward once more.

Here are the city's buildings. Large, two-story buildings rising from the cover of snow. There is dead silence in the air. Only the crunching of the snow beneath our feet breaks the silence. We arrive at the road. We march extra-carefully since the road is covered in thin, slippery ice. We cautiously pass a first group of houses. We arrive at the second one. Maybe we should perform the mission here? Seems like a completely suitable spot. While I contemplate the matter, my feet slip, tripping on the ice, and I fall full length on the ground.

A couple of dogs wake up from their slumber and start barking ferociously. An Arab sticks his nose out of the next house and starts whistling to the alarm. Now we must act quickly. There is no room for contemplation. I pick out a nice house at the heart of the neighborhood. A dog greets us with barking howls. We notice a man approaching the window. I aim, a burst of shots slices through the air. The Arab screams and immediately falls down. We jump out. Two stay behind for cover. We detonate a breaching charge near the door. The iron door does not move. A second charge thunders and the door finally opens, and I burst in. There is chaos and a thick darkness between the rooms. I try to look for the man of the house and avoid spraying the house with bullets so as not to hurt the wife. There are horrible screams coming from outside. I go out. The entire neighborhood has woken up. People are running between the houses. Shots slice the air. We have to hurry, there's no time. I go into a room and spray it with fire. I go out and order a retreat. There are terrible roars coming from the upper houses: "*Idbach al-Yahud.*" The blood freezes in the veins. We press against the terrace and try to get away, while screams haunt us from all around. We rain fire. An Arab appears above us and a burst brings him down immediately. I look back and, horrified, see there are only three of us left. What should we do? We press ourselves against the terrace and the voices around us grow louder. Who knows what might happen at any minute? Kochva roars: "Eitan! Eitan!" No response. Killed? A grenade blows up and shots echo. Eitan, where are you? An image suddenly appears from behind. There he is, what happened to him? He is leaning on the terrace wall and sighing. Hurt? I am struck with horror. I run to him worriedly. No. He is not hurt. He lost contact with the unit, and when he suddenly found himself alone in the face of the terror around us, he lost control. I order Kochva to look after him and follow us. We keep retreating. An Arab man runs in front of us. I lay him down with a burst of shots, and Katcha removes a magnificent pistol from his hand. Horrifying roars get further away, become weaker and weaker. The mission is completed.

Now we must retreat as quickly as possible. There is a new vigor in our veins. We are overflowing with joy. We made it; we completed the mission! Where are the doubts, the worries, the fatigue? Where is the fear? A feeling of victory and power overtakes us. We are powerful. We do not fear anything now. The tommy-guns are ready and we are going through the buildings walking tall. No one would dare confront us! The road is so easy now. A kilometer chases another, an hour follows another. Here are the two villages. Will we hide between the terraces now? I order to take off the safety catches –that is how we quickly march on the moonlit road, ready to quickly "persuade" any enemy.

The time is 04:30 in the morning. These are the last few meters. There is a car looming black before us. Arik meets us with a big smile on his face and excitedly shakes my hand.

The force led by Meir Har-Zion, which included three more men – Shimon "Katcha" Kahaner, Guy Kochva and Eitan "Hanabat" Bentov – performed a complex and challenging action of the highest order. It was a raid executed on-foot on a cold, wet and snowy December night in 1953. Meir Har-Zion led the squad through forty-two kilometers, round trip, on a mountainous route all the way to the heart of the city of Hebron in order to hit a wanted terrorist's house. Armed Arabs arrived from all sides and the gunfight lasted for a long time, but the force came out unharmed. Operation "Silk Gloves" is considered one of the toughest and most complicated missions in the history of the IDF.

The actions by the rest of the teams in "Silk Gloves" rightfully did not enter the report of the 101 commander, Ariel Sharon, but are only mentioned in the intelligence summary of Central Command, which was mentioned above. Neither mission was carried out, and there is no telling what the commander of Unit 101 had to say about them.

Meir Har-Zion set an unprecedentedly high bar at Hebron, one which would be very hard for the soldiers of the unit as well as the rest of Battalion 890 to measure up to. He took a chance by marching on, despite the instructions he had received to go back if they did not reach their destination by midnight. Although his insistence on setting off another explosive charge after the first one failed to breach the door did eliminate the element of surprise, it magnificently expressed the supreme value of adherence to the mission. The effort to locate Eitan "Hanabat" Bentov, who had lost contact with the squad in all the commotion, is an example of the value of not leaving men behind. Ariel Sharon, who went overboard in praising operation "Silk Gloves," placed it on a pedestal as an immaculate example for all soldiers, from then on.

When the Chief of General Staff, Moshe Dayan, decided to absorb Unit 101 into Paratrooper Battalion 890, he saw it as his obligation to come personally to the Sataf base, where the unit members were, and talk to the men. Zeev Solel describes the encounter, which was quite charged:

> It was Chief of General Staff Moshe Dayan's idea to incorporate 101 into Battalion 890. Even though he initially objected to the establishment of the unit, when he saw how 101 performed, he obviously changed his mind. He claimed that such a thing should not be limited to an elite squad, but was for the entire IDF. He said, we'll bring them into the paratroopers and then it will transfer to the entire army – and so it was. The decision to disband 101 as a separate unit and annex it into Battalion 890 – we took that very hard in the unit. Dayan came for a visit with the unit in November of 1953, there were forty to fifty of us in a tiny mess hall. They fixed it up, brought plates and made dinner. That was special for us kibbutz members. We sat in a circle and the first thing he did was ask each one to introduce himself – first name, last name and where he was from. Then he gave his speech, talked about the military-political situation and finally said, "The decision is that you will join Battalion 890." There was crying and lamenting. Then Dayan said that anyone who had something to say should stand up and do so. Those who do not wish to stay, do not have to. They could go back to their unit or ask for a transfer.
>
> One of the men got up, Moti Gemer, and said: "Say, would we have to shave every morning?!" Dayan said, "Yes, there would be a roll call every morning and you would have to shave." So Moti said, "If that is the case, I'm out." And he really did leave.

Along with the successes of Unit 101 and those of Paratrooper Battalion 890 into which it was absorbed, there were less glamorous sides. There were failures of discipline, and behavior which deviated from IDF orders and norms of conduct. For instance, the direct subordination of the unit to the General Staff caused Central Command Headquarters to be in complete ignorance when it came to Unit 101's operational activity, even though operating within its jurisdiction. It is possible that the expansion of the al-Bureij refugee camp operation, from what was initially defined as a preparatory patrol by the General Staff, and later became a multi-casualty action involving the camp residents, was a result of the unit's lack of discipline.

An extreme expression of this lack of discipline and the internal justice process of the unit could be seen in a case which occurred on a Saturday night in December 1953. Yitzhak Jibli, who was a combat soldier and driver in the unit even before he officially joined it, drove the troops to their homes at the northern kibbutzim. He made his way up to Kibbutz Afikim to spend the Saturday with his unit's commander, Yair Tel-Tzur. On the way to Tiberias, he was pulled over by military policemen since he was out of uniform, lacked military papers and had no permit to drive a military vehicle on Saturday. He was taken to the Tiberias police station where he was beaten and humiliated. Jibli was able to contact Shmuel Nisim, "Hafalach," at the Sataf camp, and he notified Ariel Sharon of the incident. Sharon reported to Rehavam Ze'evi, who then turned to Moshe Dayan, who in turn ordered the immediate release of Jibli. On Sunday morning, Jibli picked up the unit's soldiers from the kibbutzim at the Sataf base and told them of what he had been through at the detention center. Sharon, probably with Dayan's permission, authorized the unit to retaliate against the military policemen. And so, at the end of December 1953, 101 troops left for action under the command of Shlomo Baum. They raided the destination (the military police station), cut the phone lines, surrounded the building and beat the military policemen who took part in Jibli's beating. Following this incident, the head of the Manpower Directorate of the General Staff, Major General Zvi Zur, demanded that the commander of the Jerusalem District, Mishel Shacham, act strongly against the personnel of 101; however, Shacham refused. Sharon had to eventually apologize for the incident, and on Dayan's orders, the affair was over.

The "unacceptable" way in which Unit 101 conducted itself made its way into Battalion 890, as could be seen from Aharon "Erol" Eshel's story of how he joined Battalion 890 shortly after its unification with Unit 101.

> The Beit Daras's squad commanders' course held its graduation party at Beer Tuviya. And who showed up? The savior! Meir Har-Zion, along with Arik Sharon and a few more guys. I told them of my failed attempts to join Unit 101.
>
> Arik told me, "You are going with my driver to Beit Daras now, and bring whoever you think is good enough back with you." I woke up Gadi, Musa and Dan, and there was a command car waiting for us in the morning. We threw our backpacks in and drove straight to Tel Nof, to see Pini Greenberg, who was the battalion's adjutant, and he got all the paperwork ready for us. That way, just when Unit 101 was annexed to Battalion 890, I arrived there and was directly assigned to the reconnaissance unit under Meir.

7. ARIEL SHARON AND MEIR HAR-ZION

We cannot properly summarize the story of Unit 101 without talking about the special relationship between Ariel Sharon and Meir Har-Zion. Sharon had an extraordinary knack for evaluating people. His appraisal of his subordinate commanders was based primarily on their conduct on the battlefield. As a result, several officers found themselves on their way out, almost without prior notice. Sharon, an intelligence officer himself, knew how to appreciate Meir Har-Zion's qualities from the very first moment. His unsurpassed navigational skills, the way in which he would change routes, select destinations and uncompromisingly persist in achieving the mission, have been acknowledged and supported not only by Sharon, but also by Chief of General Staff Dayan and Prime Minister Ben-Gurion as well. An expression of this appreciation can be seen in the introduction Sharon wrote for Har-Zion's unique and personal account, *Pirkei Yoman*, in 1968:

> The way in which we operated in 1953 pointed to future solutions, both in unconventional thinking and also organizing units for this type of fighting, as well as in planning and executing special operations. In years to come, "specialized warfare" will also serve as the main answer to the issue of terror. The milestones set in the 1950s, as told in Meir Har-Zion's book, very much aided the consolidation of this approach.
>
> However, reprisal actions did not start in 1953, but a few years

earlier. Most of these missions failed, and even those that succeeded did so on a fairly limited scale and were not enough to substantially change the situation.

The IDF that emerged out of the War of Independence was powerless in the face of infiltration. The army, which had stood strong in the face of all the armies of neighboring Arab countries, was now helpless in dealing with this type of fighting, and suffered many failures in cross-border operations. Many factors contributed to these failures, among them the fact that the army was in the midst of a major reorganization at the time. Then, priority was mostly given to operating large military units. In addition, the reprisal actions taken during peace time were carried out under severe political restrictions. The IDF was obligated to go to extreme lengths – even more so than during wartime – to prevent civilian casualties.

The paratroopers carried the weight of reprisal actions between 1953 and 1956. During this period, the army gained experience and self-confidence, while the political echelon[16] also developed confidence in the IDF's abilities. Reprisal actions prior to the Suez Crisis significantly decreased the scale of Arab terror attacks and reduced them from large-scale unorganized actions to narrow but more organized ones guided by the Arab governments. Our reprisal objectives gradually turned toward deterring those governments. The rulers of Arab countries feared that our reactions would compromise their stability and so they largely halted the terror attacks.

The people who carried the burden of the reprisal actions almost

---

16 This term is used in Israel to describe the elected, political leadership in contrast to the military leadership, which is often referred to as the "defense establishment."

singlehandedly were not hardened and bloodthirsty warriors. They were boys who grew up excelling in youth movements, members of kibbutzim from all political streams, sons of towns and moshavim, youth from underdeveloped towns, from Haifa, the suburbs of Tel Aviv and Jerusalem. They were extraordinary youths who had great conviction and courage.

Among the paratroopers at the time, the one who stood out above all others was Meir Har-Zion. Har-Zion arrived just as we were establishing Unit 101, as a Nahal corporal who could not find an outlet for his tumultuous temperament, his will to get things done, his belief that we should and could find a way to overcome the Arab terror actions.

Within a short while, Har-Zion became Unit 101's and the paratroopers' most daring fighter, and an excellent scout, perhaps the best the IDF ever had. His leadership skills surpassed all the others, and his accomplishments on the battlefield only increased. He commanded many actions himself. Har-Zion had an excellent grasp of tactics and took part in planning and setting up the paratroopers' fighting methodology. He was a natural leader of the highest quality.

Har-Zion was injured twice in battle. His second injury was severe and forced him to resign from active duty. As a person he was honest with himself and others. Despite his successes, he remained a humble and simple man; an accomplished outdoorsman, a lover of nature who knew the country and its trails like the back of his hand.

And yet his achievements did not come effortlessly to him. He put in immense work to reach a perfect level of performance. He was not the type to socialize or lounge about; not one for public relations at all. He was a real warrior, the greatest we ever had.

His activity spanned a relativity short period but left an indelible impression on the IDF and its fighters for many years, if not generations, to come.

Chief of General Staff Moshe Dayan's decision to disband Unit 101 after only a short period of time – about five months – was in fact a return to his previous position of objecting to the establishment of the unit. Lieutenant General Mordechai Maklef was the chief of general staff who received and authorized the recommendation of Colonel Michael Shacham, commander of the Jerusalem Brigade (and the Jerusalem District). University student Ariel Sharon was a reserve battalion commander under Shacham, and he was the one who recommended that Maklef establish a special unit, which would carry out cross-border operations. The idea to absorb Unit 101 into the Paratroopers' Battalion 890 would not have caused a change in the IDF's combat spirit had it not been for Sharon's appointment as Battalion 890's commander. The change was not immediate, but was achieved by switching out the existing commanders – who were trained under the previous battalion commander, Yehuda Harari – for ones who had arrived mostly from the Nahal and had a completely different approach to combat. Two who were not switched out were Arie Biro, a fearless fighter, who remained as company commander at the battalion, and Aharon Davidi, who had joined Harari's battalion not long before and had already taken part in the Qibiya action, led by Ariel Sharon; he was appointed deputy battalion commander. We will return to the outstanding relationship between Sharon and Davidi later on, a bond that contributed to the creation of the battalion's warrior spirit. A few of Unit 101's graduates were sent to officers' course, while Har-Zion received his commission when the chief of general staff made the extraordinary decision to excuse him from the course.

The reconnaissance platoon, established within the battalion and consisting of former Unit 101 troops, was commanded by Har-Zion, and continued to conduct cross-border missions while also taking part in larger scale actions and even leading them. The battalion's platoons switched to a method of small unit reconnaissance operations, just as was customary in Unit 101 in the past. These excursions, which could be called "raids," demonstrated to the paratroopers that the border could be crossed, even a few dozen kilometers deep into enemy territory, and they could still come back in one piece. Those raids, as far as Sharon was concerned, were the definitive measure of the commanders' skills. Those who did not pass the navigation test and complete their mission were immediately dismissed.

We can learn from Brigadier General (Ret.) Zuri Sagi, who served as a sergeant in the paratrooper battalion when Lieutenant Colonel Yehuda Harari was in charge, about the process of metamorphosis Battalion 890 went through, from showcasing and exhibiting visually pleasing drills to patrolling and fighting:

> I enlisted in the paratroopers because I thought it would be something better, but I was quickly disappointed. I arrived at the paratroopers' battalion, which Yehuda Harari commanded. Harari had this worldview that the more people were violent and aggressive, the better soldiers they would make.
>
> When Arik became the Battalion 890 commander, we started a period of reconnaissance patrols. One of the examples from that time showed me how different the perception was [between Harari and Sharon]. The patrols were now more of a test than being of any value in terms of actual intelligence. Yermiyahu "Yirmi" Bardanov, who was a very good friend of mine, went on patrol with someone and they got lost, came back without finding the objective. Bardanov was afraid Arik would kick him out, so the next morning he went on a successful patrol with me and got to stay.

Sharon realized Har-Zion's value from the very first moment and set navigation as a major value for Unit 101, as well as Battalion 890 later. The ability to reach destinations beyond the border for intelligence-gathering purposes, or to perform military operations, seemed to Sharon an indispensable value. In addition to the navigation standards, Sharon embraced uncompromising adherence to the mission, the value that Har-Zion demonstrated throughout all the operations he performed.

8. OPERATION SHOSHANA: THE QIBIYA ACTION, OCTOBER 14, 1953

On the night of October 12, 1953, a Palestinian terrorist gang infiltrated Moshav Yehudiya (Yehud). Its men broke into a house, tossed a grenade inside and murdered a family: Susan Kanias and her children, Binyamin (eighteen months old) and Shoshana (three years old). The father and firstborn son, Eli (seven years old) escaped the slaughter. The tracks of the murderers led to the Arab village of Qibiya, east of Beit Nehemia and Kfar Truman. The following day the Israeli government convened, and David Ben-Gurion ordered the IDF to execute a reprisal mission. The action, named "Operation Shoshana" after the little girl Shoshana Kanis, was tasked to a combined force under the command of Ariel Sharon. That was the first joint action of Battalion 890 and Unit 101.

The Qibiya action would prove to be a turning point, due to the domestic and international criticism that followed the massive attack and civilian fatalities.

Sharon planned a multi-pronged action, with blockades in neighboring villages designed to isolate the scene. This would become the method of operation he would use for all reprisal actions in the future.

Documents in the IDF archives show that the General Staff's order to Central Command was given by Colonel Meir Amit, who at the time was the head of Operations Division at the General Staff. Amit noted that Major Ariel Sharon would command the operation and that it should be carried out no later than the night of October 15–16, 1953. Amit also emphasized that during the Qibiya action "all arrangements should be made to prevent leaving behind any identifying traces. Arrangements should be made to prevent the identification of the operating units." The head of Operations Division instructed the command to submit the action plan for approval by October 14 at 08:00. Following that instruction, Central Command published a detailed command order on October 13:

> <u>General Staff's aim</u>: executing severe reprisal actions by way of sabotage and casualties, against Arab villages beyond the Armistice border. *Meaning* [emphasis in the original]: attacking Qibiya village, temporarily occupying it for demolition and causing as many casualties as possible in order to drive the residents out of their homes. Raiding the villages of Shukba and Nilin in order to sabotage a few houses and kill residents and soldiers… the commander of Unit 101 should submit the action plan for the approval of the Operations Branch of the command by October 13 at 22:00.

"Shoshana's" operation order, submitted by Ariel Sharon in writing, makes reference to the General Staff's aim, "executing severe reprisal actions." Sharon stated that, under 101's command there would be a paratrooper company, a platoon from 57 Battalion, two 81 mm mortar sections, as well as an ambulance, a doctor and two medics.

The operation was scheduled for October 14, 1953 and Zero hour was set for 21:00.

> Four sections of paratroopers commanded by a Paratrooper Company commander (Aharon Davidi), would occupy and base itself in the northwestern end of the village.
>
> Two paratrooper sections + PIAT [anti-tank weapon] + two 101 sections, commanded by Sergeant Major Shlomo Baum, would break into the village.

One paratrooper platoon would serve as porters and reserve force to occupy the objective.

All the aforementioned forces were under the direct command of Sharon, commander of the 101.

A squad of five men, commanded by Sergeant Har-Zion, would raid and sabotage the village of Shukba.

A squad of five men, commanded by Sergeant First Class Arik Schleien, would raid and sabotage the village of Nilin.

Two mortar sections, commanded by the head of the artillery division, would harass the village of Bodrus.

One platoon from the 57 Battalion at Shiek Ismayil.

A blockade on the Qibiya-Bodrus road – under the command of Second Lieutenant Gozny.

In the Command's report to the Operations Branch there was a summary of the outcomes of the reprisal action:

Qibiya village: Forty-two killed, fifteen wounded, forty-one houses destroyed.

Shukba village: A police sergeant and several others were injured.

Budrus village: Forty-three bombs landed inside the village area and several houses were hit.

In Sharon's report on the Qibiya action, he mentioned that he had ordered the force not to open fire "unless you are met with resistance which does not allow you to move forward." The force entered the settlement, as Sharon reported, and by 22:30 had managed to go through the entire village, break into most of the houses and clear them with fire and grenades. In his report, Sharon stated there was a general flight of residents from the village even before they opened fire.

In the Central Command's report to the Operations Branch, it was also stated that the Jordanian government had convened to listen to the message from the chief of general staff of the Arab Legion regarding the incidents, as well as a memo the Jordanian government was about to submit to the United Nations Security Council. It was also reported that the joint Israeli-Jordanian Armistice Commission had condemned Israel – by proxy through its chairman, the representative to the UN – at its meeting on October 15, 1953.

It is also important to hear criticism of the Qibiya action from "Hafalach," one of the veterans of Unit 101:

> The action at Qibiya was not a restrained action. It came after preparations which, in fact, made it clear how big the operation was going to be. I heard Arik, with my own ears, order half a ton of explosives to be loaded into the command car. I was there and told Arik: You only need two gelignite sticks for two huts – why would you take so much? He said: You have an exam in Legal Procedures at the university, go do it and shut up.
>
> They simply extended the scope of operations in the Qibiya action to make a last impression. I think there was no relation between what they planned and the General Staff's order.
>
> Arik decided not to rely on me too much in this matter. He pushed me aside a bit because he saw I wasn't thinking the same way he was – he never liked to be criticized.
>
> In this kind of action, what the 101 did was to go to a destination and blow up a bridge or shoot at some village to show them they would not be able to sleep quietly at night as long as we were being harassed; that was designed to bring the IDF's confidence back. These things had been done before, more than once, during

the War of Independence by small teams from the Palmach. All we had to do was go back in history to show us that it was not impossible and that we could do it.

We were the students of the Wingate school, which really must be given credit for taking us "out of the fences." The Palmach did those things, following Wingate, while the 101 was the reply to the complacency that had spread through the army after the War of Independence.

When the 101 was disbanded and brought into Battalion 890, I went to a parachuting course with them, and when that was over, I had a conversation with Arik. He said: Come, I'll let you command a platoon or even a company, as long as you stay. I replied that I had happily given all I had to the unit, but I was not interested in a military career but to go and study.

Arik was very enthusiastic, an endless stock of vigor. He had some charm, but essentially, he was a lonely person. He had dreams, visions, many positive qualities, but he never really had good friends who loved him. He didn't really believe in people. He would share with people but, in a way, he was examining the way in which his stories influenced them.

By reading what Sharon said about the Qibiya action in his farewell speech[17] to the brigade after the Suez Crisis, we can see what was really on the mind of Unit 101's leader before it was annexed to Battalion 890.

Sharon gave great importance to performing the action on a scale that had never been seen before by Unit 101. It was also his opportunity to prove Unit 101's combat ability to the IDF's high command as well as, of course, Sharon's part in the planning and execution of such large-scale and complex actions. There is no doubt that the Qibiya action was a significant milestone,

---

17 See Chapter 33, (below) for a transcript of this speech.

both militarily and politically. It was, as mentioned, also a test for Ariel Sharon's abilities as the head of Unit 101, who planned and commanded the force that took part in the operation. For the first time, a large-scale action took place here, which had to be coordinated between forces acting in different places, while performing diverse tasks. It is safe to assume that Ariel Sharon proved his unique ability with the detailed and complex planning, as well as successful execution of the action, paving the way for his appointment to commander of Battalion 890, when Unit 101 was absorbed into it after this operation. Despite the fact that Schleien's and Har-Zion's forces were not very successful in their tasks, the operation was considered an overall success from a military perspective. This became the foundation for confidence in the army's ability to perform large-scale operations.

From then on, the IDF's reprisal actions would focus on choosing military or police targets, in an attempt to motivate the governments of the neighboring countries to prevent infiltrations and attacks on Israeli civilians.

9. THE DIPLOMATIC CONSEQUENCES OF THE QIBIYA ACTION

The global response to the Qibiya action was worse than expected. The great powers –the United States, USSR, Britain and France – denounced it, as did the UN. The UN Security Council severely condemned Israel for the attack, Britain transferred a symbolic shipment of weapons to the Jordanian National Guard and the US suspended their financial aid to Israel. The Ministry of Foreign Affairs reported severe reactions to the operation from all over the world. "The operation brought Israel's image to the edge of the abyss," Israeli Ambassador Aba Even wrote to the Minister of Foreign Affairs, Moshe Sharett, while Israeli diplomats in England reported a similar mindset. The British embassy in Israel was outraged by the action and noted that it was, without a doubt, a planned military action. The French representative also expressed its nation's dissatisfaction with the operation as well, and called upon Israel to refrain from any provocative actions in the future.

The major newspapers in the US and England mostly sided with the great powers' position, which, as mentioned, condemned and placed the full weight of responsibility on Israel for the action, and demanded severe punishment for those in charge of the action, as well as compensation for the Jordanian side. The *New York Times* mentioned that the US was appalled by the action and sympathized with the Jordanian casualties' families.

We will see later how David Ben-Gurion, Moshe Dayan and Ariel Sharon reacted to the commotion within Israel, as well as on the international scene.

The government refrained from taking responsibility for the action, and at Ben-Gurion's initiative, published a message saying: "No one is more sorry that the blood of the innocent was spilled during the Qibiya action than the Israeli government." Avoiding a clear and distinct confession did not lessen the consequences of the operation nor the harsh reactions it aroused. Although those did cause much embarrassment in Israel, not claiming responsibility for such actions was a policy set in stone. The government also relentlessly rejected the "asinine and fantastic" theory, according to them, that six hundred IDF soldiers took part in the Qibiya action. "After meticulous examination, we determined that no military unit – large or small – was absent from its base on the night of the Qibiya action." In retrospect, Ben-Gurion's transparently false denial does more than raise eyebrows. It is safe to assume that Israel avoided claiming responsibility in order to evade being reprimanded by the Armistice Commission and perhaps the Security Council as well. But many parties in the international arena, including the British and American governments, took Israel's responsibility for granted.

The Operations Branch concluded that reprisal actions in general, and the Qibiya action in particular, were fruitful in achieving the goal of preventing infiltrations. However, the Ministry of Foreign Affairs analyzed the data differently and claimed that, although there were fewer infiltrations, the effect was limited only to the area around Qibiya village, while there was no change at all in other sectors. The Ministry of Foreign Affairs' claim was unfounded, since by comparing the infiltration data of 1953 with that of 1954, there is a clear decrease in infiltrations due to the reorganization of the two internal security sections in Jordan and an aggressive line by the Hashemite Army, led by the commander of the Legion, Lieutenant General Sir John Bagot Glubb. The Qibiya action also had consequences on the IDF's operational doctrine. In future, all reprisal actions would be directed at military objectives, and not as collective punishment against civilian targets. Chief of General Staff Dayan was not happy with this turn, and over the years he constantly claimed that the transition to attacking only military targets made the actions less effective.

Dayan said, following the Qibiya action:

> The IDF's lesson is the most important one of all. The government's decisions and the chief of general staff's orders would never again be mere wishes, but minimal predictions. Instead of units returning as before, making excuses for not being able to execute what they were assigned, from now on, after each action, the paratroopers would have to explain why they did not do more than was expected of them. A surge of self-confidence had been injected into the IDF's veins.

Dayan was referring to the repeated failures of reprisals prior to Qibiya, except for a few successful actions undertaken by Unit 101.

Dayan's reaction is reminiscent of his comment regarding the criticism of Ariel Sharon, head of the Paratroopers Brigade during the Suez Crisis, for diverting from the orders of the General Staff by inserting a large force from the brigade into the Mitla Pass. Dayan then said, "It is better to struggle to restrain the knights' mounts, than to push and goad the lazy bulls with the cattle prod."

Dayan did not see the Qibiya action as significantly different from the other reprisal actions, which were meant to cause casualties as well as to damage property. Dayan had presented this belief of his to the leaders of the ruling Mapai party in the past, saying: "That is the only way which has proven to be effective, not justified or moral, but effective. When Arabs place a mine on our side... we bombard the nearby village with all its women, children and elderly people. That is what makes their public protest against the breaches, awakening the Egyptian and Jordanian governments to act in preventing such events."

Dayan's words may not have been his most polished, but concluded with a sobering and memorable punch line, "The collective punishment approach has proven, for the time being, its effectiveness."

The following, from Ben-Gurion's journal during one of the "vacations" he took at Sde Boker,[18] concerns the complex political relationships following the Qibiya action.

February 13, 1954

Ziama[19] is fearful for Lavon[20] and Dayan's plans. I told him that Dayan was not responsible. On the contrary, he objects to most of Lavon's plans, but he is a soldier and must therefore follow orders, even as he attempts to undermine them. I have advised that a small-scale committee be established – Sharett,[21] Pinhas Lavon, Ziama and Golda,[22] when she returns – to consult on all foreign and security issues. I have voiced my concerns about the Ministry of Foreign Affairs. By the way, I have asked Moshe [Dayan] if he remembers the order regarding the Qibiya action. He was the head of the Operations Branch and Motke Maklef was chief of general staff. Moshe wrote up the order and gave it to Arik, who detailed the operation. When the government asked questions about it, he remembered that Lavon – who was filling in for me as minister of defense, as I was away – struck out a paragraph from the order. He believes the material is still somewhere in the Operations Branch or General Staff…

At nine, Moshe Dayan came to see me. I asked him about his statement to the newspapers regarding the Qibiya action. The army did almost nothing in terms of reprisal actions until then.

---

18 Ben Gurion had retired from politics in January 1954. He returned to the cabinet and, subsequently, the premiership in 1955, retired again in 1963, and once again returned to politics in 1965.
19 Zalman Aran, Minister without Portfolio.
20 Pinhas Lavon, Minister of Defense.
21 Moshe Sharett, Prime Minister.
22 Golda Meir, Minister of Labor.

Yehuda Hararri of the paratroopers had managed the operations in a lackluster way and he was replaced by Ariel Sharon. When Arik and Har-Zion came to the paratroopers, they started proper actions. Lavon ordered the operation but did not detail whether they should be conducted differently than before. Arik's unit performed the action but did more than was expected. Sharett later asked to see the order, a copy of which was sent to Lavon. Moshe does not know whether Lavon read it or not [before the action]. When Moshe Sharett asked for the order, Lavon then read it and ordered that a paragraph be stricken from it. The Qibiya action was a kind of reaction to the IDF's previous operations. [Meir] Amit was then the head of the Operations Branch.

One has to read between the lines regarding the top decision makers in security matters. Ben-Gurion, despite having resigned and being a private citizen at this point, was never really detached from influencing security policy.

Tensions began to mount along the Jordanian border as early as the morning after the deadly Yehud attack, but following the Qibiya action there was a real fear of escalation between the two countries. Israel put IDF and Border Police units on alert for possible escalation and infiltration of Jordanian forces into Israeli territories; the Legion, for its part, reinforced its forces, especially around Jerusalem. Israel conveyed a warning on the matter via foreign representatives in Israel, but the delegates of the three Western powers were skeptical about the threat posed by the Jordanian mobilization. In addition, the head of the Arab Legion made clear that their actions were defensive and that Jordan had no plans to attack.

At the same time, Israel was involved in other incidents: on the Syrian border, where the canal around the Benot Yaakov bridge was being dug; and on the Egyptian border, a skirmish in al-Auja and the attack on the al-Bureij refugee camp. The representatives of the three Western powers, as well as other countries, assumed that Israel – concerned about the impending evacuation of British bases in Suez, the upcoming withholding of American aid, as well as the increased Arab boycott and a subsequent worsening of its financial condition – had decided to light an even bigger fire under the conflict.

Although the desire for revenge also motivated the decision to retaliate, none of the foreign powers doubted that the Israeli government's primary goal in launching reprisal actions was to fight off infiltration. Further analysis shows that the policy guiding the actions was aimed at spurring the governments of Israel's neighbors, from where the infiltrators originated, to take more effective measures to eradicate the phenomenon altogether or reduce the number of infiltrations.

Throughout the entire period between 1953 and 1956, the heads of Israel's security forces refused to depend upon any outside party, such as the great powers or the UN, in contrast to the Ministry of Foreign Affairs led by Sharett. The army's perception was that the diplomatic approach had failed in the fight to maintain Israel's borders and sovereignty, while the military approach had proven effective. There were also domestic considerations that influenced the decision to continue carrying out reprisal actions, mainly to provide the public in Israel with the sense that their security was being taken care of and that the IDF was handling the difficult and disturbing issue of infiltrations. The policy of reprisal actions also aided commanders of the IDF in inspecting the mixed units' operational capacity and drawing conclusions which would be used to improve operational abilities.

I cannot help but wonder, while writing these lines, about what is currently happening in the settlements in the south of Israel, mostly those in the Gaza Envelope (the area around Gaza). Much as in the 1950s, the people who live in the south of Israel still expect the Israeli government to find effective and safe ways to provide them with peace and security in the face of rockets, incendiary balloon attacks and fire aimed at them by the Hamas and Islamic Jihad from the Gaza Strip.

The differences in Israel's and Jordan's reactions to one another's counter-measures to infiltrations created a danger – as mentioned – of escalation to armed confrontation. Even though the heads of the security forces in

Israel knew of Jordanian efforts to prevent infiltrations, they still insisted on judging the situation based solely on outcomes, which is why that as long as the infiltrations lasted, so too did the reprisal operations. Yet the escalation, derived from mutual distrust, was relatively restrained, since both sides were not interested in starting a war. The commanders' agreement, signed as part of the armistice agreements, which contributed significantly to management of border relations between the two countries, was reinstated and relations between the two countries seemingly returned to "normal." However, the Qibiya action continued to resonate in both the Israel-Jordan arena and within Israel itself.

In the meantime, Unit 101's immediate operational successes impressed the IDF's senior command. The operational and perceptual shift of the army could be seen in meetings, conferences and reports. The Qibiya actions could certainly be credited with a fundamental change in how the IDF's commanders viewed Unit 101 and its capabilities. During Unit 101's existence, its fame was limited mainly to the senior ranks – due to the shroud of secrecy surrounding its actions – but its unification with the Paratroopers Battalion and subsequent assimilation of its values brought the knowledge of its successes to the army at large. This exposure also contributed to the shaping of 101's image as a military example for generations to come. The achievements of the Paratroopers Brigade in the future were, in fact, a natural extension of the raiding policy forged in Unit 101.

10. ISRAELI MEDIA FOLLOWING THE QIBIYA ACTION

The Reaction of the Press to the Yehud killings

The Israeli media, despite all its political diversity, reacted to the murder in Yehud with unanimous and unprecedented anger. The following day, the murder made the front page of almost every newspaper. Reports described the anger and frustration in the border settlements and called on the government to increase security measures on the country's frontiers.

Yedioth Ahronoth (center left) published a headline across its front page, on October 13: "The twelve-year-old boy reported to the police: 'They threw a bomb at the house! Everyone is dead!'" These words, along with the chilling description of the horrible death at the Kanias family's house, touched everyone who read it.

Maariv (center left) that same day provided a prominent place for a horrific description of the interior of the Kanias family's house. The newspaper implied a need for retaliation: "There is a way to increase the Jordanians' desire for a quiet border, and this way does not always go through emergency meetings with them."

"The lantern provided the killers with light," stated the labor union's *Davar* newspaper in its article headline from October 14, 1953, chillingly detailing the grenade thrown through the grated window and ending the lives of the mother, Susan Kanias, and two of her three children. "The oil lantern remained lit even after the murder," the newspaper added. "The IDF Spokesman," it further said, "provided updates on the terrorist's trail, revealed by surveillance of UN observers and Israeli representatives, with the aid of dogs." The trail, according to the report, led to the Arab village of Rantis.

"A mother and two children were murdered by infiltrators from Jordan," the *Haaretz* (center left) headline declared on October 14, 1953. "The Kanias family home," wrote the newspaper, "is found in an area of dense housing at the edge of the village of Yehud, near the Lod–Petah Tikva road, twelve kilometers from the border. The deadly grenade exploded in the middle of the room where Susan, the mother, slept with three of her five children. The two babies were killed on the spot, the son Yitzhak and mother Susan were injured. The injured child," the newspaper said, "survived, while his mother died in hospital."

"A grenade in the middle of the room," said the headline of the *HaBoker* (center right) newspaper, which described the deadly and murderous attack on the Kanias family of Yehud on October 14. The reporter described the room in which Susan Kanias and her two children were murdered. The mother's hand had been severed and the doctors could do nothing to save her. The reporter describes the shock, anger and frustration of the neighbors in Yehud, who remained agitated as a result of what had happened in their town.

The *Herut* (right wing) newspaper also published an article on October 14, titled "A Mother and Her Two Children Murdered by Infiltrators." The Petah Tikva reporter described the following: "An armed Arab gang that infiltrated Israel's territory early yesterday morning murdered a woman and two of her children as they slept in their apartment in the village of Yehud, south of Petah Tikva. The gang, seemingly operating according to a precise military plan, had an electronic connection to their home front in the eastern border mountains. While retreating, the gang attacked a taxi driving from Lod Airport on its way to Haifa." The reporter, who visited the family's home, emphasized the appearance of the white painted house and the flower patch as a contrast to the horror inside the house. *Herut* also printed a picture of Ben-Gurion with derisory quotes attached to his title: "Defense" Minister. In the editorial, under the headline "To Jordan," the newspaper declared: "The heart explodes with anger, the hands are clenched into fists, the mind is agitated and devoured by the image, so distinctly reminiscent of a pogrom." The newspaper accused Ben-Gurion of no longer keeping Israel safe, and closed with the call to occupy the West Bank, and perhaps even the entire Kingdom of Jordan.

The same day, *Al HaMishmar* (left wing) published the following headline, "A Mother and Her Two Children Were Murdered in Yehud Village by Infiltrators from Transjordan."

"A Mother and Her Two Children Murdered" was the headline of *Kol HaAm*, the daily newspaper of the Israeli Communist Party, on that tragic day. After describing the murder at the Kanias family's house in the village of Yehud, causing the loss of the mother's life along with two of her young children, the newspaper published the IDF Spokesman's announcement that the murder was carried out by "armed Jordanians," whose trail led to the Arab-Jordanian village of Rantis.

"Once again innocent victims have lost their lives due to the intrigues carried out by the American Observers who work across borders to organize conflicts and bloody clashes," claimed the newspaper. "This murder is not the first of its kind. There were similar murders before it, within Israel's territory, by armed forces from across the border, as well as murders committed in the Gaza Strip refugee camp and other places by Israeli forces. The governments of both sides are playing the game of the imperialist warmongers, for the pleasure of 'the third party.' The solution is expelling the foreign 'observers,' those who incite provocations at our borders. The newspaper concluded, "Mutual saber rattling and mutual murders...is contrary to the security interests and the will of the peoples of Israel and of the Arab countries alike."

All the newspapers described the details of the lethal attack in an almost identical manner. It seems they were all briefed by a single source, and focused on the description of the murder. With the exception of the more extreme papers, *Herut* and *Kol HaAm,* none of them expressed any call for revenge at that time.

The Reaction of the Press to the Qibiya Action

The newspapers implicitly referred to the Qibiya operation in their evening editions on October 15, a few hours after the action concluded and the troops had returned to Israel's borders. The reports were published hours after Arabic radio stations and Western media had already reported the action. It seems that the military censors were more heavy handed than usual. The initial reports in the evening editions talked about loud explosions and gunfire in Arab villages across the border, in the region of Beit Nabala. *Maariv* published a more explicit headline: "Jordanian Villages Under Attack" with the secondary headline "Arabs Claim: A Reprisal Action for the Yehud Murder." The newspaper also named Qibiya as the focus of events, while others were satisfied talking about the area east of Beit Nabala. *Maariv* recounted other fatal Jordanian assaults carried out in Israeli territories in addition to the Yehud murder.

It was not until the morning editions of October 16 that somewhat authoritative accounts of the operation were published. For instance, the newspapers reported the Armistice Commission's decision to condemn Israel for the action in its meeting on October 15. The reports were all based on Arab media and the publication of the condemnation decision by the Israeli-Jordanian Armistice Commission. At that point, there had not yet been any Israeli comment regarding that action.

By the morning of October 16 the Israeli press already knew about the scale of the action and the killings, mostly of civilians, from foreign news agencies' reports, BBC broadcasts and Arab radio stations. It was clear that the action significantly deviated from previous reprisal actions. At that time, newspapers were still hesitant to publish the full details regarding the action, even though most had already reported on the destruction of homes and the high number of dead in Qibiya.

HaBoker published the following headline on October 16: "Forty-Two Dead in Attack on Jordanian Villages." The newspaper relied on reports from radio stations in Ramallah and Damascus and noted, based on these sources, the large number ("hundreds") of Israeli soldiers who took part in the operation.

Herut published the following headline, "An Israeli Force Killed Forty-Two Arabs at the Border" with the sub-headline stating, "Three Arab Villages Were attacked With Mortars." The article quoted the UN spokesman in Jerusalem, saying that forty-two Arabs were killed, fifteen were injured and forty-two houses had been blown up in the villages of Beit Likiya, Qibiya and Budrus. The spokesman reported 600 to 700 Israeli soldiers there, using forty-three 3" mortars and a large amount of explosives. The newspaper quoted the official announcement by the Jordanian Government Press Office, reported on Ramallah Radio. *Herut* related the searches made by UN officers for "the tracks of unknown assassins." At that point, *Herut* too had no figures about the action from Israeli sources. The newspaper returned to the matter the next day, quoting the text of the condemnation proposal presented by the three great powers to the UN Security Council. The headline declared, in large print, "Extremely Harsh Criticism Over the Qibiya Operation." The only softening of the text that Israel was able to achieve was that the word "criticized" would be used instead of "condemned."

Kol HaAm, the newspaper of the Communist Party, published the following headline: "We Will Protect the Peace! No More Bloodshed!" The sub-headline read: "Mass Murder at Qibiya Village." The newspaper quoted Ramallah Radio's announcement about the action, that forty-two people had been killed and forty-two houses completely destroyed. According to the newspaper, the prime minister of Transjordan claimed that it was a murderous operation which killed dozens of peaceful Arab residents of a village across the border. The newspaper added that the attack had been carried out in the middle of the night between Wednesday and Thursday, by Israeli forces armed with mortars, rifles and explosives. *Kol HaAm* did not forget to mention the condemnation issued by the Israeli-Jordanian Armistice Commission.

"The Storm Over Qibiya and Israel's Response," was the headline of a long op-ed article by Moshe Jacque in *Maariv* on October 16. The sub-headline declared, "An Arab Village Has Pushed Aside All International Issues – the Israeli Government Faces a Decision."

Jacque opened with the dramatic surprise awaiting government ministers as they were returning from a visit to the work on the Jordan Canal in north of Israel. It was a sharp letter of protest from the British government regarding the clashes at the Israel-Jordan border. Before the Israeli minister of foreign affairs even had to chance to read the letter, which had been delivered to him by a representative of the British Embassy who had come from Tel Aviv, the British Foreign Office published the highlights of the letter. Britain demanded the punishment of those responsible for the attack on Qibiya village, and that Israel would pay compensation for the damage caused to the Arab village, both in property and human lives. Jacque described the coordination between the three great powers and their appeal for an emergency meeting of the Security Council. He stressed that Israel, despite extended activity in Western capitals and the upcoming discussion with the Security Council, made do with issuing two short announcements from the Foreign Affairs Ministry spokesman and the IDF Spokesman, emphasizing that the original sin lay with the infiltrations that led to the border incidents. Jacque criticized the three Western powers that, in May 1950, had guaranteed the borders of Israel and its neighbors, yet took no action during the entire three years in which hundreds of Israeli civilians were killed in attacks originated in Jordan. Jacque also stressed that Israel did not seek to escalate hostilities with neighboring countries, and took no pleasure in reprisal actions. He emphasized the threat posed to Israel's existence. That, according to him, was the challenge that Israel had to respond to, not just the infiltrations.

Yedioth Ahronoth waited until October 19 to publish an editorial about the action. Under the headline "Jewish Blood Cannot Be Shed for Free," the newspaper decided to focus on Jewish casualties caused by infiltrations, without even mentioning the dozens of Arab casualties at Qibiya. The article stated that "Jewish blood does not have a value on the global stock market, but it can be had for bargain prices… Britain and France only awoke when the [Israeli] frontier residents' patience exceeded its limits, and those who would not be murdered at night administered an epic dose of their own medicine back against the raiders by infiltrating the nests of the Arab assassins." One can clearly discern a strategic leak here from the minister of foreign affairs as well the Prime Minister's Office, who claimed it was not the IDF that performed the attack but rather Israeli frontier residents. Most newspapers at that time cooperated well beyond merely accepting the conditions imposed by the censors.

On October 18, *Al HaMishmar* published a long article about diplomatic moves on the international scene, especially at the UN Security Council. "According to the demand of the Western powers, the Security Council will discuss the Qibiya action tomorrow." The paper reported that Britain had submitted a strong protest against Israel, and went on to say that the US President, Dwight D. Eisenhower, had sent a personal emissary to get an update and learn about the situation in the Middle East following the operation. A meeting of the three Western foreign ministers, convening in London, discussed the situation at Israel's borders with its neighboring countries. According to *Al HaMishmar*, although Britain was leading the efforts to condemn Israel, all three countries were acting in unison to censure Israel at the Security Council. The newspaper reporter presented the British claim that the action was the most serious violation of the Armistice Agreement to date and that it might undermine peace in the region. The newspaper added its own commentary to the extreme British position, stating that its goal was to strengthen the position of the British Chief of Staff of the Arab Legion, whose standing had been compromised by the inaction of the Legion in protecting the Arab villages. According to *Al HaMishmar*, Britain also intended to view Jordan's request for help to the UK in terms of their Mutual Aid Treaty, thus further strengthening its grip on Jordan.

Although *Haaretz* avoided publishing an editorial about the matter on October 16, it did publish an article on page two, which had been prepared in advance, before the Qibiya action, and openly discussed the criticism of Unit 101's action at the al-Bureij refugee camp in the Gaza Strip, where about 20 Palestinian refugees were killed. The journalist was able to slip in a reference in defense of the Qibiya action into the article, writing about "the horrifying murder at the village of Yehud and the reprisal action which followed," claiming that direct retaliation after a fatal attack should not be considered an act of provocation. *Haaretz* also published an article about the United States' reaction to the Qibiya action. The title of the article was "US Announcement on the Qibiya Action: Those Responsible Should Answer for It." The newspaper's US correspondent wrote that diplomatic observers believed Israel now faced one of its most difficult times in the international scene since 1948.

In their editorial on October 19, the editors of *Haaretz* wrote that the world had found Israel guilty and that it was easy to understand why, due to the many casualties among the village residents. "Any reasonable person in Israel would also be sorry for such a tragic outcome," they wrote, "however, it was forced upon us due to the damage caused by infiltrations. This case must be viewed as part of a chain of infiltration terror attacks, a direct continuation of the war on Israel by Arab countries using unconventional means." Nonetheless, the newspaper condemned "the arrogant frivolity" with which "certain elements" in Israel – meaning Ben-Gurion and his government's ministers – dismissed global reactions to Israel's policy. The newspaper stated, "the opinion of Western governments should be taken into account while planning military actions." In short, the editors of *Haaretz* claimed that that there should be a balance between security needs and foreign policy. They stated that in the matter of Qibiya, the status quo was undermined and our international position had been significantly damaged.

"We Will Not Accept That the Lives of Our Civilians Are Worthless," was the headline in *Davar* on October 20, quoting the statement given by the prime minister live on Israel Radio. The sub-headline of the article read: "The Jordanian Government Is Responsible for the Reprisal Action at Qibiya" and quoted more of Ben-Gurion's words: "For over four years armed units have been infiltrating across the Jordanian border and those of other Arab countries, into Jewish frontier settlements and the city of Jerusalem for the purpose of murder and pillage. Hundreds of Israeli civilians – men, women, old men and children – have been murdered or severely injured during the years by armed gangs. (…) All our appeals to the Armistice Commission, all our attempts to cause Arab governments to stop this flood, have failed miserably." Ben-Gurion blamed Arab governments for exploiting the Arab refugees' plight and inciting them to act against Israel. The prime minister went on to claim that the patience of some border settlements had simply run out, and that after the murder of the mother and her two children at the village of Yehud, they decided to attack the village of Qibiya across the border. With that said, Ben-Gurion was careful to state that the Israeli government was sorry for the spilling of any innocent blood during the Qibiya action. However, he immediately added that full responsibility lay with the Jordanian government. As previously mentioned, Ben-Gurion declared: "We have conducted a precise examination and found that no military unit, not even the smallest one, was absent from its base on the night of the Qibiya attack." The *Davar* newspaper accepted Ben-Gurion's entire statement and almost blindly supported the false version regarding those who performed the action.

HaBoker chose to present Major General Vagn Bennike's[23] testimony before the Security Council on October 28, which was less than complimentary toward Israel. The words of the Danish commander of the United Nations Truce Supervision Organization were quoted in the headline, "The Situation in the Middle East Is On the Verge of Exploding." The sub-headline continued, "The Qibiya Incident, as Well as Other Incidents, Should Not Be Seen as Separate Incidents – Jerusalem Is the Main Dispute." The

---

23 Vagn Bennike was a veteran of the Danish army and the underground resistance to the German occupation of his country. He attained the rank of Major General and lead the UNTSO from June 1953 to September 1954.

newspaper quoted extensively from statements from the head of the United Nations Truce Supervision Organization (UNTSO), who described what was happening on all of Israel's borders with its neighbors. Bennike claimed that Israel used a large military force while attacking the village, which used mortars and large quantities of explosives to damage the dozens of houses in the village that were completely destroyed.

In the following days, and for a few weeks after that, many details were leaked to Israeli politicians and journalists – in the familiar Israeli way – regarding the units who took part in the action and how it was decided upon. The newspapers in Israel refused to deal with the matter and did not publish follow-up articles regarding the events of October 14–15. The Israeli public was left solely with the information published in the original articles from October 16, in which foreign and Arab radio stations were quoted, as well as the declarations of the Armistice Commission. Only *Haaretz* saw fit to share certain details of the action. It was able to bypass the censors by quoting "foreign sources." The newspaper must have pioneered this method, which later took root in all Israeli media.

11. WHIPLASH OPERATIONS, FEBRUARY 1954

Following the outcomes of the Qibiya operation and reactions to it, both on the international scene as well as within Israel, there were several Israeli cabinet members who objected to large-scale reprisal actions that could result in civilian casualties. Consequently the IDF decided, for the time being, to switch to a policy of targeted reprisal actions carried out by small retaliation squads, much like the ones Unit 101 used to perform. From the beginning of February 1954, there was a series of reprisal actions, which were named "Whiplash Operations," carried out by squads from the Paratroopers Battalion 890. Whiplash Operations 1–4 took place at the beginning of February in Gaza, and Whiplash Operation 5 was carried out at the same place at the beginning of March of that year. Whiplash Operation 6 took place on May 26, 1954. It was a raid by a band of paratroopers on the Bedouin village of Khirbet Janiba in the Judean Desert in order to confiscate the tribe's cattle. This operation took place following the pillaging of the livestock from Kibbutz Ein Gedi.

The operational order for Whiplash 5, presented below, is addressed to the Southern Command and the commander of Battalion 890, and was sent "Immediately by Messenger." The order, signed by Lieutenant Colonel Rehavam Ze'evi, the acting head of the Operations Division, provides much discretion in choosing targets and timing of the operation. For some reason, a stop order from the Operations Branch was attached on top of the order, which was probably only temporary.

Subject: "Whiplash 5" operational order

<u>General overview</u>: There is still infiltration activity aimed at stealing and sabotaging the settlements in our territory. The aim of this operation is to damage infiltration bases and pressure them by confiscating property in the Gaza Strip.

<u>Intent</u>: Performing robbery of herds, agricultural property and so on, throughout the Strip.

<u>Method</u>: Responsibility for implementation lies with Southern Command.

<u>Executing Forces</u> – Battalion 890.

The operations will be carried out throughout the entire sector of the Strip, at various times, both day and night, and will continue from April 2, 1954 to April 9, 1954.

<u>Communications</u>: UAR (Updated Action Report) will be sent directly after each activity. A detailed summary report will be sent once every 24 hours and should reach Operations Branch by 10:00.

Brigadier General (Res.) Tsuri Sagi humorously describes this operation "Whiplash" which took place in the Gaza Strip:

> One day, they told us that there's a *khirbeh* (ruin) near Kissufim Outpost and that the thieves stealing the equipment – everything was out in the open in those settlements – are hiding it there. We were tasked with stealing the materials back from them, which also included agricultural equipment. They called it "Operation Whiplash." Then, Gandhi told me that he had written the operational order. So, I took a squad and went over there to steal back from that *khirbeh*. Just before we crossed the border, we met First Lieutenant Moshe Gruber with Arik and they told us:

We're joining you. Oh great! The problem was that the entrance to the *khirbeh* was in the direction of the outpost, so we had to be careful. It wasn't easy. So we did it by sneaking in one man at a time. We went in, Arik and Gruber with us. I was sergeant and I had a first lieutenant named Moishe Goldberg, from Haifa. It was pitch black in the *khirbeh*; we couldn't see a thing, no equipment, nothing. Then Arik started losing it and started lighting matches, and that is when the [Israeli] outpost opened heavy fire on us. I sent two groups. I said, let them [the outpost] finish their ammo and we will circle around to the eastern side of the *khirbeh*, meaning we would use it as a shield. They kept heavily firing at us, so I told Goldberg: Take the section to the bottom of the wadi, Wadi Salqa, the dead area, and I will follow with Arik; because Arik was heavy and could not keep up with us. He would trip over every bump in the trail and fall flat on the ground, so I let all the guys go ahead. We reached the bottom of the wadi, I counted everyone and they were all there. I asked: Arik, do you have anything to tell them? And he said, "Alright, alright."

Despite the dubious outcomes of the Whiplash operations – seizing herds in retaliation for stealing our livestock – the trend of such operations continued. Whiplash Operation 6 was meant to confiscate a herd of cattle south of Mount Hebron, near Jordanian Police Station 912. The operation failed because the herd was simply not where it was previously observed. It turned out that the action was unknown to the Operations Branch. As we will witness later on, in the correspondence between the head of Operations Branch and the chief of general staff and the reports sent to him, as well as to the defense minister – which severely criticized the operation – there was a discipline issue here, which was typical of the way Ariel Sharon prepared for missions.

Report of the commander of Battalion 890 to the General Staff, Operations Branch and the Southern Command Headquarters on the failure of operation "Whiplash":

1. Purpose of the operation: Stealing a herd in the Jordanian sector, near Police Station 912, following a daytime observation.
2. Executing force: Two squads (twelve men); I accompanied them myself.
3. Course of action: The force left Khirbet Kritin at 19:15 and moved toward Khirbet Janiba, east of Police Station 912. The force entered the area quietly and took control of a group of Arab men. The Arab men were interrogated and, according to them, were the only ones there. They also said that there is a small herd at Khirbeh Shahna. One of the squads patrolled the *khirbeh* while the other one held the Arab men. Suddenly, three Arabs appeared, armed with rifles. Because the area was paved, they had managed to come to within a few meters of us. Since there was an order not to open fire unnecessarily, they were told to stop and raise their hands. They responded by opening fire, and we returned fire. Two of them were killed on the spot, and the third one was injured but escaped (in the subsequent search he was discovered close to death, about 200 meters away). Their weapons – two English rifles and an ammunition belt – were seized. During the gunfight, one of the Arab men we caught earlier was killed. He wasn't handcuffed and had tried to run away. The force continued to search the other *khirbeh* as well. There were signs of a herd and it is safe to assume it was moved away from the border during the night. The force returned to origin base at 23:00.
4. Casualties: The enemy had four men killed.
5. Our forces returned safely.
6. Booty: Two English rifles and an ammunition belt.
7. Note: The mission was not carried out due to the herd not being at the location; we should attempt much deeper penetration into the territory (not so close to the border).

Ariel Sharon mentions the Whiplash Operations in his farewell statement to the Paratroopers Brigade – following the Suez Crisis and before his retirement – which the battalion undertook at a time when no authorizations were granted for large-scale military operations. He said that at the beginning of 1954, it was obvious the battalion had to become a combat unit as quickly as possible. Operations and reconnaissance patrols, Sharon emphasized, were the way to get the battalion into combat mode.

The exchange of letters between the head of the Operations Branch and the chief of general staff, and between the chief of general staff and Defense Minister Pinhas Lavon, shows the tension that had existed between Dayan and Lavon. It appears that the wording of the operational orders sent from the General Staff to the executing unit were sufficiently vague to allow for deviations, resulting in criticism from the political echelon about the operations and lack of discipline.

The IDF Archives contain a request from Chief of General Staff Dayan to Meir Amit, the head of the Operations Branch, from May 30, 1954, in which Dayan asks him to submit a report titled "Operations and Incidents – Guidelines and Reporting." The chief of general staff required the report to be ready for him, in writing, for the upcoming meeting with the defense minister. Among other things, Dayan asked to know why Unit 890 operated against Operations Branch orders during the execution of "Whiplash no. 6."

Chief of General Staff Dayan replied to the letter from the head of the Operations Branch on the subject in the following manner:

1. I acknowledge receipt of your letter.
2. We are all, of course, each responsible in the areas of our authority and role for military operations.
3. As for the incident at hand, I favor initiative and overachievement, even if that inevitably leads to mistakes here and there, over the passivity of "sitting and doing nothing" and covering ourselves in paperwork and seven permits for each operation before every action.

Moshe Dayan, Lieutenant General
Chief of General Staff

Defense Minister Lavon's letter to the Chief of General Staff Dayan, which was preserved at the IDF Archives and presented below, reveals yet another portion of the tension between the Ministry of Defense and the IDF during Pinhas Lavon's term as defense minister. Lavon complained about the execution of the action in a way that had contradicted the orders he gave. The written order by Operations Branch, Lavon claimed, was very general and does not mention the restrictions that Lavon had sought to impose. It appears that Dayan claimed to the defense minister that the action was carried out without his knowledge. It is conceivable that in this case too, as in many others, it was actually Sharon who dictated how the operation should be executed without bothering to inform his superiors.

To: Defense Minister, May 31, 1954

Subject: "Whiplash no. 6"

I view operation "Whiplash no. 6" as one of the army's recent failures, even though our unit emerged victorious and certainly did not disappoint when it came to its military capability. The execution of the action in such a manner is a blatant disciplinary violation at the highest ranks of the army, as well as a total lack of understanding of the conditions surrounding the operation. For myself, the action itself came as s a surprise, since it seemed to me that when your bureau chief informed Major Gazit that the Beit Likiya action was cancelled, this action was also included in the cancellation. But, as it turns out now, this detail was not clearly stated. Had I thought this action was about to be executed, I would have postponed it, and it is certainly my fault for not clarifying. However, I view the failure to lie in the fact that it was carried out in a manner contrary to the orders issued. The order was to avoid killing, to use only a small number of troops, to operate close to the border and at the right time. And, if such an opportunity did not present itself, it would be better to not carry out the operation at all.

I thought it appropriate to bring these things matters to your attention and to emphasize that I see myself responsible for this failure, as a function of my position. As for those who are directly involved, I will bring this matter before you once the inquiry is over.

Moshe Dayan, Lieutenant General
Chief of General Staff

In fact, Chief of General Staff Dayan admits that the killing of the Arab men during the "Whiplash 6" action exceeded the intentions of the General Staff and the instructions of the political echelon. This amounted to an admission that Battalion 890 was allowing itself to act on its own accord and without authorization.

The defense minister replied to the chief of general staff with the following short letter:

Strictly personal.
HaKirya, May 31, 1954

Chief of General Staff,

I hereby acknowledge receipt of your letter of May 31, 1954, which deals with the "Whiplash no. 6" operation. It was obvious to me, and was only verified by your letter, that the action was carried out in a manner which contradicts orders, as they were given to you and the head of the Operations Branch.

Two points trouble me:

a. The written order, given by the Operations Branch, was too general and does not mention at all the limitations which should have been made clear, which you yourself mentioned in your letter to me. This is most concerning, for it might rebound and cause complications.

b. I very much fear that this case will get blown up, both at home and abroad, to the proportions of the Qibiya incident. It is clear to me that some sort of preemptive measure must be taken to eliminate this danger, or at least to reduce it. I unfortunately have no suggestion on that front. I would be extremely happy if you could find a way to explain the matter in order to soften the impression made.

As for the matter of who is responsible for this failure, I shall await the outcomes of the inquiry you have commenced.

P. Lavon
Defense Minister

The army's low operational standard in general – and in the reserves units specifically – was made visible not only in training and their operation along the armistice lines and beyond them. The low level was also subjectively measured by the heads of the political echelon, which had the authority to instruct the exercise of military force. The conversation between the prime ministers and the defense ministers points to issues of low quality at all levels of command.

A typical, harsh and trenchant argument broke out between the defense minister, Pinhas Lavon, and the highest command of the IDF, at a General Staff meeting in July 1954, with the subject at hand being the IDF's standards of performance. Among those who took part in the disagreement were the various command generals, the division heads or their deputies, the commanders of the air force and navy, the chief of general staff's financial advisor, as well as the director general of the Ministry of Defense and the minister's bureau chief. The Chief of General Staff Dayan, on a tour of the US at that time, was represented by the head of the Operations Branch, Major General Avidar, the acting chief of general staff. All of the officers who attended the meeting were veterans of the 1948 War of Independence. Some of them had been generals on the General Staff during the war while others were decorated veterans of it. By then, Pinhas Lavon had already completed thirteen months as the defense minister, but the shadow of Ben-Gurion still hung over the Ministry. Examining the way Lavon had conducted himself, we could see that, on certain topics, he would act in the same way as Ben-Gurion had done. However, it was quickly made clear that neither the other cabinet members nor top-ranking military officers were willing to take from Lavon – or any other senior official – what they would have been willing to take from Ben-Gurion. Therefore, Lavon's term as defense minister in the Sharett administration was full of disputes, some political and others based on policy.

That instructive discussion between the defense minister and members of the General Staff, as to the state and quality of the IDF officer corps, presents a very unflattering image of Israel's military. As the discussion progressed, Minister Lavon opposed the policy of targeting civilians in reprisal actions on both military and political grounds. He expanded this point by relating to the first year of the reprisal actions. The main points of his remarks to the IDF leadership were the following:

> Since the middle of 1953, the IDF had initiated forty combat missions beyond and alongside the armistice lines. The IDF had utilized every combat method: deliberate attacks on Arab civilians beyond the lines, sniper fire, navy actions, deep patrols, and more. The initial actions were meant to indiscriminately harm civilians in order to deter them from infiltrating and attacking Israelis. Later, our forces turned to attacking the military forces of our neighboring countries, in order to deter the authorities and force them to take action to prevent the infiltrations and attacks inside Israel's territory.
>
> Evidence: the actions at the village of Qibiya, Nahlin (northwest of Hebron) near Kibbutz Kissufim (where an Egyptian outpost was occupied and held for several hours), in the city of Hebron itself, as well as artillery bombardments.

"From the beginning of 1953 and until June of that year, every action that the IDF initiated, with a single exception, failed. Each failure had its own reasons," Lavon emphasized.

> One time it was bad planning, a second time it was due to someone higher up destroying the original plan, a third time it was simply the wrong force, coupled with fear and lack of control over their men by the officers, and this time it was simply the lack of ability of the officers themselves to withstand the test of such an operation.

Lavon mentioned that if they were to look at the previous two years, they could see that almost all initiated actions were considered military failures. Lavon went on:

> Since June 1953, there has been an increase in the success of the initiated actions, and the army developed a sense of smugness. This is supposedly to be welcomed. However, alongside this improvement, there was virtually no initiated military action which was conducted without deficiencies arising from intent and planning, and furthermore, they failed to comply with the orders from superiors. These faults did not originate in the desire to over-perform, but rather from a failure to do what was required.

Lavon spared unit 101 from his harsh criticism:

> The successes that did take place were credited to one unit only, the 101; the failures lay with the rest of the IDF. However, it is unimaginable that an entire army should exist solely on the ability of one unit. If you compare the individual cases to the general picture and the dangers we face, the situation is extremely worrying. I know of a case of an entire battalion which was sent on a mission, failed to execute it and came back midway. The battalion commander sent a report saying everything was done, morale is high, and the battalion was awaiting new orders.

Lavon stated the conclusions he thought it necessary to draw from these failures:

> There has to be a strict and precise adherence to the orders of those in charge, in this case the defense minister and chief of general staff, without altering the intention of the order to such an extent as to create a gap between expectation and realization. We cannot accept that competence will be the property of one paratrooper battalion. We must reach a state in which each and every military unit will be operational, so much so that the chief of general staff could order it to do what he had ordered the paratroopers battalion to do. The entire (active duty) army has to be able to train and elevate its standards.

In the matter of discipline among the General Staff officers, Lavon reminded those present that, according to the law, a military action should not be launched without the knowledge of the defense minister, who has the authority to approve, postpone or reject it. He sternly referred to the cross-border the action, which he had only learned of after the fact, and which was probably not even authorized by the chief of general staff or the head of the Operations Branch. He was referring to Lieutenant Colonel Rehavam Ze'evi, the head of Operations Department at General Staff/Operations Branch, who initiated an action beyond the border without his superiors' knowledge. Lavon ordered Ze'evi relieved of his duty, and Chief of General Staff Dayan did so. The minister made sure to stress he would take severe actions in similar cases, since the country and its leaders have to trust its commanding officers to not present them with *faits accomplis*.

12. AZUN ACTION ON JUNE 29, 1954 – "OPERATION BARUCH"

Operation Baruch at Azun was in retaliation for the murder of a farmer in the Ra'anana-Kfar Sava fields on June 27, 1954. The mission was given to Battalion 890 and Sharon, the battalion commander, put his deputy Aharon Davidi in charge of the action, leading a seven-man force. The plan was to attack the Legion soldiers encamped near the village of Azun, on the Qalqilya–Nablus road.

Israel was satisfied that those who committed the murder were part of the Jordanian army. Prime Minister Moshe Sharett and Chief of General Staff Moshe Dayan decided that a reprisal action must be carried out, involving going deep into enemy territory to hit the murderers or those who had sent them. The force consisted of commander Aharon Davidi, Meir Har-Zion, Yitzhak Jibli, Yoram Nahari, Amiram Hirschfeld, Elisha Ben-Zur and Gilad (Jerry) Harel.

The force left Kibbutz Eyal as night fell. They encountered a patrol of Jordanian soldiers north of Qalqilya and drove the Jordanian troops away with a burst of fire before continuing on their way. An Arab man who stumbled upon the force and threatened to put the operation in jeopardy was killed with a knife. The force went on to encounter a motorized Jordanian patrol. It was late, almost 1 a.m., and they debated whether to stick with the mission and face the risk of being exposed in daylight. They decided to keep going. The force arrived at the encampment at 01:30. Several Jordanian soldiers were killed in the firefight inside the camp, and Yitzhak Jibli was severely injured. Meir Har-Zion and Yoram Nahari carried him on their backs, but that delayed the retreat and there was a fear that the entire force would be exposed and attacked by Jordanian reinforcements that had started to arrive. Davidi and Har-Zion made the fateful decision to leave Jibli there in order to make it to the border in time. After a thirty-kilometer journey, the men arrived at Kibbutz Eyal early in the morning. Yitzhak Jibli was taken captive, transferred to a Jordanian hospital, and when his medical condition improved, to Zarqa prison.

Intelligence reports submitted to the Operations Branch at the General Staff provide more details about what happened in the encounter between the Israeli force and Jordanian army units. It was reported that at 20:00 there was a skirmish on Jordanian soil between an Israeli patrol and a Jordanian one, which consisted of two legionnaires. According to the report, one of the Jordanian soldiers was wounded and the two went to Qalqilya. The Operations Branch report also stated that an Arab peasant was found dead as a result of stabbing. The Legion camp, found east of Azun village, was attacked at 01:30 according to the intelligence report, and six Jordanian soldiers were killed by machine gun fire and grenades thrown by the attackers. There were also several wounded among the Legion soldiers. The report stated that a patrol from the Jordanian force went after the attackers and encountered a wounded Israeli soldier. The soldiers provided the wounded man with first aid and he was unwilling to answer any of their questions. The report states that the UN observers and the Legion officers relate all three incidents to the same Israeli unit.

It was obviously a Battalion 890 force, which was not deterred from its mission after the first encounter. The injured soldier, Sergeant Yitzhak Jibli, arrived at the Bitunya military hospital where he acted bravely and cleverly during his interrogations by Legion officers, and did not give away any military information.

The personal story, as told by Gilad (Jerry) Harel, reliably describes what happened during the Azun action:

We got civilian shoes and clothes from the quartermaster's store. We received special weapons which were uncommon for the IDF at that time, a tommy-gun, a commando knife and a large number of hand grenades. On the day of the action, June 29, 1954, we went to Central Command Headquarters in two command cars, accompanied by Ariel Sharon. There we received a detailed briefing about the action from both Arik and the Command's intelligence officer. We had a certain amount of time to learn the route, the location of the Legion camp and the retreat route, using maps and aerial photos. During the late afternoon, we went to Kibbutz Eyal (near Kfar Sava) and had some light refreshment, and we each personally said goodbye to Arik, who escorted us almost up to the border.

It was a dark and moonless light. There were faint lights from Arab villages in the distance. Movement was difficult and was done painstakingly slowly, to make sure we did not set any stones rolling down the slopes. We mostly moved along the side of the mountain, with Meir leading the way.

Meir Har-Zion led the squad. He had long legs and big steps. Davidi walked behind him, also tall and taking big steps. We all jogged after them. We moved quickly because we knew we had a long way to go and we had to come back before dawn. Suddenly, we heard singing a few meters from us; we immediately crouched down to the ground, looked around and saw an Arab man, probably watching the fields. He had heard footsteps and possibly started singing out of fear. In a quick judgment call, we decided to eliminate him quietly, without firing, since we were worried he would call the Jordanian army. Jibli crawled over to him and took him down in just a few minutes.

We found we were walking in a watermelon patch. I don't know what made us happier, the fact we had a break or the sweet taste of watermelons. When we walked behind Meir, we felt confident and knew we were on the right path.

We arrived at the entrance to the Legion's encampment; it was pitch black. We didn't notice any guards around the perimeter, which allowed us to really get inside it. Davidi divided us into sections and when he gave the order, we ran to the tents quietly. There was a firefight along with the blasting of grenades. The execution was brief and effective, and we really made the best of our element of surprise. Within minutes, we fell back toward the rally point to return, when they kept firing at us from the encampment. Suddenly we heard Jibli say: "Guys, my leg's injured." We stopped at the rally point. We temporarily and quickly bandaged Jibli's leg and got out of the line of fire as swiftly as possible. It turned out that Jibli could not walk on his own. The second one of us lifted him up, to carry him away, he was hit once again in the neck. We quickly bandaged him and kept moving with Jibli on our backs, and his heavy equipment was distributed between the rest of us. It was very heavy and made it harder on everyone. Wending our way between the rocks was very slow and we feared we would not make it to the border before dawn. We began to hear the sounds of vehicles starting and understood the Legion was getting ready for a chase, which would include blockades and ambushes along our retreat route. We knew we had a very long way to go and we had to get to the Israeli border before first light.

During a rest break we took, Jibli was lying next to an olive tree and suddenly asked us to leave him there, at the orchard, and keep going. He asked that we leave him with a watch and a hand grenade. When we asked him what the grenade was for, he said that when they got to him, he would blow himself up, along with all of them. That's how Jibli was. Davidi called Meir and Yoram for a consult, and it was decided there was no other way than to leave him there and retreat.

We had no doubt about what Jibli's fate would be and it weighed heavily on us. We said goodbye to him with our last looks, without words, and started a hurried retreat back west, homeward.

We crossed the border at first light. Ariel Sharon was waiting for us at the rendezvous point and told us they'd been worried for us because we significantly exceeded the ETA, and we did not even have a radio to let them know about the delay. Even before serious debriefing, Davidi spoke to Arik alone for about an hour and reported all the mission details to him.

The event had a severe effect on the battalion, and they decided to capture Jordanian soldiers in order to trade them for the injured Jibli.

Sharon mentions the Azun action in the personal accounting he offered when he said goodbye to the Paratroopers Brigade following the Kadesh Operation (Sinai War), in 1957. He emphasized that the action was a tough one, which is why deputy battalion commander Davidi and Meir Har-Zion were selected to lead the force. The capture of Sergeant Yitzhak Jibli would herald the future vital decision that no man was ever to be left on the battlefield.

Arik would not give up on the principle of small unit operations, both for patrols across the border and reprisal actions, even when he rose to plan more complex engagements involving many more troops. The interrogation report of Sergeant Yitzhak Jibli by the Legion arrived at the Intelligence Branch of the IDF General Staff, and the captive soldier received accolades across the board for the way he had handled the interrogation without giving away any information. The Azun action set a record of persistence, perseverance and willpower. It served as an example of adherence to the mission until its completion. It also aroused frustration at the bitter failure of leaving a wounded man in the field, who would obviously be taken captive.

13. OPERATION "EYE FOR AN EYE," JULY 10-11, 1954

The border with Egypt along the Gaza Strip was not calm. At the same time as the "financial" infiltrations declined, attacks by the Egyptian army increased. The following operational order, signed by the head of the Operations Branch of the General Staff, Lieutenant Colonel Rehavam "Gandhi" Ze'evi, illustrates the situation at the border. The order for operation "Eye for an Eye" was sent to the Operations Branch of Southern Command as well as the commander of Battalion 890:

> General: An Israeli patrol, moving along the Strip, encountered an ambush arriving from the Egyptian border and was fired on from an Egyptian outpost. The General Staff's aim is to retaliate for the above with an action attacking an Egyptian outpost.
>
> Plan: A unit from Battalion 890 will attack an Egyptian outpost in the Kissufim sector.
>
> Method: Responsibility for execution lies with Southern Command.
>
> Execution time: The night of July 10–11, 1954. Roadblocks can be established close to the outpost.
>
> Type of activity: Attacking an outpost.
>
> Communications: Report – in accordance with operational report.

Like many other operational orders, this one leaves the battalion with some freedom as to the choice of objective. However, the emphasis that any roadblocks should be "close to the outpost" shows the vigilance of the General Staff with regard to the paratroopers battalion extending the action on their own initiative, as had happened in the past.

On the night of July 10, 1954, the Battalion 890 troops, led by battalion commander Ariel Sharon, left for a reprisal action in the Kissufim sector, south of Gaza. The objective was a fortified military outpost, surrounded by two double-sloped fences, trenches and landmines. While the structure of the compound was known, combat tactics for such an objective had yet to have been designed.

Five platoon-sized forces took part in the action:

> Force A: Led by Sa'adiya "Supapo" Elkayam – who had recently moved from the Nahal to Battalion 890 – commanded the force tasked with penetrating the outpost. The actual breaching of the fences would be the responsibility of Amikam Rachelin.
>
> Force B: A reconnaissance unit led by Meir Har-Zion, who led the troops to the correct location.
>
> Force C: Led by Eli Gozni, an ex-101-man, breaching squad no. 2.
>
> Force D: Led by Marcel Tobias, commander of the battalion's recruit platoon, roadblock squad no. 1.
>
> Force E: Led by Marcus, roadblock squad no. 2.

The forces cleared the communication trenches, occupied the buildings and various facilities, and blew them up. When the forces returned from the action, there were many lessons implemented to improve the tactics for attacks on such objectives, the position of the commander during the raid, breaching the fences and navigating through mine fields. Ariel Sharon suffered a leg injury during the action, was bandaged up and sent to an evacuation point. He was promoted to lieutenant colonel following that action.

A report on the conquest of the Kissufim outpost is given, in short, in a chapter from Meir Har-Zion's autobiography, *Pirkei Yoman*, in August 1954:

> The main activity of the Egyptian outposts in the Gaza Strip was shooting at Israeli guards. An Egyptian outpost across Kissufim was attacked in retaliation for these incidents. The enemy force at the outpost had about fifty men, scattered around trenches. The attacking force had forty-five breaching men divided into three small platoons and a reserve of fifteen additional soldiers behind them. Roadblocks were set up on the roads to impede potential reinforcements. The outpost was occupied following some resistance, and the enemy suffered about nine to ten casualties, several wounded and two captives. The rest were able to escape. We seized light and medium weapons. Our losses – one killed and five wounded.

Meir Har-Zion's report is brief and dry. But the personal chapter about the battle at the Kissufim outpost in his book is a far cry from that. It is couched in a sensitive style with colorful language, which was quite unusual for him. This is what he wrote:

> Nighttime at Kissufim. The motorcade stops. We get organized and set off. The village kids watch the endless line going past the fence with curious eyes. A few of the senior officers look on from the side with smiles of delight as they watch the platoons silently pass by, their weapons ready for action. The webbing is tight, faces are tense yet confident. There is no doubt, one of them whispers to another, that these paratroopers are "alright." A spark of hidden pride kindles in those who had heard it. This time we are a force; we are not a tiny gang of four or six sneaking around in fear, attacking with caution, leaving any wounded behind. We

are a force. We are strong. It is enough to glance back once onto the long and silent column to be completely convinced of that. The tension heightens the senses. That feeling of a great will to strike. Strike with all your might. Demolish and destroy anything in our path. Soon the tommy-gun in my hands will join a choir of dozens just like it.

I march ahead. It feels great. I veer right and the column follows me. I crouch and the entire file crouches, as if it were under a spell. The column trusts me. I join it with all my heart…there is the border. There is that sorghum field we saw at the lookout earlier today. Here is where we go around the outpost and reach it from the back. I stop at a deep trench. Arik approaches: "Har, wait a minute. I'm sending the roadblock team." A few minutes pass. The calls of farmers shouting from their huts are coming from the west. We have to hurry. The file, now slightly shorter, follows me. The outpost overshadows us about 200 meters away. A watermelon patch specks some green on the white sand. I take out the knife and call Elisha to join me. "There has to be a guard here," I whisper an explanation. We silently get closer to a single shed on the perimeter. An Arab farmer suddenly rises from the field.

"*Ahlan waSahlan*," I greet him and tightly clench the knife.

"*Min hada?*" [Who is it?] He is shaking with fear and before we could leap onto him, he takes off barefoot. I try chasing him, but it is no use. We could hear his terrible cries from afar. There is a single shot in the air coming from the outpost.

Order: "Get ready to charge the outpost!"

The file is silent but powerful, spreading out and moving onto the hill. The moon lit the dark figures silently leaping onto the light sand. Barbed wire stops the advance. The outpost went silent. Could it be that we had not yet been noticed? I send the breaching squad. The Bangalore torpedoes are ready, and the shears cut the barbed wire. The fence is breached. Go! Charge. Bullets start ringing out. The machine gun spews short bursts. A grenade is heard going off somewhere. The trenches are ahead of us. We clear them with grenades and fire and move forward quickly toward the center of the outpost. A medium machine gun starts shooting long and frightened bursts at the eastern end. Supapo charges on my right. Heavy fire comes from the left. Tracer bullets raise dust all around us. Grenades are blowing up in thunderous blasts. Elisha is injured. Hananik calls out: "I'm dead." A bullet takes down Amikam and another soldier of Supapo's. This damn fire has to be silenced. "Everyone get over here," I roar and gather the men behind a dirt mount. "Open fire on the Bren and get ready to charge!" Concentrated fire splashes on the enemy's positions. Now we have to jump out and destroy it. Supapo comes running: "Har, stop. We'll shoot a PIAT shell first." The PIAT rings out and we leap after it to the station. The place is empty. They got away.

The fire dies down. I get the platoon together in the abandoned positions, in case we are counter-attacked. We gather up the abandoned weapons. We go through their positions and wonder about the spread-out linens and the backpacks left behind. Only a few minutes ago, the enemy soldiers were sleeping here peacefully, and now… a dark-faced Egyptian soldier is lying in the communication trench. There are single shots heard from the adjacent outposts, but the blockades are silent. They dare not come close. The night is ours even within their territory. I am called to report to Arik. He is lying there, bandaged. "He's injured," someone whispers to me. I report the situation and go to the outpost's center. Things are a bit chaotic here. Yet somehow the gathering of the wounded and the abandoned equipment takes place and some of the force is starting to move out with the baggage. Supapo and I stay behind to cover the outpost and take the chance to blow up some of the positions with the explosives we had left. A few more minutes and we will leave the occupied outpost and march back with the rest of them, back to the border, to get some rest. A great calm comes over me. "Wow," Supapo whispers, "it went so well this time." I completely agree with him.

Operation "Eye for an Eye" was among the first actions aimed at military objectives. The success of the actions did not stop Battalion 890 from drawing conclusions and learning lessons, including improving the method for attacking a fortified outpost. Meir Har-Zion's journal section describing the process of the operation must have been used in the lesson-learning process, which was later done routinely following every reprisal action.

14. BEIT LIKIYA ACTION, OPERATION "BENJAMIN B," SEPTEMBER 1954

On August 28, a Jordanian squad opened fire on Moshav Ramat Raziel in the Jerusalem Mountains, killing one guard and injuring another. Major General Yosef Avidar, head of the Operations Branch at the General Staff, estimated that it was the fourth act of its kind by the same gang and that the IDF knew who its members were and who was leading them.

Following the murder, Defense Minister Lavon received a "green light" for an action from Prime Minister Sharett. At the cabinet meeting on September 5, the two mentioned having discussed the issue between themselves and specifically the fear of internal storm in Israel about the killings and its possible consequences. They agreed to act on the assumption that, should the government refrain from retaliating against the terror attack at Moshav Ramat Raziel (a settlement established by Etzel veterans and named after one-time Etzel commander David Raziel), there might be "private initiatives" by the Herut and Etzel people living there. According to the head of the Operations Branch at the General Staff, "the aim was to hit a few guards in that village. The objectives were selected according to the gang's trail, which led to the Beit Likiya village, north of the Latrun enclave. There the target would be National Guard personnel." However, there was a significant gap between the prime minister's policy and instructions, which apparently reached the General Staff through Lavon, and the "private" plans of Ariel Sharon – to free Yitzhak Jibli from Jordanian captivity, which he had endured since Operation Baruch 1 at the Legion base in Azun, on June 28, 1954.

It was to be the first battalion-scale operation following Unit 101's absorption into 890 Battalion and the appointment of Sharon as its new battalion commander. The action was planned by Sharon and executed against the 7th Battalion of the Jordanian Legion, which was occupying the outposts around the villages of Beit Ur a-Tahta and Beit Likiya. The main idea of Sharon's plan was to perform a diversionary attack on the outposts and infiltrate the villages in order to draw out the Jordanian Legion's reinforcements from Ramallah. Roadblocks would be in place to hold off enemy reinforcements and allow our forces to charge them and take as many prisoners as possible in order to exchange them for Jibli.

The order of battle of the forces in this action was as follows:

> Force A: Veteran Company B of Battalion 890, led by Aharon Davidi and Elisha Shelem. They would enter the outposts and the village of Beit Likiya.
>
> Force B: commandos led by Meir Har-Zion, whose role was to establish roadblocks on the western and eastern approaches.
>
> Force C: Company A, led by Shlomo Baum, establish roadblocks on the northern approach.
>
> Force D: Company C, led by Marcel Tobias, establish roadblocks on the southern approach.
>
> Force E: Company D, led by Motta Gur, to stand close by as a reserve force in case of complications.

The roadblocks were all set up with the "double ambush" method, an innovation of Sharon's. Their task would be not only to prevent enemy reinforcements reaching the battle zone, but also to initiate encounters with the Legion soldiers in order to capture prisoners to exchange for Yitzhak Jibli.

Elisha Shelem recounts:

I had all sorts of jobs in the battalion. Shimon Pekh, who was both an intelligence and demolitions officer, went to an intelligence officers' course, so they appointed me in his stead. I was in Arik's headquarters for about a month. While I was filling in for the intelligence officer at the headquarters, I realized that when authorizations from the General Staff would come in, he would always expand the scope of the actions as much as he could.

The Beit Likiya action was meant to take prisoners in order to secure the release of Yitzhak Jibli, who was imprisoned during the Azun action. I joined Company B, the company led by Davidi, and we went to the village of Beit Likiya. In fact, we only had to make it look as if we were attacking Beit Likiya in order to get the Jordanian army reinforcements to come to us. There were two ambushes meant to deal with the reinforcements, one by Meir Har-Zion in the east and the other by Shlomo Baum in the north.

But Arik told Davidi and I to occupy the Beit Likiya hill since there was a Legion encampment there. That is how the operation was expanded and became an entire battalion action.

Here are a few excerpts from the IDF archives about the initial report sent to the Operations Branch, as soon as the action was concluded:

> Force B encountered an ambush at 22:15 and returned fire. As a result of this encounter, one of our men was injured in the shoulder. The Arabs kept shooting at the force from a distance until they were silenced.
>
> Force A, led by deputy battalion commander Aharon Davidi, encountered resistance from the southern houses of the village at 23:15 (it seemed the village was ready after encountering Force B an hour earlier). The force charged the southern part of the village and blew up the fence, reaching the outer houses. The

force opened fire on the houses (without throwing grenades at them, in order not to harm the women and children). At the same time, there were shots fired from within the village, a machine gun from the south and two others from the north. The southern machine gun had already severely injured three of our soldiers at the beginning of the action. The force attempted to enter the village twice more and encountered fire from individual rifles and three machine guns. Due to the severely wounded soldiers, the commander of the force decided to pull back and leave a squad on the field to continue to harass the enemy. The force started to pull out, with two of the severely wounded soldiers dying in the process, with the third man's situation a source of concern.

Force C, which set up a roadblock south of Beit Ur a-Tahta, took up position without any issues. A while later they saw an APC approaching from Beit Ur a-Tahta toward Beit Likiya which was carrying reinforcements. The roadblock crew ignited the flame fougasse and the APC stopped. The force opened fire on the APC, three Jordanian soldiers were killed and the other three were taken captive. In response to orders, the force returned safely to base.

The action encountered certain difficulties due to the alertness of the National Guard in the village and the confrontations between the roadblock forces and the Legion. There was a heavy price to pay as well: four IDF soldiers were killed, with five dead on the Jordanian side, as well as three of their men taken captive, as mentioned.

The operation resulted in an unexpectedly severe reaction. The United States reprimanded Israel for the raid and demanded that the captive Jordanian soldiers be returned. The British Ambassador to Jordan warned that the Legion's patience was about to wear out. At the same time, the British implored the Jordanians to show restraint. Israel was appalled by the severity of the United States' reaction and returned the Jordanian prisoners. It also returned to participation Armistice Commission. Sharett wondered whether these small scale reprisal actions, which he himself had initiated, had any effect: "Experience shows, at least using the tricks we have employed so far, that we are not really capable of performing small actions… the bottom line is that the world has the impression there is Israeli aggression." Sharett also pointed out the disadvantage in not taking direct and official responsibility for these actions. In total, and according to everything that has been said above, the Beit Likiya action is not considered a success story.

15. MOTTA GUR ESTABLISHES COMPANY D

The story of the transformation of Battalion 890 continues with the eight-month officers' course in January 1954, in which Levi Hofesh, Moshele Stampel and other cadets participated. The participants heard many stories about the deeds of the paratroopers and Unit 101, and the revolution that was about to take place. Since almost the entire previous command who served under the removed battalion commander, Lieutenant Colonel Yehuda Harari, had opted to leave Battalion 890.[24] Sharon had to immediately rebuild the battalion's command staff. Although he appointed Aharon Davidi, a company commander left over from Yehuda Harari's time, as his deputy battalion commander, he decided to replace the rest of the command staff with new blood. It was a decision that immediately proved its importance in reshaping the battalion's fighting spirit, and later that of the entire IDF.

The source of the best commanders in the IDF was always the Nahal, which in its first years was considered David Ben-Gurion's special project and attracted members from kibbutzim, moshavim and settlement groups

---

24 One of the young officers who left, probably due to his loyalty to Harari, was Arik Regev. Regev stayed in the IDF and returned to Battalion 890 two years later as a company commander, and later took over command of the battalion. Regev served as the Operations Branch's officer of the Central Command during the Six-Day War and then replaced Rafael (Raful) Eitan as commander of the Jordan Valley Division. Regev was killed, along with his Operations Officer Gadi Manela, in a chase after PLO terrorists in the Jordan valley in 1968.

who volunteered or were sent to serve in the military and in officers' courses. These settlement groups were meant to join the agricultural settlements of the kibbutzim: Motta Gur, Sa'adiya "Supapo" Elkayam, Danny Matt – one of the last Gush Etzion soldiers to be captured by the Jordanians in the War of Independence – and others. Ariel Sharon also took care of the future generation of commanders, and as Unit 101 was absorbed into Battalion 890, he sent several soldiers to officers' courses. The tradition of "bringing a friend" remained, and Sharon would arrive, as we will see, at officers' courses to recruit graduates to the battalion.

Levi Hofesh, a platoon commander under company commander Motta Gur, tells:

> There were emissaries coming to Camp 80, where the officers' course took place, on Arik Sharon's behalf, asking those who attended the course whether they would want to volunteer for the paratroopers. A few of Unit 101's veterans were there, and we knew them all. I joined a small group of guys who volunteered, and we transferred to the paratroopers right after the course was done. Motta Gur arrived straight from the Nahal, Arik recruited him, and he established Company D. All his soldiers were recruits who joined before the time of 101, when Yehuda Harari was in command, and all the officers were new. It was a very interesting combination.
>
> The entire company's staff underwent a parachuting course with the soldiers. All the soldiers were "pre-Arik" and the commanders were already "post." A very interesting combination. In fact, it took about a year to merge the two groups.
>
> In the first few training courses, some of the veteran soldiers would run away at night. They'd had no intention of serving in this kind of unit when they were drafted. The previous model in the paratroopers' battalion was marches, special uniforms, red

berets, brown boots – and no combat activity at all! None of them had intended to take part in this kind of activity when they were drafted. Then we turned up, out of the blue, and there was a great commotion. It took us a year, maybe a bit less, until we made that gang into a group of real paratroopers.

The platoon commanders were Dan "Lif" Lifshitz, Moshele Stampel and I. Motta said, "I'm not letting anyone go. I'm going to make them all paratroopers." And indeed, they eventually became one cohesive body.

Levi Hofesh describes the battalion's highly unconventional routine:

In every action, even those the company wasn't part of, Arik would take officers and incorporate them into different forces just to get them into the atmosphere of navigation and combat. The first action I took part in was outpost 100 in the Gaza Strip. I was assigned to it as a PIAT carrier. They formed a section of officers from several units. The action was under Arik's command, both the battalion as well as the auxiliary units. Meir Har-Zion led us; he was always in the lead. That was a serious action! Outpost 100 was one of our first major actions. Unfortunately, we lost one of the new officers who had gone on this first action, like I had, to taste what it meant to be present in a new area. We occupied the outpost; it was overall quite easy.

Ze'ev Solel, who transferred to Battalion 890 with most of the members of the 101, talks about the merging process with the 890:

The merger was a dramatic step which kind of went unnoticed, since it happened while we were fighting; but it could just as easily have failed. We were kibbutz members, good kids with good education, from good schools, members of the Youth Battalions,[25] and by the time we graduated from high school we already had been trained in the basics. We knew what night was and what day was. We each had the basics, even though we did not come from combat units. We knew how to operate weapons, how to navigate at night using the stars. That was all from school, not the army. We had great preparation for the military.

They called us "Tzfonbonim" ["North Tel Aviv bon-bons" an allusion to the more affluent suburbs they originated from] – the veteran soldiers were different. Most of them were Moroccans or other new immigrants, and those who were not came from South Tel Aviv. There were maybe five or six in the entire battalion who came from kibbutzim. They were Uzi Frumer, Micha of Mizra, Tzuri Sagi of Moshav Herut and Elisha Kalay of Tel Yosef.

Arik was more interested in the aspect of "selling" reprisal actions to the General Staff and planning them. Davidi was more of the minister of the interior; he dealt primarily with the military-operational aspect, but helped the commanders organize the companies and train them. Davidi was mostly influential thanks to his character, knowledge, bravery and example.

We were called the "Tzfonbonim" and they called themselves "Mau " out of a sense of contrast. Those of us who came from Unit 101 already had experience, so they looked at us with a certain admiration, they wanted to be like us. We didn't reject their admiration; on the contrary, we encouraged them. The integration worked thanks to Davidi, his sharp mind and composure, his winning personality; otherwise, it wouldn't have worked.

---

25   Gadna (Youth Battalions) is a program for high school students to prepare them for military life.

They also wanted to be heroes and we let them. Motta had a company of Moroccans (Company D), and I give them all the credit they deserve. There was no feeling of discrimination. In Harari's battalion, on the other hand, the Romanians and Hungarians were the officers and the "commoners" were not allowed to enter their mess.

Davidi was the beating heart of the integration. It worked out mostly thanks to him.

Second Lieutenant Uzi (Eilam) Trachtenberg
Currently: Brigadier General (Ret.) Uzi Eilam

Moshe Dayan greeting the troops from Unit 101 after their return from action. (Photo: Abraham Vered)

Motta Gur, Battalion 88, at a briefing before the operation
(Photo: Abraham Vered).

After the Qalqilya operation — Arik Sharon in the center with troops from Paratroop Battalion 88. Avraham Orly, first from the right, in the second row. (Photo: Abraham Vered)

Lt. Col. Arik Sharon briefs Battalion 890. (Photo: Abraham Vered)

Unit 101; Meir Har-Zion leads, followed by Yishai Zimmerman.
(Photo: Asaf Kutin)

Arik Sharon consults with Meir Har-Zion to choose the correct route of march for an action of Unit 101. (Photo: Asaf Kutin)

Moshe Dayan, Arik Sharon and Tibi Shapira. (Photo: Abraham Vered)

Arik Sharon and Aharon Davidi – Operation Elkayam.
(Photo: Abraham Vered)

Disembarking from the boat after the Kinneret operation.
(Photo: Abraham Vered)

Ar-Rahawa Action, "Operation Jonathan."
(Photo: Abraham Vered)

Qalqilya police station. (Photo: Abraham Vered)

Paratroopers on the Gaza Strip border at a night party.
(Photo: Abraham Vered)

16. THE EGYPTIAN FRONT COMES INTO FOCUS

Relations between Israel and Egypt started deteriorating in 1954. Until then, the tone of discussions in the Armistice Commission had been moderate. Unit 101's action to evacuate the Bedouins from the demilitarized zone of Auja did not "break the rules" or escalate the situation; the Egyptians settled for bringing the subject up at the Armistice Commission. The infiltration issues along the armistice line in the Gaza Strip were dealt with within the committee.

However, in late 1954, several events occurred which, when combined, created a difficult atmosphere that clouded the relations between the parties. There were a number of clashes between Israeli patrols and Egyptian outposts on the Strip's border. The encounters escalated, and on March 25, an Egyptian force attacked an Israeli patrol moving along the border, with one of the IDF soldiers being taken captive. Israel retaliated with an action to capture hostages, during which three Egyptian soldiers were killed and one prisoner was taken. In April, there were six ambushes of IDF forces inside Israeli territory. Defense Minister Pinhas Lavon wanted to retaliate by blowing up a bridge inside the Strip, but Prime Minister Moshe Sharett objected. Sharett's policy was "calm is the first priority" and usually sought American aid to influence the Egyptians to lower the level of tension on the Strip's border. The Egyptians refused to return the captive soldier and were also unwilling to discuss the matter in the Armistice Commission. The Egyptian Ministry of Foreign Affairs claimed that the soldier's capture, as well as other actions previously committed along the border, was the act of Palestinians seeking revenge on Israel for their unrelenting war against infiltrators, as well a reaction to the IDF's attack on the al-Bureij refugee camp. Notwithstanding the above, the Egyptian government aspired to minimize dealing with the Gaza Strip as much as it could and shift its focus to internal issues and fighting the British with the objective of persuading them to withdraw their forces from the Suez Canal.

Between April and September of 1954, the IDF reported at least five sabotage actions initiated by Egyptian intelligence. There were also many attacks by the Egyptian outposts on IDF patrols logged. On July 10, 1954, an IDF command car drove onto a mine and its passengers were fired upon by the Egyptians. Israel's response came swiftly: a raid by a paratrooper company on an Egyptian outpost in the Dir al-Balah area, across from Kibbutz Kissufim, in an action called "Operation Eye for an Eye." The force occupied the outpost, killed some of the Egyptian soldiers and wounded many of them, blowing up the outpost's fortifications before retreating.

Egyptian President Nasser was unwilling to deal with the Gaza Strip, because he was worried about the establishment of a regional alliance, the Baghdad Pact, which was to operate under the auspices of the Western powers. The Egyptian President acted to bring Syria, Saudi Arabia and later on even Jordan into the framework of military agreements. Israel saw all these developments as an alarming potential danger, and its sense of isolation only deepened due to the actions and initiatives taken by the Western powers. It was clear to Israel it would not be accepted into the Baghdad Pact, and it gravely feared the flow of weapons to Arab countries in the alliance. Another worry Israel had concerned the British leaving Egypt due to the agreement that granted Egypt control over the Suez Canal. Israel saw this as a violation of the status quo between the Jewish state and Egypt, mostly due to the transfer of the British bases there, along with large amounts of equipment and weapons, to the Egyptians. The IDF estimated that, following the British evacuation, Egypt's aerial abilities would significantly improve, as would its ability to conduct long-term wars. The decision by President

Eisenhower in August 1954 to extend American aid to the Egyptians for military expansion, as opposed to only training purposes, was just as troubling.

Israel's concern regarding the British exit led to a crazy idea, which was later on nicknamed "the mess" or "the affair." The intent was to perform a series of attacks in Alexandria and Cairo, executed by groups of Jewish youth controlled by Israeli intelligence. The actions were supposed to sabotage Western facilities and make it look as if they were being performed by an Egyptian nationalist underground. The initiators of this move in the security structure – perhaps Defense Minister Pinhas Lavon and/or head of the Intelligence Branch Binyamin Jibli – thought this would damage the relationship between Egypt and the Western countries. The attempt failed and the young Jewish people were captured, interrogated and severely tortured. Moshe Marzuk and Shmuel Azer were sentenced to death and the rest to long prison terms. The entire affair severely damaged Israeli-Egyptian relations.

At the beginning of August 1954, Chief of Staff Moshe Dayan visited the United States and discussed, at length, the Israeli-Egyptian relationship with the heads of the State Department. The Americans expressed their concern for the IDF's actions along the Strip's border. Dayan, known for his eloquence, explained that Israel had to deal with three types of incidents across the border from Egypt: infiltrators coming to steal and rob, trigger-happy soldiers at border outposts and organized raids for murder and sabotage inside Israel's territory. According to Dayan, dealing with the first type was the responsibility of the country of origin. The shooting from the outposts would be dealt with by direct contact between senior commanders. As for the third kind, the chief of staff claimed the solution could only be reprisal actions. Dayan's words convinced the State Department, leading them to try to get Israel to sign local commander agreements, not only on the Egyptian border but also along the long and problematic Jordanian border. Gaps between the Israeli and Egyptian positions, among them the different understanding of the UN's status in the proposed agreement, delayed implementation of the arrangement.

Israel took the murder and sabotage actions of the Gaza Strip infiltrators very seriously. There was proof that the sabotage groups were recruited and briefed by Major Mustafa Hafez, head of Egyptian intelligence in the Gaza Strip. As mentioned, there was an attempt by Shmuel Merhav's 101 Unit to assassinate the Egyptian officer, but he was not at home and therefore survived. A few months later, on July 11, 1956, Israeli intelligence used a double agent to send Hafez a book as a birthday present. The gift contained explosives and killed him.

The events at the Strip's border also intensified internal pressure within the Israeli political system. Prime Minister Sharett and the leadership of the Ministry of Foreign Affairs had high hopes that American pressure would work on Egypt, but the ongoing killings of Israeli civilians placed Sharett in an uncomfortable position domestically due to his perceived inaction. For once, he was aided in his policy of restraint by the position of Defense Minister Lavon, who displayed uncharacteristic moderation. Chief of Staff Dayan requested authorization for a major reprisal action against a central objective in the Strip, following yet another murder of a civilian from Beit Shikma on September 25, 1956. Moshe Sharett did not authorize Dayan's suggestion and even voiced his concern regarding another Qibiya-style action.

The worsening security situation was also expressed by further restrictions in movement along roads in the south of Israel. In certain areas, cars were allowed on the road at night only if there were at least three people in them and they were armed. In some areas, this provision applied even in the daytime. There were a few places where a minimum of two vehicles were required to travel together at night.

The head of the UN Observers, Canadian General "Tommy" Burns, decided to intervene when he realized the failure of Israel and Egypt to communicate properly. Burns was in the midst of arranging a "Local Commanders' Agreement" between Israel and Jordan and believed it would be the correct model for relations between Israel and Egypt. Chief of General Staff Dayan was the one Burns came to with his offer, for which he was rewarded with a resounding rejection. Dayan claimed that not only were the Egyptians not doing enough to prevent infiltrations, but Egyptian intelligence in the Strip was responsible for initiating murder and sabotage actions. The contact between Israel and Egypt officially came to an end following Israel's attack on the camp of the Egyptian Military Command in the Gaza Strip on February 28, 1956. In fact, contact had stopped even before that, mostly due to the exposure of the Jewish underground activity in the "Lavon Affair" and the hanging of underground members Azer and Marzuk. Shortly afterwards, and also after a period where the Gaza authorities relentlessly worked to prevent infiltrations, there was yet another turn for the worse in the situation all along the Strip's border.

IDF intelligence was unsure whether Egyptian intelligence or the Muslim Brotherhood were ultimately responsible for these actions, but there was no longer any doubt concerning the growing involvement of Egyptian forces in hostile actions against Israel. Egyptian outposts provided covering fire for infiltrators running from IDF forces, and on February 26 there was written proof of official Egyptian involvement. The squad that murdered an Israeli civilian near Rehovot was captured, and a document was found on one member revealing him to be an Egyptian intelligence agent. Another squad was intercepted near the armistice line while trying to enter the Strip; it too proved to have been sent on a reconnaissance and espionage mission by order of Egyptian intelligence.

These attacks completely contradicted the official Egyptian policy at that time of not aggravating border relations with Israel. The Egyptian leadership were well aware of the situation on the Israeli-Jordanian border and how clashes had almost sparked a war between the two countries. In 1953, Egyptian President Mohamed Naguib and his then Vice President Nasser made it clear – in a written exchange with Israeli officials – that Egypt would persist in its publicly hostile policy toward Israel, while expressing a discrete desire to keep an open channel of communication with Israeli leadership. Ben-Gurion regarded this as Egyptian opportunism and felt that Israel would not benefit from it. Yet the Egyptian rulers had indeed lowered the tone of their verbal attacks on Israel, increased the actions taken to prevent infiltrations from the Gaza Strip, and looked for a way to minimize friction due to the ban of Israeli ships from the Suez Canal.

Egyptian authorities did not regard the Gaza Strip as an integral part of Egypt and did not formally annex it into Egyptian sovereignty. Thus the central government in Cairo was not especially troubled by the effect of IDF actions on the population there. Egyptian intelligence operatives were therefore allowed to make use of the refugees' frustration and send them off on espionage and sabotage actions.

In the meanwhile, as the infiltrations continued – both the economically motivated banditry and the state-directed terrorism and sabotage – Israel's patience was wearing thin. As a result, and given the fears mentioned above regarding the evacuation of British forces from the canal and Egypt, it is understandable why Egypt became Israel's main strategic concern.

On March 29, the Security Council condemned Israel for the "Black Arrow" Gaza action. The decision, supported by the United States and Britain, marked a path toward possible settlement between the two countries and put General Burns[26], head of the United Nations Truce Supervision Organization, in charge of it. This was also an attempt to try to strengthen the UNTSO's position. Burns suggested that, to ease the tension along the border, the IDF would push its patrols back from the border or incorporate Egyptian soldiers and UN personnel into the patrols. Burns' proposal, as expected, provoked controversy among the Israeli leadership. Dayan and Ben-Gurion rejected his proposal, in contrast to Sharett's opinion. Due to Dayan and Ben-Gurion's decisive objection, Sharett was forced to reply to the UN that Israel had rejected the offer. Egypt, on the other hand, agreed to the joint patrol suggestion and was even willing to include UN observers in them.

Burns's attempt to arrange a meeting between the representatives of both

---

26 Eedson Louis Millard "Tommy" Burns was a senior officer of the Canadian army, eventually rising to the rank of Lieutenant General. He commanded the UNTSO from August 1954 to November 1956.

sides to settle border relations was due to a distinct escalation of events along the frontier. Firing on IDF patrols along the border had become a regular matter, as was the placing of mines on patrol routes. The more incidents there were, and with them casualties, the more difficult it became for the IDF.

In the beginning of April, an IDF patrol moving along the border was attacked with mortar and machine gun fire not far from Kibbutz Mefalsim. The force took casualties, and its men, along with reinforcements that came to their aid, charged the nearby outpost. They occupied the outpost and retreated. A few weeks later, an IDF vehicle drove over a landmine; nine officers were killed and another injured. Immediately afterwards, the defense minister and chief of general staff presented the reprisal action plan mentioned above to the closed security cabinet, targeting an Egyptian outpost across from Kibbutz Kissufim.

The Kissufim action had a significance that preceding actions had not had. This had been a direct clash between Egyptian and IDF military forces along the border. The operation had been aimed at damaging Egypt and making a statement regarding the relationship between the two countries. This had also been the first reprisal action for which Israel officially took responsibility.

From 1954 onwards, the focus of the conflict between Egypt and Israel shifted from dealing with the issue of infiltration to a confrontation with strategic significance. While Israel saw the infiltrations as a significant national security issue, the strategic threat from Egypt was perceived as a much more difficult, even existential, issue. This flowed from the British evacuation of the Suez Canal and the alliances with its fellow Arab countries that Egypt had advanced.

17. OPERATION "BLACK ARROW" – GAZA ACTION, FEBRUARY 28– MARCH 1, 1955

A few days before the Gaza action, Sa'adiya (Supapo) Elkayam's company A was in a series of squad commander training sessions outside Gush Lachish (Khirbet Sura). The squad of Second Lieutenant Uzi (Eilam) Trachtenberg – the author of this book – noticed two Jordanians carrying weapons, probably National Guard soldiers, sitting on a hill within Israeli territory. The squad got ready to attack by flanking them; they quickly killed one of the Jordanians and the other one, who was injured, managed to escape, leaving his rifle behind. Sharon, the battalion commander, arrived on the scene less than two hours later and asked to hear about the incident. Later on, and in a way that was typical of Sharon, he ordered two other platoons from the regiment to come to the area and set up ambushes.

Uzi (Eilam) Trachtenberg's account of how he made his way to Battalion 890 includes his recollection of this action:

> In the pre-draft physicals I was given an insufficient fitness grade. It was a crisis for me, after all the sports I was involved in, not just sports but Youth Battalions as well, I couldn't understand why I'd been handed down such a sentence. I went to another medical committee and also didn't get great results. When we were drafted, I went to a third medical committee, and they told me it wasn't going to change – my physical evaluation would remain

the same. So instead of going to the most sought after combat unit back then, the Nahal, I went to the Youth Brigades.

I do not exactly recall how I heard the rumors about Unit 101. I obviously wanted to join, but instead of going to the Sataf base on my own – where Unit 101 was – as many of my classmates did, I filed a regular Request for Reassignment (Form 55). A few weeks or months passed, I went to my base commander, who was a major, and asked him about my transfer request status. The commander replied, without batting an eye, that he did not put it through. I was so furious with myself for messing up. I looked for any way out of the Youth Brigades, to bypass this block set by my base commander.

I had the option of joining the Academic Reserves.[27] I wanted to go there even before I was drafted, because of my physical status. I thought of going to the university, to study math or physics, subjects close to my heart. I arrived at the Academic Reserves' acceptance tests; I passed the officers' course test and got accepted to the Technion to study electronics as part of the Academic Reserves. Then the Youth Brigades base received an order to release me. And so, instead of going to Unit 101 to be among my combatant classmates, I went to the Technion.

In the summer, an officers' course was held for the academic reserves. During the course, I checked in with the general secretary of my kibbutz and found out I was designated to be an agriculture teacher. I said, that's it. I'll finish the course and complete my military service, then we'll see. And that's the way it was.

---

27 The "Academic Reserves" is a special program in which the IDF postpones the compulsory military service of a select group of high-school graduates, sending them to get academic degrees before completing their compulsory service.

In the last week of the officers' course, I went to another medical committee and received full combat fitness status. When the course was over, and I was a second lieutenant with the red beret we used to wear back then, I arrived at the acceptance and assignment base and said I wanted to join the paratroopers. Why? I knew my friends from Unit 101 had already joined the paratroopers. Gladly enough, they agreed. I went to Tel Nof base, straight to the office of the battalion's commander, Major Ariel Sharon. When I arrived at his office, he told me, without any introduction: "I heard about you from your friends; you have instructing experience, you'll be alright. You can be an instructor in Supapo's company A, at the squad commanders' course. Off you go." And that's how it began.

Two or three events from the squad commander's course stand out as milestones for me. The first, which I believed placed me on both Sharon's and Supapo's radars, was this: We were in squad commanders' training, not far from the border, around the Lachish region. The designated squad commander was Ze'evik Sverdlik. We went as a squad into the hills, suddenly Ze'evik tells me: "There are legionnaires there, there are armed Arabs there, a few meters from us. What do we do?" I said: "Do what they taught you to do. Lay down covering fire – establish a base of covering fire with a machine gun – we'll flank them and attack." And that's the way it was. We left the machine gun crew as a holding force, started moving to the flank, the machine gun opened fire and we charged. One of the armed guards was killed and the other was injured but got away. We took the dead body and the two weapons, brought them to an area a bit further [from the border]. Two or three hours later, Sharon was already there. He came over because he wanted to hear exactly what went on. That week, he ordered two more companies to arrive at the area and set up ambushes.

A short while later, they planned a reprisal action against the Jordanian Police at Surif. Meir Har-Zion was tasked with attacking the police station with the reconnaissance platoon, which were mostly still 101 people. Supapo and company A had a small role, "just to block," and Supapo was really disappointed at that, to say the least.

The cherry on top was, as always in Battalion 890 under the new command, to be the main force raiding the police station. This role was given, as mentioned, to Meir Har-Zion because Arik knew exactly who he could count on. Supapo, who even shed a tear, said that he deserved to do it, that company A deserved to do it, but Arik decided that company A would lead the column crossing the border on the way to Surif village and the police station. There was always a leading squad at the front, it would take care of any ambushes along the way if there were any. Who did they choose for the leading squad? Trachtenberg. Why? Because they saw what he was capable of back then. It was obvious to me that I was known in the battalion by then. It felt very good.

I led the column and slightly behind me were Arik and the command staff. Arik's radio operator approached me and told me that he'd received a message saying: "Turn the wagon around." I went to Arik and updated him. He told me: "You heard nothing."

A few minutes later, the radio operator came to me again and said: "They're saying we need to turn the wagon around and they're waiting for confirmation." I went to Arik again and he repeated: "We heard nothing." The third time, Arik had no choice. We stopped before the attack on the police station and went back. We were already 1.5 kilometers deep inside Jordan. I started realizing what Ariel Sharon was all about when it came to completing objectives. We later learned that the Jordanians knew what was about to happen and had a rather unpleasant welcome planned for us. Arik promised Supapo that, in the next action he would get the role of attacking the main target, and so it was.

The Gaza action, or "Black Arrow" as it was later nicknamed, on February 28, 1955, was a major crossroads both for the IDF and Israel, as well as for the relationship with Egypt led by Nasser. We will later discuss the argument between Prime Minister Sharett and Defense Minister Ben-Gurion before the action was decided upon. (Ben-Gurion replaced Lavon after he resigned due to the scandal proceeding from the clandestine operation in Egypt.) We will also find out and elaborate, in a separate chapter, why this action is considered a political turning point.

Following a penetration of *fedayeen*[28] into Rishon LeZiyon and the murder of Henry Levi of Rehovot, Defense Minister Ben-Gurion and Chief of General Staff Moshe Dayan decided – with the authorization of Prime Minister Sharett – on a large-scale action against military targets. Battalion 890 was tasked with penetrating a military camp near Gaza City and blowing up facilities there. Close to the military target lay the water supply facility and the train station, which were also incorporated into the mission. The operation was given the codename "Black Arrow" and it took place on the night of February 28, 1955. It included, as most of Sharon's activities did, an ambush to prevent Egyptian reinforcements from arriving on the scene. It was a complex action, with various objectives planned by Ariel Sharon, Aharon Davidi and the commanders of companies A and D.

The forces taking part in the action:

> Force A: Led by Sa'adiya (Supapo) Elkayam along with auxiliary forces led by Hillel, Uzi Eilam and Tibi Shapira. This force was composed of members of company A in the squad commanders'

---

[28] An Arabic term for various military groups willing to sacrifice themselves for a larger campaign. In the period we are discussing the term was synonymous with terrorist in Israel.

course, mostly from kibbutzim and farms. The role of the force was to break into and occupy the camp, which housed the Egyptian army headquarters in the Gaza Strip, and to demolish its buildings.

Force B: Led by Moshe Yenuka, would be held in reserve near the border. Its job was to secure the infiltration zone of the attacking forces that passed between the Egyptian outposts to prevent surprises from the rear.

Force C: Led by Captain Danny Matt and Shimon (Katcha) Kahaner, included the battalion's reconnaissance platoon and consisted mainly of ex-Unit 101 troops. Its role was to block the Gaza-Rafah road and stop any Egyptian reinforcement that might arrive from the south.

Force D: Led by Motta Gur, included the company D soldiers who were divided into three sub-forces commanded by Levi Hofesh, Dan "Lif" Lifshitz and Moshe Stampel. The force's role was to occupy the train station and the camp next to it.

The role of force E, led by company D's Company Sergeant Major Avraham Halawa, was to serve as a close reserve to the battalion commander. The General Staff's Training Department sent observers, Major Michael Kartan and Lieutenant Colonel David "Dado" Elazar;[29] they were at the headquarters with Ariel Sharon.

For the first time in IDF history, some of the troops received "Uzi" submachine guns as well as "bazooka" anti-tank launchers.

Below is the story of the Gaza action, according to articles based on the operation's debriefing and materials from the IDF Archives:

"Roy, a tractor driver and a member of Kibbutz Ein HaShlosha in the

---

29 He went on to serve as chief of the General Staff during the Yom Kippur War.

Negev, died tonight and his friend was injured in an encounter with a group of infiltrators," the main headline of the *Yedioth Ahronoth* newspaper read on January 25, 1955. "Automatic fire was opened on the two tractor drivers who were busy plowing the farm's fields." The following day, it was reported that "the Egyptian-Israeli Armistice Commission will convene for an emergency session to discuss Israel's claim."

Israel didn't put much hope on Canadian General Burns, who led the armistice commission that had been established after the War of Independence (War of 1948). The series of attacks by the Egyptian *fedayeen* on the civilian population begged for a response. It was decided to hit the Egyptians with a heavy blow, to make them realize that the terror attacks would take a toll on them as well.

The reprisal action was planned shortly thereafter, under the codename "Black Arrow." It was almost automatic that the defense minister and chief of general staff should task the paratroopers battalion commander Ariel Sharon, and his deputy Aharon Davidi, with the operation.

"The objectives of the reprisal actions," Dayan later wrote in an article he published in 1964, "was not revenge or punishment, but deterrence. To bring the authorities of the Arab countries which operate the anti-Israeli terror units to the realization that it would be more damaging than beneficial for them." The road to deterrence, even if not specifically mentioned in the operations order, ran through hitting enemy soldiers on their own territory: a fitting punishment, as far the Israeli security leadership was concerned, for those who believed that Jewish lives were cheap.

Taking part in actions and operations of this kind was the greatest ambition of the paratrooper commanders. Their volunteering spirit, operational prestige and, of course, ego were on the line. There are some who still remember, to this day, the tears coming down Sa'adiya (Supapo) Elkayam's cheeks when he was told he would not be attacking the main objective at the Surif police station operation, and how Sharon promised him he would make it up to him next time. "Black Arrow" was a good opportunity to please everyone. Sharon selected officers from companies A and D for the mission. Each of them commanded a small force and so everyone took an active part in the attack.

The "Black Arrow" file in the IDF and Security Forces Archives contains the operational orders, as they were given to Sharon and Davidi. "IDF's aim is to react to murder and intelligence missions based out of the Gaza Strip," it said. "Guidance – infiltrate the military camp in the Gaza area and blow up its facilities. The enemy soldiers must be harmed only in a case where they interfere in the completion of the mission." As for casualties on our side, the operation order was unequivocal, "No man is to be left behind."

The intelligence file given to Sharon included information about the area and the enemy's forces and their deployment. However, most of the information about the area was based on aerial photos which turned out to be outdated, a British report on the camp from 1947. The remaining information was based on officers' contemporary knowledge of the area, mainly Sharon's. "The battalion did not conduct a preliminary patrol for fear that might only enhance the enemy's alertness," the operation's debriefing said.

"The Command's intelligence officer offered to send out an aerial patrol but the battalion commander [Sharon] trusted the interpreted aerial photos as well as his personal knowledge of the area." The interpreters of the aerial photos had marked the fence around the camp, which was supposed to be lit, as a landmark. When they arrived at the fence, they would breach it and infiltrate the camp. "Mistakes regarding the location of the fence and the lighting later became very important in the course of events"

Uzi (Eilam) Trachtenberg relates:

> I learned, being alongside Ariel Sharon as his intelligence officer, how he would "get" operations, how he convinced the General Staff, or Southern Command in this case, to authorize them. We at the battalion knew there was to be an action. Supapo would be compensated for not really having had a central role in the Surif police station operation. Company A got the "cherry" on the Gaza action, attacking the Egyptian forces' headquarters north of the city of Gaza.

We started combat preparations and the way they built their forces was very typical of the paratroopers back then. There were five forces participating: company A, Supapo's, was almost as big as a platoon; company D's force, led by Motta Gur, was also about the size of a platoon; there was Danny Matt's force, a blocking force south of the city of Gaza, with the reconnaissance platoon, most of whom were "relics" of Unit 101. "Katcha," Shimon Kahaner, was the platoon commander, but Danny Matt was appointed the force's commander; there was a small northern blocking force led by Sergeant First Class Halawa and a reserve force led by company A's deputy commander, Moshe Yenuka, which stayed across the border as a rescue force.

Supapo chose three force commanders and they each had about ten men. One force was led by Hillel, my platoon commander; the second was commanded by Tuvia Shapira, "Tibi," and I was entrusted with the third force. Motta Gur built his force from company D men, with an officer – Motta's platoon commanders – leading each of the squads. Ariel Sharon, the battalion commander, left with a minimal staff, which naturally included Aharon Davidi, the deputy battalion commander. The entire force taking part in the action was about as big as one company.

There was much excitement. We took a truck down south toward Kfar Aza and took some of the female soldiers, who were parachute packers, with us. There were a lot of kibbutz girls, since the kibbutz boys were drafted to the paratroopers, the girls volunteered to be parachute packers and the bravest of them even went through a parachuting course. We sang songs, and for a minute even forgot we were going to battle; we were happy.

Supapo was in high spirits; he'd finally received the main objective in a battalion action. Our platoon was set to go to the front, and just like at the Surif action, Supapo chose me and my force for the lead section. We had to spread out, with Supapo behind us, Arik and his staff behind him and the rest of the force behind them.

Night fell and we were given the "classic" dinner we got before the actions: a kind of meat and potato stew, something inedible and sometimes even causing diarrhea. We weren't too hungry. Arik said a few last words and we were off to the action, walking through the fields of the kibbutzim near the Gaza Strip, until we reached the border, marked by a very deep trench. There was no fence.

We went into the trench and climbed out the other way, we were beyond the border and our hearts skipped a beat. We slowly and quietly advanced and when we were already two kilometers deep inside the Strip, between outposts on the path that was relatively the safest to walk through, there was suddenly a shout heard: "*Min hada?*" [Who's that?].

We obviously didn't reply and kept walking, but then the silent night was shaken by a gunshot and then another one. They weren't firing at us but in the air, and I, without asking any questions or wasting any unnecessary time, charged forward with my force. We went into the outpost, which turned out to be a small one, secondary to one of the larger outposts, and had a few Egyptian soldiers in it. We got into the trenches and cleared them with bursts of fire while running. Suddenly, a dark figure stood right in front of me in the trench, the first Egyptian I'd ever met, and he was armed with a rifle pointed right at me. I shot him first, from very close range, and he collapsed into the trench. We passed through all the outpost's trenches and found that some of the Egyptian soldiers had been killed and others probably escaped to the main outpost. There was no fire coming from the main outpost and it was quiet again.

Once the firing subsided, Arik came to see us with Supapo, and I witnessed a consultation he had with Davidi, Supapo and Lieutenant Colonel David ("Dado") Elazar, the General Staff observer. There was quite a dilemma, since our objective was a long way away and we had basically already exposed ourselves; the question was, how to proceed from here? Arik decided we would keep going. The decision was approved by the two observers who came with us. Dado, the General Staff's observer, seemed to me to be really old back then, almost an "old man," and I wondered why he would want to take part in an action beyond the border. Years later I learned that it was a well-known and acceptable protocol for General Staff officers to be given the right to take part in actions and draw conclusions through personal and direct impressions. The other observer was a major, also from the Training Department, Michael Kartan, who unfortunately died on our way back to the border after the action was over.

We kept going with my force leading once more and Supapo right behind me. We arrived close to the camp's headquarters, which was our destination. Motta Gur's force was headed to the train station, which was west of the headquarters, and Motta split from the main force to go there. Simultaneously, Danny Matt and Katcha, along with the patrol platoon, arrived at their roadblock-ambush position south of the city of Gaza and reported their arrival to Arik. This entire thing took place in an orange grove north of the city of Gaza. Arik decided to set up his staff position in the corner of the grove, a few hundred meters north of the Egyptian headquarters camp, and Supapo started leading our force toward the camp.

Our plan was to attack the camp from the west, with two forces – mine from the right and Tibi's from the left – the force led by Hillel, my platoon commander, was a reserve and his men carried bags of explosives in order to blow up the camp after we occupied it.

We followed Supapo past the train tracks. Those were remnants of the British Mandate and led north from Gaza. We passed the cluster of train tracks and quietly went west alongside it. On the cluster itself, right on the train tracks, there was an Arab civilian walking and we quietly waited with the dilemma: *Do we eliminate him or not? Maybe he saw us and will notify someone, or maybe he didn't?* The man kept walking, we held our breath, standing still, and he just went on his way.

We kept going south toward the camp, and according to the plan, we were to arrive at the breaching point west of the camp. At a certain point, Supapo started "drifting" east. We saw a road and beyond it there were fences, Supapo whispered: "That's the camp!" We used a Bangalore to breach the camp gate, and kept going into the camp while firing bursts. There were a few tents there and we noticed a few soldiers. We pushed on, in the heat of battle, and shot into the tents. It turned out we only attacked a small camp which guarded the water pumps for the city of Gaza. The Egyptian forces' headquarters was much bigger and was west of the road, not east of it.

Tibi and his squad also came in from my force's right and engaged in a firefight. During that shooting I felt a strong pinch in my right hand, sort of like a blow. I was wounded in my right palm, and when the firing died down a bit and it was quieter, I asked one of the soldiers to bandage me.

Suddenly we heard Davidi, the deputy battalion commander: "Supapo, this is the wrong place!" Supapo came to his senses and realized he'd identified the wrong camp, and immediately called out: "Follow me!"

We left the water pumps camp and quickly went single file along the road south. There were fences to our right, lights and positions spread out along it. Supapo hurried and he kept walking along the fences, lit by the fence lighting. Supapo's entire small force's column – a machine gunner and two bazooka carriers – as well as my force, were exposed to the Egyptian soldiers at their positions, we were "sitting ducks," which resulted in many casualties. All the Egyptian positions along the road opened fire. Within less than a minute, I heard Supapo yell 'Ahh' and saw him go down. I ran to him; the machine gunner and bazooka carrier were lying next to him. I could hear cries of "Medic! Medic!" from my force as well, I leaned over Supapo and saw he had a large hole in his head, in his forehead. He'd been in the head hit by a burst, and it was obvious to me that he was no longer alive.

I asked the medic to treat the wounded men in the ditch. I myself went down to the ditch and tried directing fire against the positions that were attacking us, to somehow break ourselves free from the fire that had us pinned down. And then, out of nowhere, Aharon Davidi appeared next to one of the Eucalyptus trees beside the road. Since I felt bad not joining him, I stood up as well. Davidi asked: "Uzi, what's going on here?" I said: "Supapo is dead and there are quite a lot of wounded." Davidi continued calmly, as if there was no fire raging around us: "What are you doing?" I said: "We are firing back, trying to pin down the Egyptian forces in their positions." Then Davidi took out a hand grenade from his webbing and threw it at the nearest position; when I saw him do that, I also took out a grenade and threw it at one of the positions beyond the camp's fence. Davidi continued his questioning, "What are you going to do now?" I replied that I would take anyone from my force who wasn't hurt and enter the camp from the north side.

The wounded were already bandaged and relatively safe in the shelter provided by the ditch beside the road. I called those from my force who weren't wounded to follow me. About three soldiers got up and came with me to the north side of the camp. There was barbed wire there and we had to use wire cutters. We quickly breached the fence and went inside, when I noticed, from the corner of my eye, Hillel with his squad and the explosives, which we would only use later.

I ran forward, first clearing the firing positions, then the buildings and finally the headquarters. When I reached the middle of the camp, Micha Livni, from Kibbutz Genosar, who was right next to me the whole time, was hit and died at my side. I kept running with the guys behind passing me grenades and clips for my Uzi the whole way. I ran without allowing myself to think of the dangers before me, completely focused on the mission of clearing the camp.

When I reached the headquarters building, I only had two soldiers with me, Ze'evik Sverdlik and another soldier whose name I cannot remember. The headquarters building was deserted and suddenly everything went silent. It was a strange silence, almost screaming after all the shootings and explosions, after all the injuries and the cries of pain.

I sent Ze'evik to tell Davidi that the camp was cleared, and we could start blowing up the structures. Hillel, the platoon commander, and his force entered the camp through the north breach along with Prizant, the battalion's sapper, who blew the charges on the buildings. Prizant was efficient and practical and seemed like he enjoyed every minute of his role. Motta, along with his force and his wounded, came back from the action at the Gaza train station. Sharon also came over from his corner in the orchard. We loaded our dead and wounded, along with the weapons that we had collected, onto the truck.

Meanwhile, I received an order from Davidi to go and blow up the water pumps at the small camp as well. I took Prizant and Peretz – a soldier from my force who wasn't hurt – with me, we piled sacks full of explosives on ourselves and went to the water pumps. Prizant quickly laid the explosives and lit the fuses while the three of us quickly ran for cover. We didn't get far enough because the fuse was too short, and we immediately heard the explosions. Rocks went flying everywhere and one of them hit Peretz in the back of the neck, and he lost consciousness. We thought he was dead and Prizant and I carried him to the truck where we loaded him up with the dead. A few minutes later, Peretz woke up, saw he was in the wrong place, rose and calmly got off the truck, as if nothing had happened....

There was another hectic consultation between Arik, Motta and Davidi in which they debated whether we should take the truck we had seized out of the camp and breach through the Egyptian border station across from Kibbutz Kissufim, or walk with the wounded and dead on foot. In the end they decided to travel on foot and go back along a route close to the one we came in through, between the large outposts. We took the dead off the truck and improvised additional stretchers from rifles and shirts. I again got the job of leading the point unit, in addition to carrying the wounded like everyone else. We already had seven dead by then, the eighth was Michael Kartan who was killed on the way back, and quite a lot of wounded, and we had to carry them all. There wasn't anyone who wasn't carrying a stretcher or supporting a wounded man.

We were on our way back, but all the outposts were on high alert by then. We walked between them, the way we came in, only this time they fired on us. Luckily, they used tracer bullets, so we could see the burst coming and drop down immediately; when the firing stopped, we kept walking. We finally reached the border.

Then someone told me that there was someone injured and left behind, in the Wadi we'd passed through. My men were already across the border, in Israeli territory. I ran back there and found there was indeed an injured man there. I picked him up on my back in a "wounded carry" and brought him back across the border. I realized it was Major Michael Kartan, who caught a burst in the stomach and was no longer alive. All in all, we had one ambulance with a medic waiting across the border. When I saw all my men were back and being treated, I went to the ambulance and told Dr. Shibolet, the medic: "Doctor, look, I have a wound here." He took off my bandages and said: "Straight to the hospital!"

Force D, the blocking force led by Danny Matt and Katcha, waited at the planned ambush site and had roadside charges and a gas jerry can called "fougasse," in order to stop the Egyptian reinforcements that would arrive at the battle zone from the north of the city of Gaza. 23 Egyptian soldiers were killed by the blocking force's fire on the two trucks that were hit from the roadside charges.

The "Black Arrow" action ended. The death toll: all in all, thirty-six Egyptian soldiers had been killed and twenty-eight more were wounded. The water supply was destroyed, as was most of the Egyptian camp. All the mission parameters defined for the operation had been fully accomplished, but there was a harsh price to pay – eight of our soldiers had been killed and thirteen were injured. The following day, the newspaper *Yedioth Ahronoth* reported on the many Egyptian soldiers killed in the action and that there were also a few Israeli casualties. Our eight dead soldiers were not mentioned, not even the next day.

In his farewell speech to the Paratroopers Battalion following the Sinai War (Suez Crisis), Sharon stated that the battalion's real actions had begun with Gaza. The year 1954, although it was not full of operations, was still essential for drawing initial conclusions and forging the battalion.

Referring to operation Black Arrow, Sharon said, "In planning the operation, the possibility of reinforcements arriving, especially south of Khan Yunis, was also taken into account. The conclusion was that a serious blocking force should be placed six kilometers south of the city."

The operation itself, as Sharon said, was among the most massive the battalion had ever undertaken. With that said, success was highly questionable at certain moments. The target was not studied well enough, a neighboring position was initially attacked, and the enemy thus had time to organize.

Sharon said that, after the main target had been misidentified, there was an attempt to breach the camp through its eastern gate. The company commander was killed but the camp was not breached. Not only was the entire action in doubt, there was also a serious fear of high casualties. At that moment, Second Lieutenant Uzi (Eilam) Trachtenberg reached the real target and, following the failure that occurred by the camp's eastern gate, he succeeded in breaching the camp with his men from the north. When his men started penetrating the enemy positions, the balance of power shifted. When the troops breached the Egyptian positions and engaged in hand-to-hand combat, the enemy's resistance ceased and they started fleeing. Following the Gaza action, and talks that took place in the battalion's headquarters, we concluded that we should choose commanders like these, who the men would run after into battle. Platoon and company commanders, who would personally lead the charge, had to be the best fighters in their units.

For composure under fire, identifying the grave mistake and leading the operation to its completion, deputy battalion commander, Major Aharon Davidi received the Medal of Courage. Captain Sa'adiya (Supapo) Elkayam and Second Lieutenant Uzi (Eilam) Trachtenberg were also rewarded with the Medal of Courage for their part in the action.

Following the action, Defense Minister David Ben-Gurion, together with Sharon and Davidi, visited the injured men of the battalion at Tel Hashomer Hospital. He went from one soldier to the next in order to congratulate the wounded men. In an extraordinary letter to the chief of general staff, Ben-Gurion asked that the following would be told to the members of the unit, following operation "Black Arrow":

> At the cabinet meeting on March 6, 1955, I gave a detailed account of the battle that took place in Gaza, and the government unanimously decided to let the unit that took part in the battle know – all its soldiers and commanders and the entire Paratroopers Battalion – that we value and admire their spirit of exceptional Jewish courage shown in this battle, as well as the great planning and execution by the Paratroopers Battalion.

Ben-Gurion added:

> I am sure that the government's feeling is shared by the entire country. The love and admiration of the people of Israel are directed at the Paratroopers Battalion, which once again publicly proved the primacy of Jewish heroism and added a glorious page to the book of victories of the Israeli Defense Force.

18. OUTCOMES OF THE GAZA ACTION

The reprisal action against the Egyptian military camp north of the city of Gaza, later nicknamed "Black Arrow," stirred up considerable controversy. The Israeli force, which was as large as a company, had eight casualties and thirteen wounded, but the losses on the Egyptian side were thirty-six casualties and twenty-eight wounded. As the details became known, Prime Minister Moshe Sharett defined the action as an event that might cause international complications and future dangers. Though Sharett had agreed to the operation, he did not conceal how appalled he was by its outcomes. Nonetheless, he actually regretted that the approval of the operation and its execution would be credited to David Ben-Gurion, who had recently returned from Sde Boker to the helm of the defense ministry, and reaped all the glory. Ahead of his return to government, Ben-Gurion had announced that even though security came first, they had to strive for peace. Sharett, who knew Ben-Gurion and his style very well, realized that the old-new defense minister intended to keep the reprisal policy in place, even if that would impede peace.

Ben-Gurion was soon given the opportunity to apply his approach. Since it turned out that Egyptian intelligence personnel were involved in the murder near Rehovot, the chief of staff sought the approval of the defense minister to carry out a retaliatory action. Ben-Gurion gave his approval, following which Prime Minister Sharett also concurred and approved the operation, despite his earlier opposition that had prevented action. His reluctance dated from before Ben-Gurion's return to serve as defense minister. As mentioned above, there were more than sufficient grounds for a response to the attack. These included the execution of the Egyptian Jews convicted in the "Lavon Affair," the ban on the passage of Israeli ships in the Suez Canal and the crystallization of the Baghdad Alliance – all these contributed to the decision to launch a major retaliatory action. The policy of not claiming responsibility for the actions continued, and at the initiative of the defense minister, an IDF Spokesman's announcement was drafted, as follows: "An IDF unit was attacked by an Egyptian force near the city of Gaza. A fierce battle formed between the attacking Egyptian force and the IDF unit, which started in Israeli territory and went all the way into the Gaza Strip."

The Gaza action revealed an important issue within Israel. It was, so it seems, the opening shot of the clash between Prime Minister Sharett and Defense Minister Ben-Gurion about the aims of Israeli security policies. Sharett preferred political activity and believed that Israel should turn to the great powers for help in dealing with its security problems. Ben-Gurion, who was still very much involved with events even while at Sde Boker, saw with concern how Moshe Sharett's line was taking over security policy. Ben-Gurion saw the Sharett-led policy as a dangerous erosion of Israel's positions, causing ongoing damage to its sovereignty. Ben-Gurion's return to the Ministry of Defense heightened the confrontation between the two leaders. Sharett presented to Ben-Gurion, in writing, the damage the Minister of Foreign Affairs believed Israel had incurred: putting Israel in the dock at the Security Council, difficulty in obtaining security guarantees and military aid from the United States, and even a danger of casualties within Israeli territory should Egypt decide to respond to the action that had so damaged its prestige.

Ben-Gurion immediately responded to Sharett's letter, completely rejecting all his claims. He did not give too much weight to the decisions of the Security Council and insisted on mentioning that, even if we were to behave in an exemplary way, we would not change the balance of the

Security Council in our favor. Ben-Gurion also addressed the extremism of Egyptian leader Nasser's position and saw his declarations of aggression as a real threat to Israel's security.

In fact, the Gaza action could not have come at a worse time for Nasser. He was struggling both internally and externally; damage to the armed forces, which were the core of his power, would have further diminished his prestige. While Prime Minister Nasser had succeeded in overthrowing President Mohamed Naguib in November, the humiliation he endured due to the attack by IDF soldiers on Egyptian troops in Gaza was perceived as a personal risk for him, and even aroused fears that he might be overthrown.

At a speech Nasser gave just a few days after the Gaza attack, before graduates of the Egyptian Military Academy in Cairo, he promised he would never forget the attack on the Egyptian forces. Nasser threatened that Egypt would not depend on the Security Council to defend itself. Should Egypt be attacked, he said, it would strike back against Israel with military force, even in response to mere border clashes.

The "Black Arrow" action, in all its aspects, received massive coverage in the Israeli press. As the following descriptions show, each media platform in Israel reported it in a way that matched its own worldview.

Davar came out with the front-page headline: "Eight Israeli Soldiers Killed and Fifteen Injured in a Battle Near Gaza." The newspaper provided an update on the action, as it was reported in Egypt and the UN, and attempted to predict Britain's reaction. The following day, the newspaper published that the spokespeople of the British Ministry of Foreign Affairs used sharp and peremptory language when addressing the Gaza action.

In addition to its headline, *Haaretz* added a sub-headline which saluted the "Bravery Demonstrated in Hand-to-Hand Combat." The newspaper quoted the United Press report from Cairo of Egyptian Prime Minister Gamal Abdel Nasser declaring to the Egyptian government that they must take a stand against Israel's aggression in Gaza and respond forcefully. The *Haaretz* correspondent in London reported that the action was "a blow to the calming efforts" by the three Western powers.

HaBoker reported that foreign journalists in Israel actually praised the IDF. The newspaper criticized Israeli information services, which had been silent for too long and were not doing their job properly. According to the newspaper, Prime Minister Sharett had placed the responsibility on Egypt and believed that Israel must now decide whether to keep going down a path that would cause additional casualties or whether to completely avoid hostilities. A journalist for *HaBoker* in the United States quoted evaluations by Egyptian and Western diplomats linking the incident with the return of Ben-Gurion to the position of defense minister.

Maariv backed the decision that led to the action, without reservation. The options Israel faced, so the newspaper claimed, were either to ensure the security of the Israeli frontier or to protect our "good reputation" and simply refrain from responding to Egyptian provocations. The newspaper published an article entitled "Did Egypt Learn a Lesson in Gaza?" in which they estimated that Egypt had interpreted Israel's lack of reaction in previous months as a sign of weakness, and hence increased the terror attacks. *Maariv* stated that all casualties on the Egyptian side during the Gaza action were soldiers and that no Egyptian civilians were harmed in the operation. Subsequently the newspaper distilled the question facing Israel, the great powers, the UN and Egypt: What next?

Kol HaAm, the newspaper of the Israeli Communist party, did not content itself merely with describing the action and reporting on the reactions criticizing it around the world and in the UN. The newspaper decided to present the views of the Soviet newspaper *Pravda*. "The operation," according to *Pravda*, "is part of an imperialist conspiracy to fan the flames of hatred between Israel and the Arab countries."

The *Herut* newspaper chose to feature an article titled "The Heroes of Gaza Speak." The newspaper commenced with a paean of praise for the IDF. It went on to vigorously protest the fact that neither the affair of the Bat Galim ship, which was stopped at the Suez Canal and had its crew arrested and tortured, nor the hanging of the two young Jewish men in Cairo, nor even the endless infiltrations by Egyptian intelligence soldiers into the Gaza

Strip, had shocked the world – whereas the Gaza action, in which, as the newspaper claimed, Israeli soldiers managed to intercept an Egyptian unit moving inside Israeli territory, "shook" the world.

At the first meeting of the Israeli-Egyptian Armistice Commission following the action, Egypt expressed its desire to reestablish informal contacts with Israel. The communication was slow to develop and could not bridge the gap between the countries that had resulted from Israel's action and its outcomes. The Gaza action was a crossroad: though it had been executed according to the reprisal policy the IDF had been following for some time, it brought on a divisive change in the relationship between the two countries. Nasser did not see the Gaza operation as an Israeli tool to apply pressure on Egypt to prevent infiltrations, but rather a signal that Israel saw Egypt as an enemy.

Another bloody incident, during a wedding held at Moshav Patish in the southern region of Israel on March 23, 1955, resulted in the death of a female volunteer and the injury of fifteen people. The trail of the attackers led to the Gaza Strip and the defense minister posed some penetrating questions to the chief of general staff: How long would it take to conquer the Strip? Was the IDF ready for a war against Egypt? Was the IDF ready for war against all of the Arab countries? As a practical option, Ben-Gurion suggested "banishing Egypt from the Gaza Strip." Sharett vehemently opposed Ben-Gurion's proposal and decided not to discuss it within the reduced security cabinet, where Ben-Gurion was guaranteed support, but at the meeting of the full cabinet, which rejected the proposal.

Ben-Gurion knew that occupying the Strip would bring about a direct confrontation with the three Western powers who had signed the declaration guaranteeing the armistice lines, as well as promising to react to any breach of those lines. Israel was unaware of the action plan developing in the White House's National Security Council, in which they had discussed – among other things – withholding financial aid, commercial embargoes and even military actions, against anyone in breach of the agreement. In fact, Ben-Gurion did not really mean to change the Israeli security policy and intended to keep to the status quo. All he was looking to accomplish was a change in the "appeasement" line Sharett took when it came to preventing infiltrations and coping with murder actions backed by Arab governments. Prime Minister Sharett, Ben-Gurion claimed, supported a passive stance within the government, to which he could not agree.

The squad commanders' course, which Supapo led until the Gaza action in which he fell, concluded with a festive ceremony overseen by company commander Danny Matt, at the Tel Nof base. There, a surprise awaited Uzi Trachtenberg: the commendation for his part in the Gaza action. But a greater and more meaningful surprise was in store for him when the company returned from leave. In an interview he described what transpired:

> The squad commanders' course ended and there, at the graduation roll call, the company commander who took over for Supapo, Danny Matt, read my citation [for the Medal of Courage] from his papers and called me over to receive [the decoration]. My mother was there. I am not sure she understood exactly what went on…
>
> The entire company went on leave with some of the graduates, not many, of them being assigned as squad commanders in the battalion, in several companies. A few of them went straight to infantry officers' course and the rest stayed, as corporals, in a special company which was still called company A.
>
> When we came back from leave, Davidi called me to his home and told me that the company would remain combat-oriented, they would add the reconnaissance platoon to it and I would serve as acting company commander (until Meir Har-Zion came back to the battalion, which took five months). I skipped straight from being a squad commander to a company commander, which was unorthodox in the military back then. That is how I actually learned about Arik and Davidi's approach; to them, the thing that mattered was your personality and not necessarily your rank.

What mattered to them the most was how you would perform when faced with a serious test, how you functioned under fire. That is how I became a company commander while only being second lieutenant, and had two platoon commanders under me who were first lieutenants, Ovad Ladginsky and Tibi Shapira. They were both more senior than I was; Ladginsky had even served in the Palmach. For me, it was quite a test of leadership, authority and creativity.

Meir Har-Zion was on leave at Ein Harod, forced on him after the killing of the Bedouins he performed as retaliation for the killing of his sister and her friend in the Judean Desert.[30] That is how I came to be acting commander of company A for the full five months he was away.

I lasted in this role thanks to my command experience and had no problem with it. The one who served as my wise mentor, advising, reassuring and encouraging me, was deputy battalion commander Davidi. He helped me many times – and not just me, but everyone. We weren't in touch with Arik much except when the company undertook patrols across the border, when I would get his approval. His involvement was almost solely when it came to the operations. Arik knew how to get them approved, plan them and execute them the way Unit 101 used to. We used to perform these small-unit penetrations, then the actions got bigger in terms of the number of participants. The attack on the police station at Khan Yunis, that was already a large-scale action.

---

30 In February 1955 Har-Zion's sister, Shoshana, along with her boyfriend Oded Wegmeister undertook an illegal hike into Jordanian territory. They were captured, abused and murdered by Bedouin. Har-Zion and three ex-members of Battalion 890 carried out a lethal, private retaliation action that resulted in the deaths of several Bedouin. On their return, Har-Zion and his companions were arrested, but eventually released without charge as a result of protection from their colleagues in the army. For full details of the affair, see Chapter 32.

19. OPERATION "ELKAYAM," AUGUST 31, 1955

In this action, the IDF attacked the Khan Yunis police station, which housed forces operating against Israel. Seventy-two Egyptians were killed in this operation, following which more Egyptian troops were posted to the Gaza Strip.

Lieutenant Colonel Menachem (Menn) Aviram, the head of the Operations Branch at the General Staff, released a short one-page operational order to the Central Command's Operations Department officer.

> Background: On the night of August 29–30, 1955, murderous attacks were carried out on the country's border by Egyptian squads.
>
> The IDF's aim is to respond to these actions.
>
> Goal: Attacking the Khan Yunis police station, inflicting damage on it and its occupants.
>
> Method: To be executed on the night of August 30–31, 1955.
>
> Half-tracks will be operated across the border should it be necessary for executing the mission.
>
> Our forces should be extracted and evacuated even if doing so involves occupying any Egyptian outposts that interfere.
>
> Communications: Operation progress should be constantly reported to the Operations Division, as it occurs.

The operation order, initially code named "Avraham," was given to Battalion 890 by the Operations Division and described damaging military facilities and vehicles at the Strip in retaliation for recent violations of sovereignty by the enemy. The missions were initially supposed to be spread across two nights against Egyptian military camps and outposts, including ambushes on vehicles. However, according to the summary report of the Khan Yunis action, submitted to the Operations Division by the Central Command – still named "Operation Avraham" before becoming "Operation Elkayam" – the retaliation actually focused in one major action on the Khan Yunis camp and the police station within. The Command intended on occupying the Palestinian Brigade headquarters at the Khan Yunis police station, damaging the structures and tents around it and killing as many military personnel as possible.

To secure extraction for the operating forces, Outpost 132 at the entrance to the village of Abasan was to be occupied, and the soldiers there killed.

Among the restrictions placed upon the operation's commander was a directive to avoid hurting civilians, including women and children of course, as much as possible. The order was to harm only those interfering in the execution of the mission.

The first order, according to the report, was given by the chief of general staff to the head of Central Command, at which point the target had not yet been determined, only that it would be an Egyptian military camp or military facility. The Khan Yunis police station was selected as the objective of the action in a discussion held at the head of Central Command, which the Battalion 890 commander also attended.

The Khan Yunis action was later known in military code as "Operation Elkayam," named after Sa'adiya "Supapo" Elkayam, Battalion 890's company A commander who fell during the Gaza action. Operation Elkayam was the first armored action of the paratroopers, with the aid of half-tracks to occupy and blow up police buildings. The Khan Yunis police station was, in fact, a British Tagart fort,[31] three stories high. Such an operation was a new type of combat for the paratroopers.

The action plan, as detailed in the report by Lieutenant Colonel Shmuel Galinka, Operations Division officer at the Central Command:

The force was divided into five sub-units:

> Force A, the size of a company, on half-tracks – its mission was to occupy the Khan Yunis police station and demolish it.
>
> Force B, the size of a company, on foot – its mission was to conquer Outpost 132, digging in and standing by to rescue force A (if necessary).
>
> Force C, the size of a platoon – its mission was to establish a roadblock about six kilometers north of Khan Yunis, on the main road.
>
> Force D, the size of a platoon – its mission was to establish a roadblock south of Khan Yunis, about six kilometers north of the Rafah refugee camp, on the main road.
>
> Force E, the size of a company, on foot, plus the 81 mm mortar squad, would be held in reserve near the border.
>
> Support – a battery of 25-pounder guns and a battery of 120 mm mortars, providing direct support for the occupation of Outpost 132 and the Khan Yunis police station.
>
> Battalion Aid Station – between Nirim and the Khirbet Ma'in camp, along with the reserve company. Three command cars

---

31 A string of heavily fortified police stations had been built by the British authorities across Mandatory Palestine. They were named after British police officer and engineer Sir Charles Tegart, however the name is pronounced in Hebrew "Tagart."

would be waiting by the border, fitted out to transfer casualties to the first-aid station.

The battalion's command, along with the reserve company, would remain near the border.

A forward command post at Khirbet Ma'in would operate from 21:00 and would house the head of Central Command, Operations Division officer and intelligence officer, with the necessary measures for control and communications to higher command[32].

Departure from the assembly area – 21:00
Crossing the border – 23:00

The force would be ready to leave the assembly area by 21:00 on August 30, and with it five M3 half-tracks. The additional half-tracks from the Armory Corps would not arrive until midnight. Hence, the head of Command decided to postpone the action until the following night. In a briefing held on August 31 at dusk, deputy battalion commander Davidi noticed the tension surrounding the battalion as a result of the operational delay. Davidi told a story about a young bull that saw a loophole in a fence and asked to go through it quickly, to have its way with one of the cows, while an old bull told him he should enter slowly and have his way with all of the cows. The laughter from the entire battalion showed how well placed, and well timed, was Davidi's quip.

Force A consisted of troops from company D, commanded by Motta Gur, and was responsible for breaking into the police building.

The force was split into six units, as follows:

1. Platoon 11, led by Levi Hofesh.
2. A platoon assembled from different units, led by Tibi Shapira.

---

32 Galinka's report does not mention, at this point, the first-time use of a Piper aircraft to maintain communications.

3. Platoon 12, led by Moshe Peles (Moishale Stampel).
4. Platoon 10, led by Hagai Erlichman.
5. A force led by Doron Mor had to take over and secure the intersection on the main road, through which the battalion would proceed.
6. A sapper unit.

During the battle, Aharon Davidi replaced Motta Gur after the latter was injured when the police station was breached.

Troops from Force E, led by company commander Raful, was tasked to occupy and clear the entrenched position near Abasan village, in order to allow Motta Gur's force to reach the police station without any delay, as well as ensuring a corridor for retreat. The Force A soldiers established the roadblock north of Khan Yunis, led by deputy company commander Uzi "Trachtenberg" Eilam, as well as the southern roadblock led by platoon commander Ovad Ladginsky.

Levi Hofesh, a platoon commander in Motta's company, tells of his role:

> In the Khan Yunis operation I was navigating and led my platoon and the entire company D force, mounted on half-tracks. I am still convinced, to this very day, that I had the right route. Suddenly I heard Motta, over the radio, "Stop, you are going the wrong way." I told him: "Motta, we're on the right way," but he insisted and said: "Stop and come back." The road ran through Khan Yunis, but we went around it to bypass the area we thought was dangerous. To take care of the police, they designated one force that would go with Motta and Stampel and another force led by platoon commander Hagai Erlichman of Ein Shemer. I arrived at my area and the mission was to attack a few soldiers and tents. Motta's force got a bit confused and attacked from the wrong direction. They took severe fire; Motta was hurt and so was Stampel. The force still managed to enter the police station and execute its mission. Once I finished off the Egyptian force, I stayed to protect the perimeter until they cleared the station and

got the explosives, which our one-eyed demolitions officer Yirmi Barandov made for the occasion.

Tzuri Sagi was a platoon commander in company E, which was led by Raful. This is how he describes his company's role:

> The role of company E in the Khan Yunis action was to occupy Outpost 132, which was near Nirim, and part of Abasan. Motta Gur with his company D troops were supposed to reach all the way to the Khan Yunis police station with half-tracks. Raful said the Egyptians would place a mine every meter around the perimeter, and if they had done so here, and we started dismantling them under fire, we would take many casualties. We would charge in two columns in the standard method of attacking a fortified post. The platoons' commanders would lead us straight to the trenches under covering fire, and so we would minimize the casualties. And that's the way it was. I ran with the right column through the minefield, and nothing happened to me. But in the left platoon, Amnon Lavi from Sarid stepped on a mine and was killed, and Dan Ziv was injured. We did not repeat that method of Raful's anymore.

Doron Mor tells of the Khan Yunis battle from his point of view:

> A few months after I arrived at Battalion 890, as an officer, the battalion received a mission of a kind that had never been performed. We were to execute an armored night raid (using half-tracks) on a police station located at the heart of the second-largest city in the Gaza Strip. The raid was led by Motta Gur, the company D commander, and the commander of the sapper unit was platoon commander Moshe Stampel (who was later killed during the War of Attrition while serving as a battalion commander, chasing down a Fatah squad in the Jordan Rift Valley).

Stampel's platoon was divided in two, half went with the sappers, who were supposed to blow up the police station, and the other half had to secure the intersection on the main road. I was assigned to lead the second half, a young officer without any combat experience. The action was a success and we only had one young paratrooper from Sarid killed from our forces. Motta and Stampel were hurt, but the police station was demolished and about seventy enemy soldiers and *fedayeen* were buried in its ruins.

In the report submitted to the General Staff, Lieutenant Colonel Galinka, who was the Central Command's operations officer, noted the successful execution of all missions, with the demolition of the police station and the occupation and demolition of Outpost 132, and that the two roadblocks that were not used because enemy reinforcements never arrived.

Our forces suffered one dead and eight wounded.

The enemy suffered about sixty-one dead and forty wounded.

Galinka's report drew five main conclusions:

1. This type of action was different from anything the Egyptian enemy had known before and was therefore a complete surprise. Without a doubt, the enemy's fear of mobilizing forces at night on vehicles, in the Strip, allowed us to conquer and destroy their outposts one by one. It is possible that the next time we take a similar course of action, the enemy may react more aggressively and quickly.
2. The half-tracks are an efficient vehicle for transporting infantry at night, especially moonlit nights. The standard of the half-track drivers and the technical level of the vehicles themselves are far lower than what is required for battle.
3. In such an action, it is better to train on similar objects with live fire. This will ensure a perfect, smooth and precise execution of an action as complicated as the one in question.

4. It is necessary that a unit like the one that breached the Khan Yunis police station will have not only a commander but also an officer to replace the commander in case of injury [Galinka, for some reason, did not think the first lieutenant was good enough…]
5. We have proven the efficiency of the Piper airplane to communicate with forces that are out of radio contact (in this case, the roadblocks).

Sharon's words at the farewell ceremony from the Paratroopers Brigade after the Sinai War (Suez Crisis) stressed the new dimension – breaching the Khan Yunis police station with armored vehicles (half-tracks) and arriving at the destination as fast as possible. The aim was to attack the police forces before they could regroup, and maintain the element of surprise. The key was speed, the inherent surprise of the raid and massive fire. To demolish the police station, we did not have to occupy the whole building; it was enough for us to suppress its occupants and clear the place where the explosives were supposed to go. The fear of enemy forces that might intervene made it necessary to place roadblocks, and in light of experience of the former Gaza action, a route was selected to secure the retreat.

Indeed, as Lieutenant Colonel Galinka mentioned, it was a complex action which proved how far Ariel Sharon had gone in venturing into multi-objective and multi-participant actions. The outcome of the action, with high enemy casualties compared to only one death on our side, testified to the operative capability Battalion 890 had achieved. "Operation Elkayam" was an impressive milestone for Sharon the tactician. From now on, he would better "orchestrate" all the elements needed for the success of the reprisal actions.

20. CUSTOMS HOUSE ACTION, "OPERATION SA'IR," OCTOBER 22, 1955

Following the kidnapping of Nahal soldier Yaakov Minkowski by Syrian soldiers, the government – led by Moshe Sharett – decided to perform a reprisal action aimed at capturing Syrian soldiers and exchanging them for the Nahal soldier as well as five other troops who had been captured ten months earlier while on a mission for military intelligence. They had been attempting to maintain Israeli listening devices installed on Syrian telephone lines in the Golan Heights. The five, who were being held at the al-Mezzeh prison in Damascus, were three paratroopers: Meir Yaakobi, Gadi Kastelnitz and Jackie Lind, as well as two Golani soldiers: Meir Moses and Uri Ilan.

Deputy Chief of General Staff Haim Laskov tasked Ariel Sharon with the action, and he chose to perform a combined action with two simultaneous objectives:

A. The Customs House next to the Benot Yaakov Bridge.
B. Urpiya Outpost, a few kilometers north of the bridge.

> "Sa'ir" Operational Order, no.14/55
>
> Intelligence: Following an increase in Syrian activity, resulting in the kidnapping of a Nahal soldier from Kibbutz Gonen, the chief of general staff is planning on performing a reprisal action aimed at capturing Syrian prisoners to be used as hostages for the

four soldiers, the body of Uri Ilan who committed suicide[33] in the Syrian jail and the Nahal man, all of whom are in the hands of the Syrian enemy.

<u>Aim</u>: Capturing Syrian prisoners without causing enemy casualties, in order to take as many prisoners as possible.

<u>Method</u>: The responsibility to achieving the aim lies with Northern Command headquarters.

a. Battalion 890 will execute the operation on the night of October 22–23, 1955.
b. Our forces to return to the Israeli border by 23/04:30.

<u>Forces and tasks:</u>

a. Battalion 890 will set an ambush on the Customs House-Al-Qunaitra road, east of the upper Customs House, in order to capture any soldiers on the move on that road.
b. Battalion 890 will take control of Urpiya Outpost (Outpost 22) while setting up roadblocks to prevent any possible enemy movements and preventing the Syrian unit's retreat from the outpost.
c. Standby along the Syrian border for possible enemy reaction.

The spatial defense settlements in this section will be put on alert level C.

The Border Police battalion operating in the Northern Command's area will be operatively subject to Northern Command Headquarters as of 22/22:00.

---

33 The captured troops had suffered harsh interrogation at the hands of the Syrians. Uri Ilan committed suicide in the course of the questioning, leaving behind a note saying: "I was not a traitor."

d. The air force will be on increased alert to supply possible assistance in extracting Battalion 890 or any other developments that might arise on the Syrian front.

The ambush raid on target A, the Customs House, would be carried out by the forces of Tibi Shapira, Arie Biro, Ovad Ladginsky and Yoav Shacham. The forces of Meir Har-Zion, Danny Matt and Mussa Ephron took part in the occupation of objective B, the Urpiya outpost. A few Syrian soldiers died in the exchange of fire and five Syrian soldiers were captured, as well as a Syrian officer from the Circassian community. The prisoners were held at the Rosh Pina police station. There were no casualties on the Israeli side.

The operation itself was a success, but it was not until five months later, in which time Syrian prisoners had been captured, mostly during the Kinneret action, they were able to exchange forty-one Syrian prisoners for the five Israeli ones. The body of Uri Ilan, who committed suicide in a Syrian prison, was also returned.

21. KUNTILLA ACTION, "OPERATION EGGED," OCTOBER 27, 1955

Paratroopers Battalion 890, led by Ariel Sharon, raided the Kuntilla Police station, Sinai.

Following a penetration by the Egyptian army into the Nitzana area, the occupation of our outpost near Be'erotayim, the killing of one IDF soldier and the capture of two others, Battalion 890 paratroopers were sent on a reprisal operation. It was the first such action deep inside Egyptian territory – about twenty kilometers into the Sinai Peninsula – aiming at conquering Fort Kuntilla, across from the Faran brook, taking as many prisoners as possible and seizing weapons, equipment and military documents. The operation was given the IDF codename "Operation Egged."[34] The forces left for the operation on October 27, 1955 and were led by scout Aharon (Erol) Eshel, who got close to that police station in a preliminary deep reconnaissance.

Colonel Uzi Narkis, head of the Operations Division at the Operations Branch of the General Staff, signed the "Egged" operational order on October 23, 1955.

> <u>Intelligence</u>: The IDF intends to respond to the Egyptian attacks from October 26, south of the demilitarized area, at the Kuntilla police station, which serves as a department of the Egyptian border police.

---

34 Egged is the name of the bus company (actually, a workers' cooperative) that had a near monopoly on public transport in Israel until very recently.

Aim: Capturing about fifteen soldiers of the Kuntilla police station.

Method: Execution of the operation will be by Battalion 890 on the night of October 27–28, 1955. The forces will return to Israeli territory no later than October 28 at 05:00. The police stations should not be demolished. Any military documents and equipment found there should be confiscated.

Air Force: The air force will be on increased standby to aid with extraction or any other developments that might occur toward dawn.

Communications: Southern Command will be responsible for constant communication with the General Staff via air reconnaissance.

Report: Success – "Hapoel"; failure – "Maccabi"; back to Israeli territory – "Beitar"

The operation included the following forces:

Force A: Reconnaissance company led by Meir Har-Zion, to attack and occupy the southern structure from the south.

Force B: Company E led by Rafael (Raful) Eitan, to attack the main building.

Force C: Company B led by Mussa Ephron, to occupy the northern building.

Force D: Led by Haim Nadal, to block the road from the north.

Force E: Led by Tibi Shapira, to block the road from the south.

When Arik Sharon stepped down from command of the Brigade 202 after the Suez Crisis (Sinai War) he made a speech to the brigade officers – both in regular and reserve service – in which he devoted time to a description and analysis of the Kuntilla reprisal action. Sharon stressed that the mission of capturing prisoners was a difficult one which required much discipline and restraint.

To prevent any possibility of the enemy shifting forces from one target to another, the idea formed to attack all three goals simultaneously. Sharon remembered the tremendous pressure of organizing the scheduling when the order was received on Thursday morning and had to be executed that same night. The action, so Sharon claimed, was successful and achieved the capture of twenty-nine prisoners, the deaths of twelve Egyptians and the seizing of a large quantity of weapons. Sharon praised total discipline exhibited by the troops in penetrating the positions to extract the prisoners without killing them.

Militarily, it was the epitome of perseverance, willpower and commitment to mission. About fifteen kilometers before the destination, the force encountered an obstacle and an insurmountable wadi. According to the plan, they had to go by vehicle until they got close to the destination. The action would normally be cancelled if such an obstacle was encountered; Sharon thought the forces would be able to go fifteen kilometers on foot, perform the action and walk back the way they came before daybreak. They did indeed do so, dismounting from the vehicles and walking all the way to the fort. In a battle that lasted twenty minutes, they occupied the fort and captured twenty-nine Egyptian officers and men, among them wounded ones who were carried on the shoulders of the paratroopers. The IDF suffered two dead and two wounded men.

22. THE SABCHA ACTION, "OPERATION VOLCANO," NOVEMBER 2, 1955

Following an infiltration by Egyptian forces into the Nitzana area, the IDF attacked that area on November 2, 1955. Seventy Egyptian soldiers were killed and forty-eight were captured. The IDF suffered seven dead.

In the 1949 Armistice Agreement, it had been stated that the Nitzana area would be demilitarized. As time went by, both the Egyptian and Israeli armies had more forces in the area than the agreement allowed. In June 1955, Israel began marking the border; however, despite the marking, there were still clashes in which forces on both sides suffered casualties.

The Egyptian army began establishing defenses near the border. They placed a regular-service battalion, reinforced by artillery batteries, and dug out seven positions for them in the cliffs of Sabcha and Ras-Siram. To complete the formation, they infiltrated across the border and positioned one of their outposts ("Lily") within Israeli territory.

When the Egyptians refused to evacuate those positions, the Israeli government decided to instruct Chief of General Staff Moshe Dayan to immediately retaliate against the Egyptian violations of the armistice agreement. However, destroying the Sabcha bases required a large concentration of forces which would take time to organize. Therefore, it was decided, in the meantime, to perform an immediate reprisal action. This would serve to distract the Egyptians to a different front while preparations for the major operation could be finalized. The diversion actually took place on the night of October 27–28, 1955, and we named it "Operation Egged." The raid on the Kuntilla military camp, about twenty kilometers from the Israeli border, contributed to the surprise that came five days later with "Operation Volcano" – the Sabcha action.

The Sabcha action's order was issued by the Operations Branch to Southern Command. It was dispatched by special courier and indicated that the Egyptian military had taken over several positions in the demilitarized zone of Nitzana and was holding onto them, with an infantry battalion (3–4 companies) set to defend it.

This order defined the IDF's intention:

> <u>Intention</u>: To respond to the Egyptian violation of the armistice agreement in the demilitarized zone of Nitzana and to demonstrate the sovereign control of the State of Israel in that area. Stand by to carry out operation "Shachar" (a pre-plan of the action in the demilitarized zone of Nitzana) by order.
>
> <u>Aim</u>: Southern Command forces will occupy the Sabcha outposts, clear them of enemy soldiers and then withdraw from the demilitarized zone. After the evacuation of the outposts the demilitarized zone will be held by police forces only.
>
> D-day is set for November 2 and Zero hour – as early as possible.

Southern Command was explicitly ordered to assign the responsibility for the occupation of the Sabcha outposts to Brigade 1 (Golani) and make Paratrooper Battalion 890 subordinate to the Brigade's command. The General Staff's order included an option to activate a prior plan called "Operation Shachar" to conquer the Gaza Strip in case of a massive reaction by the Egyptian army, which could escalate to a comprehensive battle across the entire Strip.

"Operation Volcano," the conquest of the Sabcha outposts, was entrusted to Golani Brigade – led by Colonel Haim Ben-David (Chabad) – by Meir

Amit, the head of Southern Command, in accordance with the Operations Branch order. The paratroopers of Battalion 890 and the rest of the forces were also subjected to Golani command, which the head of Southern Command believed was best for the mission at hand.

During the preparations for the operation, there was a serious communication breakdown between the Golani Brigade commander and the paratroopers' battalion commander. There were two reasons for this. First, Ariel Sharon was simply offended at being subjected to the Golani Brigade commander and refused to make contact with him. Second, the difficulty was due to the multitude of targets, the nature of the terrain and the direction of movement of the forces – the paratroopers attacked from south to north while Golani attacked from north to south. These and other difficulties led to each unit operating independently. Therefore, the communication between Ariel Sharon and the Golani Brigade commander amounted only to announcements about their departure for the mission and their returning from it.

The outcome was that the Golani Brigade commander commanded only his own forces and occupied the three outposts at Ras-Siram, while the Battalion 890 commander separately commanded his own forces to conquer the four Sabcha outposts.

Among the many documents from Operations Branch, Brigade 1 (Golani) Command and the Battalion 890 Command found at the IDF archives, there was also a document called "Main conclusions and highlights summarizing Operation 'Volcano.'"

Conclusions:

1. In the preparation stage, Southern Command Headquarters invited the Golani Brigade commander as well as the Battalion 890 commander to the Southern Command planning meeting, while the Battalion 12 commander was not invited. At this meeting, two separate plans were offered for "Operation Volcano" by the commanders of Golani Brigade and Battalion

890. This led to a complete loss of control later by the Golani Brigade's command – who had overall command of the operation – over the preparations for the action and the execution of the operation by Battalion 890, which acted independently.
2. A transport plan by the command authority had to include a transport plan of the operational forces. Southern Command's quartermasters did not take part in the transport schedule of Battalion 890's convoy and that of the Artillery Corps, which included approximately ninety vehicles moving toward the assembly area.

An initial summary of the operation's command (Brigade 1 command):

1. The operation's Field Headquarters only had control over Battalion 12 during the action.
2. During the entire action's execution by Battalion 890, the operation's command had no control over the paratroopers. The Battalion 890 commander reported to the operation's command only twice, both through Southern Command Headquarters' chief of staff – reporting the beginning and end of the operation.
3. It is possible to perform a battalion-scale attack at night, with artillery support. but only by pre-arranged shelling. This requires only minor adjustments.
4. Golani Brigade's summer training allowed it to:

    a. Develop a brigade combat procedure and practice the effective movement of the Headquarters and other units in the minimum of time.

    b. Effectively coordinate between Field Headquarters and its own units, as well as the Artillery Corps' units.

    c. Maintain an adequate level of night attack performance, on the battalion level, against targets deep inside enemy territory.

The fruits of the exercises were apparent at all stages of the operation.

Battalion 12's commander remarked on the discrepancy between the intelligence data on enemy forces at the Wadi Siram outposts. The company-level plan focused on Outpost 260 A – since intelligence reported that was where the Egyptian force was concentrated – rather than their true disposition, which was at the Rivkah 2 outpost. The Battalion 12 commander also criticized the planners for failing to consider enemy lookouts (meaning teams stationed on possible access routes to raise the alarm when enemy forces were spotted on their way to attacking the outposts). He claimed that an elite unit should have been assigned to deal with those sentinels. In his opinion, the lack of such a force disrupted the entire attack, since the battalion's entire A Company charged the enemy lookouts en route to the destination. The Battalion 12 commander further claimed that the battalion did not have up-to-date aerial photos of its destinations and was not provided with enough time for its commanders to study the existing photos. The Battalion 12 commander also remarked that he had no reserves for immediate commitment. The reserve company, as he rightfully pointed out, consisted of new recruits and was meant to be deployed only for basic tasks. The lack of a suitable combat reserve delayed the occupation of the Rivkah 2 Outpost.

Initial Battalion 890 summary:

1. At approximately Zero+25 the entire enemy formation collapsed, even before official reports on the final occupation of the targets arrived.
2. During the attack, there was no firing plan executed by the Egyptians to block the breach of the outposts using machine gun fire. Their machine guns only fired at our forces when they noticed them.
3. Even though it was Battalion 890's first artillery-aided action, both the battalion's Field Headquarters as well as subordinate

command exhibited great adaptability to dealing with the problems presented by such aid.
4. The Battalion 890 Headquarters was mobile and close to the forces in the field. At Zero+45, Battalion 890 Headquarters was in place for the first occupation, which allowed it to fully control auxiliary forces throughout the action.
5. Organization and consolidation after the attack:

There was no seizure of arms, equipment, etc., nor any wounded men evacuated prior to the end of the fighting. The forces charged with seizure (force C) and casualty collecting forces (reservist company A) were designated in advance at the pre-action briefing, which allowed each force to concentrate on its main mission.

In a report he submitted, the Battalion 890 commander stated that the main factor in his battalion's success was taking maximum advantage of the element of surprise by selecting a circuitous route that went around enemy positions, allowing for an attack in the rear. Sharon also stated that the decision was made to attack all vital destinations from three directions simultaneously. Doing so had allowed for the immediate takeover of the center of the enemy's formation, its Headquarters and its ballistic support weapons. The Battalion 890 commander also mentioned taking advantage of the element of deceit, which undermined the enemy's morale. Sharon pointed out that the movement of the entire logistics convoy, thirty vehicles in total, from the assembly point at Jabel Aziz toward the Sabcha at zero-hour, with their lights on, made it look like even larger forces were moving toward the targets. Sharon also commended the artillery support, which according to him completely undermined the enemy's resistance and covered the movement of the Israeli forces right up to them reaching the enemy positions. In addition, he praised the ability of the entire battalion's command ranks in studying the intelligence problems from aerial photos and performing commanders' observations on enemy targets.

The Battalion 890 commander concluded that the battalion had demonstrated outstanding leadership at all levels of command, with a strong desire and an iron determination for success and victory.

The total disregard for the very existence of the Golani Brigade, as well as for the status of the brigade's Headquarters as responsible for coordinating the entire operation, stands out in post-action reports as well.

First Lieutenant Ze'ev Solel, formerly of Unit 101, who was already a reservist when he was called to take part in the operation, says:

> When the Sabcha action was organized, the usual truck that would pick us reservists up for all the reprisal actions came along. There wasn't a battalion of reservists yet, only companies. I was a platoon commander for Elisha Shalem's Company C, which was already a reservist unit as well.
>
> We had to take one of the positions, a sort of hill. When we got to the position, it was already empty. Arik decided to enter from the back, a classic Arik move. Always looking to surprise, coming in from another way. It was the bread and butter of Unit 101's tactics, then in the battalion, from one person to the next without having to officially teach it. The Sabcha action, the line of vehicles with their lights on to seem like a larger force, those are great Arik ideas. The Sabcha was a very successful action, genius!

The platoon commander, now-retired Brigadier General Tzuri Sagi, tells of the part played by Raful's Company E:

> I was the platoon commander in Raful's Company E during the Sabcha action. We took the central ridge which dominated the battlefield. Arie Biro with his Company B (rookies) conquered the front line. This was the plan: the surrounding force came in behind the Ezuz mountain, hidden and unseen. The position which had to be taken was the Sabcha, which was occupied by an Egyptian battalion.

Arik briefed us, the commanders, at Ezuz mountain and established the forces and their roles:

Yehuda Reshef's company of reservists had to take the rear formation of the entire Egyptian command, which was west of the ridge. Arie Biro's Company B had to attack the forward formation. And we, Raful's company, had to conquer the ridge overlooking the Sabcha. Meir Har-Zion had to go further around and arrive from the north, overtaking the small Sabcha. Tibi Shapira had to move toward Kseimeh and set an ambush there, which served as a roadblock in that direction. Tibi's force was armed with model-73 anti-tank bazookas. Tzvika Levanon, along with a Nahal company, had to attack a position situated between Kseimeh and where we were.

All the vehicles that dropped us off had to go on to Nitzana, and at zero-hour had to turn on all their lights and start driving southwest. We wanted the Egyptians to think the motorized force was about to attack them, and then we came from behind, from the flank; and that's how it happened.

Arie Biro, along with his rookie company, cleared the front line and we, Company E, cleared the high ground. Har-Zion, of course, took the little Sabcha. An armored force met Tibi's force and they fired on them with the bazookas, but it did not penetrate their armor, so he pounced on them, "by hand" as it were, and stopped them.

Later, in order to evacuate, we had to clear minefields toward Nitzana, because we were at the rear. Katcha (Shimon Kahaner) from the reservists' platoon was injured in the stomach and had to be evacuated right away. It was a tough situation. Yirmi Brandov took a platoon of prisoners, along with an officer who led them, to the opening in the minefield, and from there we could keep going without worrying about the mines. Katcha was lucky that way, that's what saved him.

"It was a brilliant action," Tzuri Sagi summed up, "a plan which incorporated classic deception, from the academy of Arik Sharon."

At the Natan base near Be'er Sheva, the mess hall had prepared a "kingly feast" for the paratroopers in advance of the operation and sent it to Sde Boker. However, the food was spoiled. Rafael Eitan describes what happened next in his book, *A Soldier's Story*, "A few hours after the meal, we all were stricken with diarrhoea. While we were walking toward the destination and during the charge on the Sabcha outposts, we had to go aside and drop our trousers and... the noise and stench enveloped the desert."

Arik did not say much about the Sabcha action, "Operation Volcano," in his farewell speech to Brigade 202, at the end of Sinai campaign. He didn't mention the fact that the head of Southern Command, Meir Amit, had appointed Golani Brigade commander Colonel Haim Ben-David, along with two Golani battalions, to lead the action. Sharon chose to almost completely ignore the commander that Meir Amit put in charge of him. He spoke of the Sabcha action as if only Battalion 890 had operated there. Sharon explained that since the enemy's position was fortified at the front, the decision was made to attack from the rear. Sharon also said that due to lessons learned from the Kuntilla action, it was decided to attack all the destinations simultaneously, and the outcome was successful both in terms of the complete execution of all the battalion's objectives and the speed in which they were achieved.

The statements of Golani Brigade commander Haim Ben-David, as well as the criticisms from the head of Southern Command, Meir Amit, reveal disciplinary violations when it came to administrative matters, which had operational consequences. Colonel Ben-David, who was formally the operation's commander, claimed that Southern Command Headquarters was in fact unable to control Battalion 890, led by Ariel Sharon, since there was no radio connection with the battalion. This was not due to a technical issue, but because Battalion 890 avoided entering the command's network, even though they were instructed to do so. The Golani commander also claimed that Sharon did not notify the operation's command about the battalion's course of operations, and only reported on the beginning and end of the action. At the end of the operation, the paratroopers battalion's operations officer compiled an operation briefing, to which the head of Southern Command, Meir Amit, reacted with anger and astonishment. Amit noted the inaccuracies in the briefing and implied that the lack of control by the operation's Headquarters – meaning, the Golani Brigade commander – stemmed from discipline issues. And so, along with the praise the paratroopers received regarding the execution at the post-action briefing, there were also some unsettling questions regarding the battalion's level of discipline and its unwillingness to accept authority or incorporate other forces in its actions.

Immediately after the combat ended and without stopping to brief the forces – that was supposed to take place the following day at the Tel Nof base – Sharon hurried to Southern Command Headquarters to get authorization for an action south of Mount Hebron the following day. Eli, his trusted driver, was tired, and the intelligence officer, Uzi (Eilam) Trachtenberg, volunteered to drive to Be'er Sheva. It is possible the late hour and the fatigue caused the accident at one of the curves, a few kilometers east of Ktziot. The jeep rolled over, and Eli the driver and Quartermaster Officer Yaakov ("Double Jack") were thrown clear, but without any major injuries, while Sharon and the intelligence officer were trapped under the jeep. Eli and "Double Jack," guided by the intelligence officer, released both him and Sharon, and an ambulance was called to drive the two injured men to the hospital in Be'er Sheva, and from there to Tel HaShomer Hospital. The action south of Mount Hebron was not executed and Sharon was disgruntled about that for a long time.

23. OPERATION "OLIVE LEAVES," KINNERET ACTION, DECEMBER 11, 1955

In the Kinneret[35] action, an IDF force raided Syrian outposts on the eastern shore of the lake. The ostensive reason for this operation was harassment of Israeli fishermen on the Sea of Galilee by Syrian troops. The operation resulted in the deaths of about fifty Syrian soldiers and the capture of thirty more. The IDF suffered six dead.

It is hard to believe such a large-scale action was justified due to sporadic shooting at Israeli fishermen, at a time where there were not many severe attacks by the Syrian armed forces. A reasonable hypothesis is that the motive was strategic. Egypt had signed a defense pact with Syria, which included a mutual defense clause should one of them be attacked by a foreign power. Some say that Israel was seeking to undermine Egypt's status: if Nasser reneged on his promise, he would appear unreliable; if he tried to fulfill it, but failed, he would look weak. In September 1955, Nasser had announced an $83 million deal with the USSR to supply the Egyptian military with modern Soviet weaponry through Czechoslovakia. The Czech weapons had not yet arrived in Egypt at this point, which made it possible for Israel to gain better strategic positions in order to defend its border and maintain supremacy over the new alliance, even after the Czech weapons arrived. From a military standpoint, this complex and ambitious action was proof of the confidence the IDF had in the paratroopers to carry out such a large

---

35 Lake Kinneret is known in English as the Sea of Galilee.

operation, in contrast to the small unit operations Unit 101 had initially performed.

An interim report by the Northern Command's Operations Branch, among the documents found in the IDF archives, does not define the motives for the action but simply presents the plan of the operational commander (the commander of Battalion 890) as given at the commanders' meeting held in Beit Yerach:

> Mission: conquering and demolishing all Syrian outposts above the northeast of the Sea of Galilee. The first paratrooper action would combine an amphibious assault and artillery support. The action would be carried out by the paratroopers of Battalion 890, Nahal parachute troops as well as soldiers from Givati's Battalion 51; the forces would be divided into six sub-forces:
>
> Force A:
>
> Three paratrooper companies [from Reserve Battalion 771] led by Major Aharon Davidi. The mission: occupying the Beit Habeck outpost, clearing the entire way up to and including Masudiya, blocking the positions in the Khirbet Dika area as well as the inner route (at datum-point 21022583). Davidi's force gathered at Pilon Camp and departed for the action from Almagor (Tel Mutila).
>
> Company E, the members of the squad commanders' course led by Rafael (Raful) Eitan, would conquer the estuary outposts in the north.
>
> Company B troops, led by Mussa Ephron, would blockade the north of the Sea of Galilee, preventing the Syrian army from accessing the estuary outposts and Beit Habeck.
>
> Company C, led by Marcel Tobias, including a platoon of

parachuting instructors led by Zalman Zamir and a rookie platoon, was responsible for transferring the forces through the Jordan River.

Company G, consisting of Nahal troops led by Elisha Shelem, were to conquer the Beit Habeck outpost.

Force B, led by Meir Har-Zion, about sixty commandos from Company A were to occupy the four outposts surrounding the village of Kursi, north of Ein Gev. The force was to leave from Ein Gev.

Force C, led by Shmuel Ran (Goldberg), including Company C from Givati's Battalion 52, was to conquer and destroy the position of Naqeb, north of Ein Gev (border posts).

Force D, led by Captain Yitzhak "Gulliver" Ben Menachem, about seventy troops from Company D, left Beit Yerach onboard navy landing crafts, and were to launch a surprise occupation of the outpost at Aqab Village and secure the beachhead (for evacuation).

Force E, led by Captain Arie Biro, blocked the Scopia-Kursi road, preventing the Syrian army from reaching the positions along the Sea of Galilee.

Force F, fifty troops led by Yair Tel Tzur, included some of Company F, and were to serve as reserves, opening the Ein Gev–Aqab route and collecting prisoners and captured matériel.

Force G of the navy, including four command cars and motorboats, would land Force D, rescue any casualties and evacuate Force D when its part of the action was over.

Artillery support: a battery of heavy 332 mortars at Ein Gev, a battery from Battalion 402 at Kati and another one from the same battalion at Capernaum. These were to help forces A, B and C according to their needs and the action commander's decision.

Headquarters: Forward command unit – at Villa Melchett. The operational commander on the navy landing craft at the top of the beach.

Changes during the execution: Force A pushed back the zero-hour by one hour, which made the action lose its element of surprise. The delay was caused by an inaccurate estimation of the difficulty in transferring the forces across the Jordan River. Therefore, the area of the action was secured by reinforcements.

Tzuri Sagi describes what Raful's Company E did:

The Kinneret operation was decided on after [Israeli] fishermen were fired upon. They decided to perform a large-scale action and conquer the entire shore of the Sea of Galilee. One force, led by deputy battalion commander Aharon Davidi, included Elisha's company, Mussa Ephron's company and our company – Raful's company E. We occupied the Beteiha Valley and the northern wing, the river mouth outpost. Gulliver, along with Tibi, landed from the water and occupied Nukeib. Meir Har-Zion, along with the commandos, went around from the south and conquered the Kursi position, while Biro, along with Tarzan[36] and Nir, blocked the road to Scopia.

Our force, consisting of three platoons commanded by Aharon Davidi, was supposed to go down from the outpost at Tel-Mutilla. We would arrive at the Jordan River, where Marcel's force – along

---

36   David "Tarzan" Ben Uziel. In later life an agent for Israel's foreign intelligence service, the Mossad.

with the navy commandos – would cross the river on inflatable boats. Our force – company E, led by Raful – would go around the flank and arrive from the east. Within our force there was a platoon from the squad commanders' course, eleven officers tutoring the trainees, and those in charge of this action were the trainees – each with his tutor. It was a battle for the river mouth position, the most fortified target there could be.

I turned my platoon over to Aharon "Erol" Eshel and acted as Raful's deputy company commander. Erol had to capture the left trench, parallel to the Sea of Galilee; Amnon Shwartzberg of [Kibbutz] Beit Alpha had the right trench, and my force and I had the center of the outpost and all the positions there. Raful obviously had to oversee the entire platoon. Elisha Shelem had to take Beit Habeck and Mussa Ephron had to block the road to the hill. This was Davidi's force. We arrived at the Jordan River and things were terrible because it wouldn't stop raining. Before the action, we were issued new crepe-soled shoes that kept slipping on the rocks. We arrived at the Jordan River and the inflating of the boats was accompanied by terrible whistling. Davidi ordered us to stop inflating the boats, they tossed a rope out and everyone crossed one after the other. We were soaking wet from the rain. We told jokes as we crossed the river and I can't remember anyone complaining about the harsh conditions. I guess the Syrian soldiers from the river mouth outpost heard the whistling of the boats being inflated, and they sent a patrol along the Jordan River. The patrol walked along the river until they encountered Elisha Shelem's force. Three or four Syrian soldiers were killed there. It was Davidi who gave Elisha the order to charge. We went on with the action and charged the river mouth position exactly as planned. There were barbed wire fences and trenches, and we cleared them all without suffering any losses. When we finished the action, we were suddenly fired upon from the north fence, outside the trench. I was with the main force, so we charged the source of the firing. Raful joined us and immediately caught a burst in the stomach. Amnon Eliaz from Beit Alpha was the one who killed the machine-gunner, he also received a medal for it.

We found a flat fishermen's boat and evacuated Raful to Capernaum. Even before the rest of the forces were evacuated, we got word from Poria Hospital that he was doing okay.

The enemy sustained fifty-four casualties and thirty wounded.
We lost six killed, among them the illustrious soldier Captain Gulliver, and thirteen wounded.
It was a major and complex action. The forces and the tasks they were given demanded precise planning, that the commanders and their units adapt to their various tasks, as well as coordination between different operational forces. Sharon "had it" and he outdid himself in that operation, showing explosive creativity. The secret to this operation's success was brilliant planning on Sharon's part and determined execution by all units. There were obviously some glitches, mostly involving Force A, led by Davidi, crossing the Jordan River. However, at the end of the day, the results spoke for themselves and the paratroopers had a lot to be proud of.
The Kinneret operation drew harsh criticism from abroad. The international press condemned it vigorously and frequently portrayed Israel as a violent warmonger. The world did not perceive the connection between the attacks on the fishermen at the Sea of Galilee and the operation. Israel's activities also infuriated several governments who protested the escalation on the northern border.
Within Israel, criticism came mainly from the Minister of Foreign Affairs, Moshe Sharett. He was infuriated at the timing of the action, which took place while he was in the United States, trying to convince the American government to supply Israel with advanced weapon systems. Sharett claimed that the action was unprovoked by the Arab side. He also claimed that the

action presented Israel as a warmonger and put American support of Israel at risk. Ben-Gurion rejected Sharett's claims and emphasized the country's duty to defend its citizens. Despite that, the prime minister admitted that the timing of the action was "not the best."

Applying the conclusions of the operation's summary report, it was determined that incorporating additional units into the action raised their standards without damaging the execution of the mission. Therefore, it was decided to go one step further by including other infantry units in paratrooper operations. Golani, Givati and Nahal brigades were ordered to each hold a company ready to join reprisal actions with Paratrooper Battalion 890. In January 1956 it was also decided to extend the paratroopers' battalion to include the Nahal Paratroop Battalion 88 within Unit 202. Eight months later, Unit 202 became a Brigade. The merging process of the Nahal battalion with the paratroopers marked the continuing process of spreading the combat doctrines and values that had been developed by the paratroopers, into other units in the IDF.

Toward the end of 1956, Moshe Dayan decided to change the policy that placed responsibility for these difficult tasks exclusively on elite units. He claimed that the army was strong enough to endure failure, which was why even when there was no complete confidence in achieving mission goals, other units should still be included in the reprisal actions and allowed to gain experience. And indeed, troops from the Givati Brigade and armored and artillery forces took part in the Qalqilya action.

24. AR-RAHAWA ACTION, "OPERATION JONATHAN," SEPTEMBER 11, 1956

In August and early September, 1956, there was an increase in clashes on the border with Jordan. Israel claimed that not only were the Jordanians not taking action to prevent the infiltrations, they were actively encouraging them. The last straw, which brought about the end of the restraint policy and a renewal of reprisal actions, was the murderous attack committed on September 10, 1956. It was a planned attack by the soldiers of the Jordanian Legion on IDF soldiers during mapping and navigation training around Amatzia (Dwima) in the Lachish area. Six students, soldiers of the Academic Reserves, were murdered in that attack, and three were injured. The editorials of September 11 and 12, 1956 in the *Maariv* and *Davar* newspapers demanded a response.

Chief of Staff Dayan flew to Sde Boker on September 11 to discuss a reprisal action with Ben-Gurion. Dayan claimed that the Arab residents of the village of Idna, which was close to the attack, should not be exempt from responsibility for the murders. He requested an immediate attack on the village and demolition of its houses once it was completely evacuated. Ben-Gurion supported the idea in principle but refused to make the decision himself, and sent Dayan to the cabinet meeting that very day, where the chief of staff suggested performing a massive punitive action against the village of Idna. The cabinet members, still traumatized by the Qibiya action, unanimously rejected the proposal to resume attacks on villages. Finally, an action was authorized, but only against the police station in the Hebron area, in order to have some sort of connection with the place where the soldiers were attacked.

Paratrooper forces led by Ariel Sharon, a force from Battalion 890 and Nahal Paratroop Battalion 88 arrived at the gathering point near Amatzia, having been told that they were about to attack the village of Idna. Having assembled, the troops was informed of a change of plans and set out to raid the Jordanian police building at Ar-Rahawa. The operational command given to the brigade took into account that the force was already organized for a mission similar to the new one. However, the change of plans did impede the force's preparation for the operation. The announcement regarding the change of destination arrived late in the day and forced the soldiers to move to Be'er Sheva for another planning session. The attack was finally set for September 12.

The intent, according to the operational order given by Operations Branch, was for Brigade 202 to attack and occupy the Ar-Rahawa police station, kill everyone inside and blow up the structure. The date of the action was set for the night of September 11–12, 1956. The method, according to the order, included attacking enemy forces stationed around the destination and wiping them out if they intervened. The forces would make their way back to Israel by first light on September 12. Women and children, obviously, should not be harmed.

Below is a section of Brigade 202's operational order, given verbally:

<u>Objective</u>: Occupying the Ar-Rahawa Police station, demolishing it with explosives while killing the forces inside.

<u>Method</u>: To be performed by Brigade 202. A night raid on the police station, including blocking the Ar-Rahawa–Daharia road north of the station, in order to prevent reinforcements from arriving at the scene. In the event enemy forces stationed nearby interfere with the action, they may be attacked and destroyed. The action has been set for the night of September 11–12. Zero-hour:

12/01:00. All operating forces are to return to Israeli controlled territory by first light on September 12.

Forces and tasks:

Force A: thirty soldiers from Company A of Battalion 890, led by a company commander, are to breach the police station and clear it.

Force B: forty soldiers from Company C of Battalion 890, led by a company commander, are to cover the breach.

Force C: seventy soldiers from Company B of Battalion 890, led by a company commander, are to serve as general reserves and demolish the police station with explosives.

Force D: twenty-five soldiers from companies C and E of Battalion 890, led by a company commander, are to establish a roadblock the Daharia–Ar-Rahawa road.

Force E: thirty-eight soldiers from Nahal Paratroop Battalion 88, led by a company commander, are to occupy the house at datum-point 14350875, kill everyone inside and blow it up.

Artillery support: Heavy Mortar Battalion 334 and an artillery battalion providing general assistance.

Communications: A command communications plane for artillery support and liaison.

Course of the Operation

The organization of the force and sub-forces was rushed due to the change in objective – Ar-Rahawa instead of Idna – only two hours before the scheduled start of the operation.

The force left the gathering area near Be'er Sheva and moved in vehicles, arranged in company formations, down the Daharia–Be'er Sheva road to a staging area about one kilometer from the border.

Force A: Commandos, led by Meir Har-Zion and his deputy Micha Ben Ari (Kapusta), guided the forces. Gideon Kressel and his men arrived at the base's gate and breached it with explosives. Gideon was immediately hit with a burst of bullets. Meir and the commandos went through the gate and breached the police building.

Force B: Troops led by David "Tarzan" Ben Uziel blew up and cleared the communication trenches and covered Company C, led by Elisha Shelem.

Force C: Sappers led by Marcel Tobias and Yirmi Brandov seized matériel and blew up the police building.

Force D: led by Arie Biro, Ovad Ladginsky and Amos Ne'eman, established the roadblocks to the north.

Force E: Company D troops from Nahal Paratroop Battalion 88, led by Ze'ev "Waxi" Wax, along with his deputy Yair Lin, occupied the military barracks across from the police station.

Immediately after the gate was breached, Meir Har-Zion was badly injured and the battalion medic, Dr. Moshe Agmon (Morris Ankelevich), spread out a field operation kit – for the first time during an IDF battle – and performed the surgery on Har-Zion then and there, on the battlefield, thus saving his life. The medic received the Medal of Courage for this action. (Dr. Agmon made a small incision at the base of the throat and inserted a curved tube into the trachea, saving Har-Zion from suffocating.) Micha Kapusta took command of the company but was also injured. Half an hour later, all the goals were achieved: the police building was demolished, the Legion reinforcements were halted, and the enemy suffered heavy losses.

Night Raiders

Uri Getz, a member of the commandos, recounts:

> Ariel Sharon gathered all the companies in the SHEKEM[37] at the Tel Nof base. We were going for a major action, the police building at the center of Idna, a large village in the Hebron Mountains. Arik spoke to the battalion, getting them excited by summarizing what lay ahead of us that night: "We'll do it, and we'll do it well!"
>
> We left for the village. Something went wrong on the way and we changed direction toward Ar-Rahawa – a Jordanian Legion police building, on the Hebron–Be'er Sheva road. Meir led the battalion by heading the commandos, and the rest of the companies followed us. It is hard for me to describe the feeling of following him, as if it were the safest thing in the world.
>
> There were a few dozen Legion soldiers at the police station, good soldiers. The first squad charged the police station's door, under artillery cover that we brought down on anyone in the way. The squad broke in and swept through the entire structure. They went from one room to the next, making sure no one was left. There, under one of the beds, was a Jordanian soldier, he took out his weapon and fired a single bullet. The bullet probably hit Meir in the neck. He was badly hurt, and in the police station's yard – right by the entrance – the battalion's medic, Dr. Morris Ankelevich (Agmon), operated on Meir Har-Zion and saved his life.

When examining the reports regarding the course of action, it seems like the Israeli forces were continually needed to improvise responses to one surprise encounter after another. Though the forces were ready for the action at the village of Idna, this was cancelled at the last moment, requiring improvisation to complete all the objectives of the new target. Completing all the objectives is a significant achievement, but the rush nearly led to its failure.

---

37 Base cafeteria, similar to the British NAFI or American PX.

The roadblock, with the deployment of two fuel fougasses and the successful choice of location, justified itself, and the execution, when the Legion's reinforcements arrived, was excellent. The company from Nahal Paratroop Battalion 88's was assigned to occupying and blowing up the single house at the last minute, but this task was also executed with much resourcefulness and completed successfully. The most dramatic event of the action was, as mentioned, the severe injury of Meir Har-Zion and the operation performed in the field by the battalion's medic, Dr. Ankelevich, who saved his life. The reprisal raid on the Ar-Rahawa police station, "Operation Jonathan," was Meir's last action and ended a long and impressive line of reconnaissance and reprisal actions.

Chief of General Staff Dayan was satisfied with the outcomes of the action. "The action was very successful. The police station went 'sky-high,' the roadblock damaged three Land-Rovers and the Jordanian army suffered more than twenty dead," he said with satisfaction.

The action severely damaged the Legion's morale – especially that of the Desert Patrol unit, which was composed of Bedouin. At an Arab countries conference held in Amman a day after the action, attended by King Hussain, the Legion's Chief of Staff, General Ali Abu Nuwar, made it clear that there was no chance Jordan would get aid from its fellow Arab states in defending the kingdom. Jordan's conclusion at the end of the meeting was that it had to do all it could to prevent Israel forcing a war on them. Jordan complained that this sort of reprisal action damaged precisely the forces trying to block infiltrations, and that the soldiers killed at the police fort had nothing to do with the Idna incident. The Jordanian chief of staff threatened that another such action would force Jordan to react with great force, which might lead to a war that the country did not desire.

25. GHARANDAL ACTION, "OPERATION GULLIVER," SEPTEMBER 13, 1956

On August 16, 1956, Jordanian forces set an ambush on the Arava road, between Ein Yahav and Be'er Menucha. Jordanian soldiers opened fire on a civilian bus and its military escort; a civilian woman and three paratroopers were killed in the gunfight, including soldiers from Company D: Yoram Trigger, Meir Toledano and Michael Meir-Hen. The trail of the Jordanian infiltrators led south. The death of the soldiers sent a shock wave through the country, and the cabinet decided to task Ariel Sharon with a reprisal action in the south of the country.

Sharon chose to attack the Jordanian police fort at Gharandal, in the Arava region across from Kibbutz Yahal. The fortified, three-story building housed soldiers from the Jordanian National Guard and a camel unit of the "Desert Commando." Elisha Shelem's Company C troops were on a navigation exercise around the Dishon River in the Galilee, and on August 18, 1956 were ordered to return to Tel-Nof Base, where Company A's troops were gathered under the command of Meir Har-Zion along with the Nahal Paratroop Commando from Battalion 88, led by Ze'ev "Waxi" Wax. That same evening, all the forces left in a convoy of vehicles toward the Arava road. About twenty kilometers south of Be'er Menucha, the motorcade stopped and the force set out to continue east on foot. The company commanders – Meir Har-Zion, Elisha Shelem and intelligence officer Uzi Trachtenberg (Eilam) – were assigned to navigate. The urgent call to action on a Saturday afternoon, and the great distance they had to cover – almost all the way to Eilat – left very little time to study the route. The forces started moving but hours passed, and the Gharandal fort was still nowhere in sight. At 02:30, a call was made to abort the action, for fear the forces would be bound to return during daylight.

About a month later, on September 12, 1956, infiltrators from Jordan murdered three Druze guards at the oil drilling camp at Ein Ofarim, near Hatzeva. Among the victims was Rafiq Abdallah of Sumei village. The Arab murderers were probably National Guard soldiers belonging to the "Desert Commando" at the Gharandal fort. That very day, the August reprisal plan was re-initiated that would, once again, include the occupation and demolition of the Gharandal police fort.

The operational order for the Gharandal action, codenamed "Operation Gulliver" in memory of Captain Yitzhak "Gulliver" Ben Menachem, who died in the Kinneret action, was issued to the head of Southern Command, the commander of Paratrooper Unit 202 and the commander of the air force. Colonel Uzi Narkis, the head of Operations Division at the General Staff who signed the order, notes that the action would be carried out without any assistance. The air force would be on standby to act against the Jordanian air force that might attack the IDF troops if the action dragged on into daylight. Because the action was located a long distance from the center of Israel, the air force was also placed on standby to land Dakota aircraft on the Arava road in order to evacuate the wounded to the Sirkin airport and, from there, to Tel-HaShomer Hospital.

The action took place the following day and was executed by companies A, B and C of Paratrooper Battalion 890, as well as a company from the squad commanders' course of Nahal's paratroop unit (Battalion 88), led by Avraham Klar. The commander of the company that would lead the assault on the fort was Elisha Shelem of Ramat Yohanan, and the commanders of the breaching units were Ami Hayut of Kibbutz Giv'at Brener and Moshe Sanya Ein-Mor of Jerusalem. Second Lieutenant Arie Hirsch was killed during the break-in and twelve other soldiers were wounded. The casualties were evacuated on the Dakota aircraft, which had landed on the Arava road.

Platoon commander Second Lieutenant Ami Hayut tells of his role in breaching the police station along with Elisha Shelem's Company C:

> Raful assigned the breaching and clearing of the Gharandal police fort to Elisha Shelem's Company C, with the company deputy being Levi Hofesh. Elisha had prearranged four or five breaching and clearing squads, with an officer in charge of each of them. Each squad was given a well-defined role to deal with each of the fort's four towers. I was in charge of squad no. 2 and I was given specialized equipment for breaking in, which included a wooden cross mounted with breaching charges in order to blow in the fort's front door. My squad's mission was to enter the fort and clear its northwestern tower.
>
> In the evening, our forces left Tel-Nof Base on our way to the Arava road. About twenty kilometers south of Be'er Menucha, the convoy stopped and the force grouped up to continue east on foot. Elisha Shelem, Company C's commander, was assigned to navigate. After about a ten-kilometer walk, the forces split, each to its objective, and my company came closer to the fence of the police building, when heavy fire suddenly opened up on us. Our covering force returned fire to eliminate the sources of the shooting. During the battle that preceded breaching the police station, there was suddenly an explosion, probably a hand grenade, that blew up next to the breaching squad. Almost all the troops in the first squad were wounded by shrapnel and Second Lieutenant Arie Hirsch died on the spot. Among the wounded was also Elisha Shelem, who was injured in his head and left hand. Despite his wounds, Elisha kept commanding the force and, in coordination with him, I approached the main gate of the fort with my squad, in order to blast my way in with the demolition cross. However, when I got there, I saw there was a wicket

gate we could just push open. I got the "okay" from Elisha to enter the fort's yard through there. To make sure there were no Legion soldiers behind the door, I threw in a hand grenade and only after it went off did I push the door open, fire an entire Uzi magazine into the yard, and enter with my men. We quickly crossed the yard and entered the police building. On our way to the north western tower, we passed by the empty office of the Police Chief, then quickly cleared the tower. From there, we went on to clear the north eastern tower as well. At the same time, additional squads entered the building in order to clear the southern towers, where most of the resistance and shooting came from. Once the breaching and clearing stage was done, they started evacuating the wounded, seizing matériel and getting ready to demolish the police fort.

The action was definitive proof of the operational ability developed and perfected by the paratroopers, in a variety of conditions and challenges, facing different enemies and diverse objectives. This ability served as a role model for other units of the IDF.

26. HUSSAN ACTION, "OPERATION LULAV," SEPTEMBER 25-26, 1956

The attack on the Hussan Police station, called "Operation Lulav," was executed according to the operational order issued by the Operations Division of the General Staff, and it is described in a detailed report sent out by the Operations Division, kept at the IDF Archives.

The political and military background displayed in the report stresses Jordan's concern about an Israeli attack following the reprisal action on the Ar-Rahawa and Gharandal police stations. Israel was aware of discussions between Egypt and Jordan about the establishment of a unified command for both armies. Although an agreement was not reached at that time, the talks formed the main topic in the Operations Division's review, and the prospect of such a pact seems to have intimidated Israel.

The report notes a number of incidents and serious acts of aggression on the part of Jordan, including:

- The National Guard occupying a building in the demilitarized zone in Jerusalem.
- Machine gun fire from the Mar-Elias Outpost on archaeologists attending a convention at Ramat Rachel, causing the death of four and injuring sixteen.
- The murder of a woman at Moshav Aminadav and a tractor driver from Ma'oz Haim.

All of these required a response, and the Hussein police emerged as a suitable target.

The report details information about enemy forces at the police station and its surroundings: a squad of police and another squad of the National Guard at the police station, a National Guard company at the Um-al-Kal'a outpost and a squad at Khirbet Hamza. There were also forces concentrated further away, such as in the village of Hussan itself, around Mar-Elias and at Hebron and Dahariya.

The report quotes sections of the General Staff's operational order to "occupy the Hussan police station and blow it up, 'Operation Lulav.'" The order mentions a nighttime attack with artillery support by Paratrooper Brigade 202, and details the occupation of the Um-al-Kal'a outpost as well as setting up roadblocks in the area. The order stresses that the action must be concluded by morning on September 26. Two batteries of 25-pounder artillery and light planes for observation and communication were also made available for the operation.

The report also quotes sections from the oral orders to Battalion 890 and Nahal Paratroop Battalion 88 (battalion commanders were Rafael [Raful] Eitan and Motta Gur, respectively), which mentioned the occupation of the Hussan police station.

The secondary forces were as follows:

> Force A: Company B, led by Tibi Shapira, would break into the police station and eliminate the occupants.
>
> Force B: Company A, led by David Ben Uziel (Tarzan), would be used as a reserve force and cover the breaching force.
>
> The brigade's reconnaissance company (Sataf commando), under the command of Duvik Tamari, would carry the explosives.
>
> Force C: Company D, led by Moshe Stampel, and Company E staff, led by Arie Biro, would set up a roadblock on the Hussan–al-Khader road.

Force D: Company F, led by Arik Regev, would set up a roadblock on the road between the village of Hussan and the police fort, and would be used as a general reserve force and to seize matériel.

Force E: Company A (squad commanders' course) of Battalion 88, led by Avraham Keller and his deputy Nathan Hocherman, would occupy the outpost at Khirbet Um-al-Kal'a.

An auxiliary company from Battalion 88, led by Micha Pikes, would occupy the Khirbet Hamsa Outpost.

A light plane from the air force, with the brigade's intelligence officer Uzi (Eilam) Trachtenberg aboard, would raise the alarm should any reinforcements from the Jordanian army arrive in the area, and would assist communication between the forces.

The description of the progress of the operation by Battalion 890 begins with the departure, on foot, from Mevo Beitar, which took over two hours and brought about a delay in the action's start time. When the forces were in position to attack and the suppressing fire was opened on the police station, a jeep emerged from it, traveling north. There it encountered the covering force and was destroyed. At the same time, there was some movement detected on the hill south of the police station. The reserve squad was sent there and, after a short battle, occupied the position. Twelve Legionnaires were killed as well as a few National Guard soldiers. The IDF suffered one dead.

The breaching force opened a hole in the fence and penetrated the police building quickly and with very little resistance. As the action was underway, the patrol aircraft spotted a long convoy of vehicles leaving Hebron, northbound. The brigade's intelligence officer called in the 25-pounder artillery batteries, which were the most powerful weapons that the IDF possessed at that time. The motorcade halted and its lights went out. The intelligence officer evaluated that the motorcade was still moving and ordered the artillery to aim the fire somewhat further down the road. That was how, according to later intelligence, the Jordanian force was stopped near Solomon's Pools.

The description of the progress of the operation by Battalion 88, according to the report, begins with their departure from Mevo Beitar, about an hour after Battalion 890. According to the brigade's plan, the occupation of the Um-al-Kal'a outpost should have started simultaneously with the attack on the police station, but was moved to an earlier time. The Jordanians spotted the battalion's movement and opened fire from an advance unit from the Hussan outpost and also from the village of Hussan. Force A, from Battalion 88, in a departure from the original plan, had to storm the outpost. Despite the enemy's fierce resistance, the outpost was occupied after only twenty-five minutes. The Jordanians suffered fifteen dead and many wounded, while the IDF suffered three dead and fourteen wounded. Battalion 88's Force E, which occupied the Hussan village outpost without any real resistance, was ordered to set up the roadblock on the Hussan–Nahlin road. While setting explosives there, a fault occurred, causing the explosives to go off, killing two IDF soldiers and wounding another.

As the action at the police station ended, Battalion 88's Force C – the general reserves – arrived there with half-tracks, evacuating the wounded and seizing matériel. This was when the force started withdrawing toward the border.

The total casualties the IDF suffered in this action were ten dead – including the two who had died from the accidental explosions – and sixteen wounded. The Jordanians suffered thirty-nine dead and twelve wounded.

The report of the Operations Division discusses some of the political reactions to the action including:

- Jordan was claiming victory, not only to save face, but also so that it would not have to engage in risky reprisal actions.
- Jordan approached Iraq for military assistance.
- The Egyptian-Syrian alliance sent five aircraft and a large quantity of weapons and ammunition.

The Hussan action was a complex and large-scale operation. Despite the mishaps that befell them, the Paratrooper Brigade achieved all its objectives. The action also increased Israeli deterrence vis-à-vis Jordan as well as neighboring Arab states.

27. QALQILYA ACTION, "OPERATION SAMARIA," OCTOBER 10, 1956

On October 9, 1956, two laborers from Even Yehuda were murdered in an orchard near Neve Hadassah. That very same day, the Israeli government decided to perform a massive reprisal action, including the occupation and destruction of the Qalqilya police fort and the killing of the soldiers of the Jordanian Legion based there.

The political and military background presented in intelligence reports indicated increasing Egyptian influence in Jordan. This not only brought extra weapons to the National Guard from Egypt, Syria and Iraq, and dispatched a delegation of military instructors from Egypt, but also operated *fedayeen* gangs for murder and sabotage. The *fedayeen* were integrated into the units guarding the border. Not only did they enjoy freedom of action, but even received authorization and guidance from the authorities, including King Hussein.

The intelligence assessment prior to the action showed that the military deployment on the Qalqilya–Nablus axis presented a new concept in Jordanian defenses. The front line, according to the new theory, was to be held by the National Guard while the regular army was retained in battalion and company compounds on the main routes that the Israeli enemy would use in an attack. Using this method, the central reserves of the Jordanian army could be reduced. The intelligence claimed that it was clear that the Jordanians were expecting an attack, probably on a police station, but they did not know the exact objective. Since the start of tensions in the area, all permanent camps, as well as all the tent camps had been dismantled. Military units not assigned to outposts were sitting in their vehicles, awaiting orders to move.

Summary of the General Staff's operational order:

Objective: Occupy and demolish the Qalqilya police station and destroy the force there.

Method: Nighttime attack, with the support of artillery, on the night of October 10–11, 1956. The occupation will be carried out by Brigade 202. The target will be illuminated by spotlights. Access routes should be blocked in order to secure the battle zone. The platoon of French AMX-13 tanks is not to cross the border. Forces should not enter Qalqilya and the city should not be bombarded unless there is any low trajectory fire from there on our settlements. The Khirbet Supin outpost can be bombarded. In the event of low-trajectory fire from Qalqilya, we are to return low-trajectory fire. The air force will be ready to provide support in case of complications encountered by ground forces. The air force will supply reconnaissance and communication aircraft to the operating force.

Forces and tasks:

Force A: Three reduced companies from Nahal Battalion 88, one of half-tracks, that would break into the police station, occupy and demolish it. The half-track platoon will secure the nearby area of operation and serve as a close reserve and will assist in carrying the explosives and sappers. Another platoon of AMX-13s (plus two spotlights) would remain at the border.

Force B: Three reduced companies from Paratroop Battalion 890 will be used as reserves at the edge of the woods, datum point

14661788, with a small force to hold down the northern pillbox of the Qalqilya police station with bazooka fire.

Force C: The battalion's reconnaissance unit, along with the forward observation officer and supported by a battery of medium guns from Artillery Corps Battalion 402 will block the Qalqilya–Azun road.

Force D: A Mechanized Infantry company from Battalion 52 of the Givati Brigade, led by the battalion's commander, will stay around Neve Yamin to be used as general reserves and to rescue the forces if need be.

<u>Artillery support</u>: A 25-pound artillery battery from the Artillery Corps' field Battalion 402 would support force A directly.

A medium battery from the Artillery Corps' Battalion 403 for anti-tank action.

Two heavy batteries from the Artillery Corps' Battalion 332 in general support (also in order to cover Khirbet Tzufin with fire).

Two spotlights.

<u>Aerial support</u>: Aerial support officer liaison at the Brigade's headquarters.

Three light aircrafts for reconnaissance and communication.

The following forces participated in the operation:

Force A: Paratroop Nahal Battalion 88, led by Motta Gur, supported by spotlights and tank fire to soften up the police station's defenses. The force breached the police station and fought the Jordanians, who resisted and engaged in face-to-face combat, which led to many casualties. In the end, force A occupied the police station, cleared it and blew up the structure at

23:30. They then went on to blow up the northern pillbox.

Force B: Battalion 890, led by Rafael (Raful) Eitan. The force left the Beit Berl assembly grounds at 20:30 and moved toward the border. At 21:30, the force reached its objective, northwest of the police building, where it was held in reserve. At 01:00, the force's commander was ordered to move on foot toward the roadblock and rescue them. As they arrived in the Khirbet Tzufin area, the force saw the half-tracks moving on the road. Raful was ordered to turn back since the blockade force had been rescued by the Givati Brigade's half-tracks. The Battalion 890 force returned to Beit Berl.

Force C: Paratrooper Brigade commandos, led by Yehuda (Reif) Reshef, established a roadblock between the villages of Azun and Qalqilya. The commandos reached the designated position at 21:40. At 22:00, the patrol aircraft – carrying the brigade's former intelligence officer, Uzi (Eilam) Trachtenberg, who had been injured and was assigned to aerial patrol and liaison by Arik – informed them of a fifteen-vehicle convoy entering the village of Azun. The Jordanian's reinforcements were the size of two companies. About ten minutes later, the leading force of the Jordanian motorcade attacked the commando unit and, in the ensuing firefight, almost all the Jordanian troops were injured. The commando force withdrew about 300 meters west of their original position. The Jordanians charged the blockade force several times, from various directions, but were pushed back by the force, which also had artillery support from 155 mm cannons. It was a long and hard battle, in which the force's commander and his deputy were injured and several of the force were killed. Ariel Sharon's communication with the commandos was facilitated by the communication aircraft, which he used to send a message to the platoon commander, Dovik Tamari, to take charge of the force. Dovik decided to move to the Khirbet Bartona hill and the force did so, with its dead and wounded. Shlomo Gal, the artillery liaison officer, operated the 155 mm cannons the entire time, with great efficiency and bravery. At 02:30, the force D half-tracks arrived to rescue the commandos. The convoy moved to the Khirbet Tzufin–Qalqilya road and suffered two more deaths in the exchange of fire at Khirbet Tzufin: Major Moshe Broyar,

Unit 202's operations officer, and Yirmi Bardanov, formerly Battalion 890's demolition officer.

Force D: A reserve force from Armored Corps Battalion 79, led by the deputy commander of Brigade 202, Yitzhak (Haka) Hofi, was tasked with rescuing the commandos.

Force E: An Artillery Corps force, including a battery of 155 mm cannons from Battalion 403 and another from Battalion 402, as well as 120 mm heavy mortars from Battalion 332, led by Alex Pereg.

Force F: A reserve force from Givati Brigade. A tank division from Battalion 9 of Brigade 7, led by Zvi Rahav, also took part in the action, as well as a mechanized spotlight unit from the Artillery Crops.

Casualties:
Dead: Israeli, 18. Jordanians, 88.
Wounded: Israeli, 48. Jordanians, 15.

When summarizing the Qalqilya reprisal action, we cannot overlook the high number of casualties sustained. Most of the casualties suffered by the Israeli side were at the police station itself. At the second focal point of the battle, the roadblock manned by the commandos, there were three soldiers killed, with two of them – Brigade intelligence officer Major Moshe Broyar and Yirmi Bardandov – killed during the rescue operation.

Israel was aware that the Jordanian military was on high alert. Even if the Jordanians did not know exactly what the objective was, there is no doubt the forces at the police station and its surroundings were ready. The commandos' battle on the Qalqilya–Azun road should also not have come as a surprise to us either. Indeed, within ten minutes, a two-company sized force from the Bedouin Battalion arrived, and the heroic commando battle began. Sharon's plan included many forces and was allegedly supposed to end the action with much fewer casualties. However, Battalion 890, led by Raful, was left inactive, except for successfully destroying the northern pillbox. The order to deploy Battalion 890 to help the commandos was cancelled once the rescue of the unit was carried out by the half-track force of Givati's Battalion 52. The Jordanians fought back hard, both inside the police station and outside of it; this might point to the limited influence the spotlights, the tanks and cannon fire had in softening up Jordanian resistance.

Uzi (Eilam) Trachtenberg tells of the way he joined the action:

> I was still at Convalescent Facility 3, near Haifa, when the Qalqilya action was about to be launched. Micha Kapusta, Meir's deputy, was with me there and was also recovering from an injury. We ran away from the military convalescent facility and drove to Kfar Sava. We knew that following the attack there [on the laborers from Even Yehuda], there would be an action. I went to Arik and he said: "Ah, you're in a cast? To the aircraft!"
>
> I was in the air for seven hours, with one break for refueling, and served as liaison between Arik and the commandos, who were surrounded and being attacked by a large Legion force. It was a very difficult story there, especially when the commandos' commander, Yehuda Reshef, and his deputy Yair Tel Zur, were put out of action due to injury. Arik had no direct communication with the commando unit and I had to relay communications between them. He asked who command should be transferred to, and I recommended Dovik Tamari, who went on to perform exceptionally.
>
> When the action was over, Arik told me to go to the Sataf (commando headquarters) and help them organize (I was about to be released and the role of intelligence officer transferred to Gideon Machanaymi). I was at the Sataf base all day, returning to Tel-Nof in the evening. I went to Arik and told him: "I was there and did all I could to help the commandos get organized. I'm still on duty, is there something you need me to do?" Without thinking twice, he told me: "Yes, one of Motta Gur's company commanders

died in the attack on the Qalqilya police station; you will get his company. Motta already knows you're coming."

That was the company I took to the Sinai War (Suez Crisis). But what was I supposed to do with an arm in a cast? There was a rumor of a big war coming. While I was at Tel-Nof, I quickly went to the intelligence department, and heard from Gideon Machanaymi that a major war was on the horizon, including the French and the English. I went back to Ness Harim, where my company was in training. I called the company medic and asked him to cut my cast off…there was still one line of sutures on the arm, but that didn't bother me. It was only after the Sinai War was over that I returned to Convalescent Facility 3 for treatment and they took out the sutures.

The Suez Crisis (Sinai War) was about to break out, so the full critique and lessons learned from "Operation Samaria" was postponed. This critique was part of Sharon's standard investigation, which he used to perform after every reprisal action, major or minor.

Chief of General Staff Moshe Dayan was well aware of criticism in Israel, focusing mainly on the heavy price Israel had paid for the operation, reflected in the high number of casualties. Dayan asked to meet leading journalists and share some information with them, which was not supposed to be made public, and he brought with him Ariel Sharon, who had planned and commanded the action, as well as Head Artillery Officer Colonel Freddie Blum. Below are a few sections of the meeting, held on October 11, 1956:

Lieutenant General Moshe Dayan:

> I requested this meeting concerning two issues, or rather two parts of the same issue, all following on from last night's action. The first is the story – what happened. The second is stating an opinion, my own, about the considerations that brought us to those kinds of actions, and examining whether or not we have

the option to perform other actions within this framework. These two questions – the first being the story of what happened and the other being whether those actions were justified – I am sure, are before each and every one of us, regardless of the ratio of our losses to those of the enemy or the military analysis of the action (…) we each have to ask ourselves, when following such an action we held eighteen funerals and had nearly fifty wounded men, ten of them badly – was it necessary or justified militarily? Was it necessary or justified in terms of purpose, especially since this is not the end of the affair? What will happen tomorrow, at the next action? (…) Could we do it differently? Can we execute these actions in a different form, which will cost less? Are these kinds of actions even necessary? Are they effective? I am sure each and every one of us has been asking themselves these questions.

This meeting is off the record, so is the account of the action, but not because it is something to be ashamed of. The decision not to publish the account this time was made with the minister of defense before the action was even executed, because he believed and stated that we have reached a point of saturation following descriptions of previous actions. We shall not recount that Force A did this and Force B did that, etc. That is why we have set this off-the-record meeting, not for publishing what happened but to bring it to your attention. What I am most interested in is for those present to know the facts as they are. This does not mean that you can't think things could have been done differently, but you must know exactly what happened. Therefore, the aim is to involve you in the matter. We will not censor the stories that will arrive from various sources, apart from military censorship.

I very much regretted hearing on the radio this morning the almost cheerful description about the "symphony and concerts," since this is a very discordant issue. Neither the action, nor its objective, nor the heavy price we have paid for it are "cheerful," and they do not resemble a concert or symphony. Actions that end with funerals and wounded men should not be described to the public in this manner. The IDF Spokesman made do with a laconic announcement, and the newspapers will do with it as they will.

I assume you are all familiar with Lieutenant Colonel Ariel Sharon, commander of Paratrooper Brigade 202, a brigade which includes Nahal as well as paratrooper units, which has been designated by the IDF for special missions. There are sometimes other units taking part in the missions, as was the case this time. I have asked Colonel Freddie Blum, chief artillery officer, to also attend this meeting. His force played a support role and he will explain their part in the action.

The order of the meeting shall be as follows: Arik will report on the action and Freddie will add to it regarding artillery support. Later, there will be time for questions if there will be any. I will then report our considerations for choosing this objective as well as the form or execution, on which I will answer any questions there may be.

Ariel Sharon's review of the complex and multi-force operational plan, as well as its execution, was detailed and fluent. It seemed Sharon was familiar with all the parts of the action, during the planning and execution stages as well as the outcomes. Familiarizing himself with the situation at hand was one of Sharon's unique abilities throughout his life. He allocated a considerable and important part of the review to the battle the commandos had fought at the roadblock after it was attacked by Jordanian Legion forces, and sustained several wounded men, among them its commander and deputy. Sharon commended the young platoon commander who took charge of the battle until the force was rescued by the half-track unit. The artillery officer assigned to the commandos was also praised for his vital part in aiding the unit, since they had been fighting for their lives. Freddie Blum, chief artillery officer, described the support components given to the force that breached the police stations and mentioned the unconventional solutions taken by the artillery officer assigned to the roadblock. According to Colonel Blum, aiming artillery fire toward targets so close to the commando force, which was under constant attack, was unprecedented and successful.

Lieutenant General Moshe Dayan (after also answering some of the journalists' questions):

> Lately, the *fedayeen* attacks have become routine. It is probably Jordan's decision to activate them on a daily basis. They took the *fedayeen* units and attached them to the Border Guards, and told them to go out and kill Jewish people. (…) We do not even have a way to prevent this thing called *fedayeen*. If an Arab person likes, he can walk into Israel, even enter the Knesset, schedule a meeting with Ben-Gurion himself; any Arab person is free to go into Israel…
>
> I would like to speak about the framework in which we select objectives for reprisal actions:
>
> a) The policy does not include occupation for the sake of possession. The army can perform operations which end by dawn or an hour after first light, and return to Israeli territory. This is therefore the first principle: an action is not for the purpose of conquest. This is the first condition and the army chooses its objectives within this framework.
>
> b) The second condition is avoid or minimize harm to women or children. This action can serve as an example of that: we feared the families of the policemen and soldiers were living in the station with them, so we gave the unit two orders: First, to break for ten minutes after completing the first shelling, assuming any

families would be evacuated from the police stations if there were any. Second, to check the police station before blowing it up and evacuate any women and children. The orders were to damage only military objectives. The pressure on the Jordanian government to cease operating the *fedayeen* is currently being made through one channel, while objectively it could come through two channels. Today the pressure is applied only through the military channel. In the Qalqilya operation the [civilian] city of was not involved. Legion Battalion 9 suffered fifty casualties and the Qalqilya National Guard suffered fifty casualties. This surely puts pressure on the Jordanian government, but had we damaged civilian settlements, the pressure on the Jordanian government would have come also through the second channel – pressure from the civilian residents.

c) The third condition is the type of weapons used. We do not operate air or armored forces against enemy objectives and, during the day, not even artillery. We could have successfully sent two airplanes to demolish the Qalqilya police station without any of our people getting hurt. The reason is that there is a political distinction and classification in which operating aircrafts has to do with wartime use. Militarily and technically, you do not have to send in soldiers to blow up a police station.

Dayan concluded his statement by noting that everything said in that meeting was due to his assumption that, without such an explanation, there might have been a feeling of failure. He did not believe Jordan could remain indifferent after everything that had happened during the Qalqilya operation. Dayan stated that if the Arabs did not stop the *fedayeen*, whether by Egyptian or Jordanian initiative, Israel would have to continue reprisal actions against them. The chief of general staff clarified that, in order to apply maximal pressure, some civilian property would have to be damaged and it would be necessary to show less concern for the lives of Arab civilians.

Dayan claimed there was no conflict with the minister of defense, and at times the latter gave them quite a bit of leeway with his authorizations.

In an attempt to understand what brought Dayan to hold that meeting with the press, we should recall that in addition to the high number of casualties Israel had suffered during the action, there was acute tension between Dayan and Sharon following the conduct of the latter and his men during the Qalqilya operation. Dayan changed Sharon's original plan of action and also instructed them to wait an additional ten minutes between the artillery bombing of the police station and the subsequent breach, to allow any civilians within to evacuate. Sharon objected to this instruction, and in a debriefing he performed with the brigade, he did not hesitate to inform the troops that the instruction had not been fulfilled. Dayan recognized the insubordination of Sharon and the likelihood of more such episodes in the future. The chief of staff knew he had to put a stop to such dangerous occurrences before they could escalate further. When Sharon spoke to the journalists, he did not mention the matter of the ten-minute pause in the shelling at all, while the Dayan mentioned that order as an example of the effort they took to avoid hurting civilians. Sharon had been put in his place. During an inquiry Dayan conducted on his own following the action, he saw the danger in the paratroopers' sense of superiority. In his harsh criticism, he claimed that each member of Brigade 202 was first and foremost a soldier in the IDF, not a member of one "gang" or another. Moshe Dayan, like Ben-Gurion, knew Sharon well, and knew the great contribution this excellent fighter and commander made toward shaping the IDF's fighting spirit, as well as how to limit the effects of his faults.

Dayan was not only a military man to the core, but also a politician, which seemed to have been noticed both by Ben-Gurion and Sharett. The meeting with the journalists described above included Ariel Sharon and the chief artillery officer for a reason. A review of the newspaper articles published after the action indicates the mood among the public.

The day after the Qalqilya action, *Davar* stated in its editorial that the blood spilled in the Qalqilya campaign "surpassed the rest of the battles in Israel since the War of 1948." Both Israeli and Jordanian casualties and wounded, as the newspaper claimed, were victims solely of Arab aggression.

Davar portrayed the heroics of the IDF soldiers as all but miraculous, publishing a headline which read: "Two Murdered by Infiltrators at Even Yehuda." The article recounted chilling details of the murders by infiltrators who mutilated the laborers' bodies.

Haaretz headlined its coverage, "IDF Forces Fought the Legion at Qalqilya." The newspaper stated the level of fortification of the Tagart police station at Qalqilya, as well as the high alert of the Jordanians, which resulted in the large number of casualties on both sides. The newspaper noted the "heroic stand of the roadblock force," which prevented major Jordanian reinforcement from arriving at the scene of the fighting at the police station.

With that said, the newspaper allocated considerable space for the criticism voiced by Member of Parliament Menachem Begin on the method of reprisal actions, which according to him did not deal with the threat to national security. In his speech to the Knesset, Begin demanded to hold elections immediately.

HaBoker quoted Ben-Gurion in its main headline: "The Israeli government will maintain its freedom to operate." The newspaper brought some of the prime minister's statements from the parliamentary debate, in which he addressed the possibility that the Iraqi military would enter Jordan. He emphasized that the only means of preventing a war to deter the enemy. Ben-Gurion disclosed that IDF forces had grown stronger since the Czech arms deal.

Herut published a long political polemic criticizing the strategy at the base of the reprisal action. Yohanan Bader called the government's explanation of the consideration for the reprisal action "primitive and childish concepts." Bader, a Herut movement leader, called for "liberation actions" (i.e. liberation from Arab rule and incorporating into Israel) rather than "punitive actions" in order to improve Israel's security. The editorial by the newspaper glorified the military on the one hand, but seriously criticized government policy in refusing to deal with the conquest of vital areas around the country's slender waist, at its center as well as its north.

Maariv commended the occupation and demolition of the Qalqilya police station and went on to praise the achievement of the troops who manned the roadblock and faced a battalion of the Jordanian Legion that surrounded them. As the newspaper wrote, the resourcefulness of the young officer Dovik Tamari, who took command after both the force commander and his deputy were injured, was to be commended. *Maariv* stated that both sides – Israeli and Jordanian – would surely learn their lessons from the Qalqilya action. This raid proved to the Israelis that, despite heavy losses, the IDF maintained their qualitative edge. Jordan, on the other hand, needed to understand that it was in its interests to restrain extremist forces operating within it. Jordan might also have become increasingly dependent on forces from other Arab states, a most unwelcome development.

In addition to describing the operation, *Al HaMishmar* reported on a meeting between British diplomats and Minister of Foreign Affairs Golda Meir. The newspaper stressed in its headline, "London Threatens to Intervene Militarily against Israel in the Matter of Iraq and Jordan," referring to a possible Israeli attack on Jordan if the Iraqi army should enter the kingdom.

28. MOSHE DAYAN, BATTALION 890 AND ADOPTING THE RAID CONCEPT

Dayan's deep involvement in the developments within Battalion 890, and his recognition of the importance of the raid as a tactic, are worthy of further examination and evaluation. Ben-Gurion greatly appreciated Dayan's way of thinking and recognized the importance of the raid as the most important tool in the IDF's "toolbox" at that time. During 1953, conditions ripened for a change that could free the IDF from the conceptual stalemate forced upon it due to the disbanding of the Palmach and the discharge of many experienced, battle-toughened troops after the end of the 1948 War of Independence. Ben-Gurion identified two main challenges, which were different in nature yet politically, operationally and strategically inseparable. The first was the risk of conventional war against one or more Arab countries. That had been Ben-Gurion's nightmare since the end of the 1948 war, arising from his concern regarding the involvement of international forces and the fear that the young country might not be able to withstand another round of total war.

The second challenge had to do with the *fedayeen* actions, supported by the Arab regimes, whose territories afforded them bases from which to carry out their raids. The *fedayeen* did not present a threat to Israel's existence but rather to maintaining a reasonable level of national quality of life and preserving the security of the entire Israeli population.

Since the *fedayeen* operated from bases within Egyptian, Jordanian or

Syrian territories, any attempt by the IDF to prevent them from infiltrating Israeli territory would have infringed the sovereignty of neighboring countries, creating the danger of clashes with their armed forces.

Ben-Gurion recognized the need for an operational paradigm capable of suppressing the *fedayeen* terror attacks without dragging Israel into an all-out war with the Arab countries. He understood that he needed a chief of general staff who could tackle two tasks: one, to shake up the IDF's underperformance; and two, to enforce accountability on the Arab governments for the responsibility Israel believed they bore for the *fedayeen*. Lieutenant General Mordechai Maklef, who accepted Ben-Gurion's offer to become chief of staff, asked to serve in the role for only a year. Although he was one of the veterans of the British army, he turned out to be entirely open to the approach to command that had been developed by the Palmach.

The search for a possible operational method to alleviate the effect of the Palestinian *fedayeen* attacks on the Israeli home front led Maklef to approve the recommendation made by Colonel Michael Shacham – the head of the Jerusalem Command – to establish Unit 101. It was a brave attempt to once again adopt the doctrines of Wingate and his Night Squads and the fighting principles Yitzhak Sadeh and his Mobile Unit, which had imbued the Palmach. The mandate given to Major Ariel Sharon was to conduct special operations against sources of *fedayeen* terror actions, thus restoring security to Israeli citizens. Dayan turned the new paratroopers unit into the engine of the High Command, which would power the adoption of a number of operational goals and strategic principles throughout the whole army.

These are the goals that Dayan sought:

A. Turning the IDF into an efficient and offensive military body. The offensive initiative had decreased since the end of the 1948 war, which was why a change had to be made.
B. Developing a military strategy better balanced between Sharon's proactive approach and Ben-Gurion's more cautious attitude.
C. Implementing the objective of the political echelon to suppress *fedayeen*

terror by deterring neighboring Arab countries from supporting them (perhaps comparable to how the defense establishment currently views punishing Lebanon in order to deter Hezbollah).
D. Restoring the confidence of the civilian community in the IDF's ability to provide security and reasonable living conditions.
E. Applying an effective method of military action without crossing the line of international condemnation.

Chief of General Staff Dayan's overall objective was that the raid become the template of a combat technique that best fit the strategic conditions of the time. Dayan's intent was to adopt the extraordinary experience of the Palmach and Unit 101, develop it through the operations of Battalion 890, bringing it from there to the paratroopers, and finally to turn it into an offensive tactic which could be implemented throughout the entire IDF. Dayan strove to change the raid from an exceptional tactic into a standard one, thus turning the entire cumbersome and inefficient IDF into a "raiding force."

The raiding tactic naturally created rich strategic potential. It made use of the relative advantages the IDF had on the level of tactical warfare. In addition, the raid fitted Israel's geopolitical conditions perfectly. Furthermore, the model of the combat raid was suitable to a wide range of terrains and diverse offensive actions. A raid could be just as effective against regular troops as against special forces. Dayan believed that professional and agile forces, equipped with accurate intelligence, could execute successful actions within limited time frames.

Between 1954 and 1956, Battalion 890, backed by Chief of General Staff Dayan, operated as the engine for developing the raid as the principal framework for IDF operations.

The raiding actions, as a maneuvering system, were based on four components during that time:

A. Penetrating deep into enemy territory by marching at night and pinpoint navigation (from Wingate's "textbook").
B. Isolating the objective's immediate area by spreading a web of ambushes that would block access to the battle zone.
C. Attacking the target, in most cases a military facility, and neutralizing its inhabitants in brief and decisive combat.
D. Disengaging and withdrawing back into Israeli territory within the time frame of that same night.

What started as a platoon action developed, in 1954, into a company action, then into raids on a battalion scale during 1955, eventually reaching complex actions that involved brigade-scale units against Jordanian, Syrian and Egyptian targets during 1956. Thanks to Dayan's insightful operational understanding, he predicted the tension between Ben-Gurion's twin imperatives: his desire to take an initiative that would improve Israel's security on the one hand, and on the other, his deep fear of escalation toward total war, which might bring the wrath of the international community down on Israel. In addition, the "strategic disgrace" that had resulted from the tactical success of Unit 101's raid on the village of Qibiya, caused Dayan to realize that an effective strategy would be one that forced Arab governments to withdraw their support from the *fedayeen*.

Unlike Maklef, whose roots did not originate in the Palmach, Dayan held the value of the elite unit in high regard, which was also a qualitative factor in spreading the raid concept to other IDF units. Dayan, who personally controlled the operation of the paratroopers, saw Battalion 890 – and later on Brigade 202 – as an institutional mechanism that generated knowledge in important and key areas of combat through its current operations.

29. AN INSIDE LOOK INTO BATTALION 890 AND THE DEVELOPMENT OF ITS SPECIAL CHARACTER

In this chapter we will try to get into the heart of Battalion 890, after Unit 101 was merged into it, to understand what happened there and why. It is impossible to understand the processes that took place in the battalion without discussing the contribution of three people – who are so unique and different from one another – who are responsible for the transformation of the Paratroopers Regiment into a combatant unit.

- Ariel Sharon, the new commander of Battalion 890, which until that time had been used for parachute training and air shows, knew he had to recruit a whole new line of commanders.
- Aharon Davidi, the commander of Battalion 890's Company B, which had been under the command of previous battalion commander Yehuda Harari before Unit 101 joined them, was made deputy battalion commander as Sharon assumed the new position.
- Meir Har-Zion, the "pillar of fire," unsurpassed in navigation, and the master of small-unit operations. It was he who established the doctrines of reconnaissance and small-scale, cross border actions in Unit 101. Meir disseminated this doctrine to the entire battalion, not by lectures but through personal example. As we will later see, this would not have worked had he not had the support of the battalion's command, Ariel Sharon, and his deputy Aharon Davidi.

Ariel Sharon, who was born in 1928 on Moshav Kfar Malal, fought in the Alexandroni Brigade during the War of 1948 and was injured in a bloody battle during unsuccessful attempts to take the Latrun police station from the Jordanian Legion. The severe injury and the time that he had to wait until his rescue were etched deep in his heart and manifested in his determination that no man should be left behind on the battlefield. Sharon was prepared for his role in the IDF, having served as the commander of the Alexandroni Brigade's commando force, then of Golani's commandos, later as the intelligence officer of both Central and Northern Commands. These roles laid the groundwork for the principles that guided him as he molded Unit 101, and later the entire paratroopers' battalion. There is no doubt that Sharon's reconnaissance and intelligence background led to the unique connection he had with Meir Har-Zion – the natural scout – which we will revisit later.

Aharon Davidi, born in Tel Aviv in 1927, joined the Palmach and was a communications technician on the home front until, after many attempts, he managed to join a combat battalion as a communications officer. The technological field no longer appealed to the ambitious officer. Davidi, who continued to serve in command roles, had great inter-personal communication abilities, which were later used to bring the members of the battalion together. Davidi trained as a company commander in the Training Camp 1 officer's course, and stood out thanks to his red beard, which remained his trademark. As a company commander in the paratroopers' battalion during the period when it was commanded by Yehuda Harari, Davidi took part in the Qibiya action and earned his place as a combat officer in the eyes of the Unit 101 troops, especially Ariel Sharon. Davidi was not one of the officers who demonstrated their allegiance to Harari when the battalion's commander was forced to step down and make way for Ariel Sharon. He was among the few officers who did not leave Battalion 890 but stayed on as a company commander in the battalion. Sharon chose Davidi as deputy battalion commander, demonstrating the keen ability to evaluate people's worth, which would serve him throughout his military career and later in his civilian positions. Without Davidi's ability to connect and bring together such different people and get them to act as one, the incorporation of Unit 101 into Battalion 890 would not have gone so well. And without the successful changes made to the battalion, the idea of spreading the battalion's combat spirit to the entire army would not have been realized.

Meir Har-Zion was the third leg of the tripod that supported the transformation of the combat value of Unit 101 and Battalion 890, and later the entire IDF. Here, Sharon again showed his amazing ability to gauge people's worth. Arik recognized Har-Zion as a combat scout who perfectly fit the nature of the actions for which he'd established the unit. Most of the 101's actions were reconnaissance patrols, and according to the level of performance of the operation, Sharon knew who among the men – recruited via the "bring a friend" approach – would fit the unit and stay, and who would be rejected. Har-Zion was a natural navigator who had acquired that skill as a boy hiking throughout country. If you read his book *Pirkei Yoman*, you will see that Har-Zion would sometimes flounder even on the patrols and that his navigation was not always successful. The image of him as a fearless warrior, according to his own book, was also not quite accurate. Har-Zion, like all of us, naturally had fears and worries before going on missions. One quality that stood out, in any case, and which probably earned him Sharon's appreciation, was his extraordinary devotion to completing the task at hand. Here too, according to Har-Zion's journals, there was certainly hesitation. It is not for nothing that Sharon mentioned operation Silk Gloves, the Hebron action that Meir Har-Zion and three other Unit 101 troops took part in. Sharon mentioned the action on that snowy night, deep inside enemy territory, as an example of a reprisal action, and showing persistence that was second to none.

Throughout the entire period in which Unit 101 was active, slightly over five months, Har-Zion and his team served as an example to the rest of the teams on how to navigate, what to do when encountering an ambush or when attacking a house. Even though Shlomo Baum was officially Sharon's deputy, Har-Zion was the one the commander actually considered his right-hand man. When the unit joined Battalion 890, several of its members were sent to officers' courses, and those who remained became the battalion's reconnaissance platoon, led by Har-Zion. In some of the battalion's actions, Sharon left the main role – attacking the main target – in the hands of the reconnaissance platoon.

Sharon maintained the use of small teams that had worked in Unit 101. Over the years reconnaissance missions across the border, limited to small teams of three to five men, remained a major part of the paratroopers' activity. This even persisted into the growth from battalion to brigade. Throughout, success in the reconnaissance patrol continued to be the main criterion for gauging the skills and level of aptitude among the commanders, with Har-Zion continuing to be the benchmark against which their performance would be measured.

Ze'ev Solel, a member of Har-Zion's platoon (along with three other Unit 101 troops from Kibbutz Ein Harod) best describes the process in which the unit and its soldiers merged into Battalion 890, back in the days of battalion commander Yehuda Harari:

> The merger was a dramatic thing that was not given enough attention. It was done while we were performing the reprisal actions and could easily have failed. We came from the kibbutzim, good kids with good education. We had been in the Youth Battalions and when we graduated from high school we were already trained. We knew what night meant and we knew what day meant. Even though we did not come from the combat units, we each had the basics. We knew how to handle weapons, walk at night, navigate by the stars.
>
> Arik mainly dealt with the aspect of "selling" reprisal actions in the hallways of the General Staff and the various commands, and planning the details of the actions. Davidi was more like the

minister of internal affairs, dealing with a lot of the operational doctrine and connecting different people. Davidi was influential mainly due to his character, knowledge, silent bravery and personal example.

The veteran soldiers, from the Harari days, admired strength and bravery. We, the people of Unit 101, brought experience, so they admired us in a way, wanted to be like us. We didn't push their admiration away, on the contrary, we encouraged them. The one who contributed most to this connection was Davidi, with his sharp mind, composure and radiant personality. Davidi was the heart of the integration and it worked well thanks to him. The veterans saw him as one of their own, since he came from the paratroopers, from the era of Harari.

Sharon's statement at his parting from Paratrooper Brigade 202, following the end of the Sinai War (Suez Crisis), appears in full in the next chapter. Sharon said goodbye to the brigade he had established and commanded during the Sinai War, and his words clarify the deliberations and conclusions arrived at by him and his deputy Davidi. These directly influenced the way in which the combat spirit of Paratrooper Battalion 890 was shaped, and later, the entire IDF.

The battalion had almost three months with no operational activity and they used the time to regroup and train. According to Sharon, the battalion was lacking two main components: good men to make into commanders and good current commanders to lead the men into action and nurture these future commanders. As part of the efforts to address these twin deficiencies, Sharon started a process of "importing" commanders from outside the battalion. That is when people like Supapo, Danny Matt, Motta Gur and others arrived.

At that time the battalion leadership concluded that they would act according to the principle of small units, where each and every soldier could be controlled. The commander of a unit traveling at night could not control more than twenty to thirty men. Nonetheless, such a small platoon could do more than a large platoon and with fewer casualties, since it moved faster, was easier to operate, was flexible and capable of immediate response. The company, the basic unit, could be evaluated, not by the number of members, but by its ability, in terms of its command, to carry out an individual mission. In contrast, the strength of the battalion was calculated entirely based on the number of command teams it contained.

Sharon and Davidi held many conversations – some of them also including Meir Har-Zion – about behavior in battle. One of the conclusions they reached was that self-respect was a key component and a valuable motivator in combat. On the other hand, love for one's country and the national spirit did not really influence fighting spirit. In many cases, soldiers were most concerned by how their peers would view them. A soldier, knowing he is constantly accountable to the social construct in which he lived, would do anything to excel, or at the very least not shame himself.

Another conclusion they reached was that there should be a body of higher standing in every unit, to spur the rest of the units on. In the beginning, it was the reconnaissance platoon in Battalion 890, comprised mostly of Unit 101 veterans, led by Har-Zion. Later it was Company A, led by Supapo (until his death in the "Black Arrow" action). It was comprised of graduates of squad commander courses who were not placed in command roles. It, along with the reconnaissance platoon that was added to it, became the flag bearers of excellence in navigation and combat.

Following the Gaza action, Sharon and Davidi debated what qualities a commander needed to have and who the platoon commanders in the battalion should be – the people who actually lead the fighting. Their conclusion was that they had to choose commanders that ran forward and who knew how to motivate their men to follow them. These platoon and company commanders, personally leading the charge, had to be the best soldiers in their units.

Davidi and Sharon were two completely different people – in their personalities, their behaviors and their actions in the field. Davidi was the calm kind of combatant. He did not rush to lie down and take cover when under fire; he preferred to stand and see what was happening on the battlefield. That was the case in the Gaza operation, after Supapo was killed. Davidi showed up and made Force 1 of Supapo's Company A breach the Egyptian camp and complete the mission to occupy it. In that way, Davidi was an extraordinary character whose serenity instilled a sense of security in all the people he commanded.

Sharon was completely different personality. He was not in the field as much as Davidi used to be, and spent a considerable amount of his time in the hallways of the General Staff and the command generals' offices. For him, the most important thing was to get the actions authorized. Even in this area, Sharon was exceptionally creative and persuasive. He did not shy away from accepting for himself impossibly short timetables to carry out actions. To achieve that, companies were sometimes on standby for days at a time, while giving up on off-base training.

Sharon excelled in his tactical thinking, which relied on his perception of the field, his acquaintance with the enemy and its abilities, and decisions based on intelligence when assembling the attacking force for each one of the missions. His creativity, which might have been linked to his affinity for music, brought his action plans to the pinnacle of harmony and allowed him to maintain the element of surprise, taking advantage of it to ensure the mission's success.

When it came to evaluating and judging his commanders' abilities, Sharon was a tough and uncompromising officer. If you did something wrong, you would be kicked out for it without a second thought. He didn't care what had happened before; "take your clothes and go home" was a typical Sharon response. He thought this was the only way to maintain operational discipline, dedication and adherence to the mission.

Meir Har-Zion was born in Herzliya in 1934. When he was three years old, his family moved to Moshav Rishpon, and as the War of 1948 broke out, when he was thirteen, his parents split up. His mother moved to Kibbutz

Beit Alpha with his two sisters, and he and his father joined Kibbutz Ein Harod. On July 30, 1952 he joined Nahal, and about a year later, when Unit 101 was formed, he transferred there. While in Nahal Har-Zion already made a name for himself due to his many hikes and reconnaissance patrols around Israel and beyond, and as a soldier with above-average fitness and tough character, though not always disciplined.

Immediately after Unit 101 was merged into Battalion 890, Har-Zion became the commander of the reconnaissance platoon. It was a kind of "mini-Unit 101" which set an example for the standard required in patrols across the border and the high benchmark Sharon had set for the execution of military actions for every soldier in the battalion. Har-Zion commanded the reconnaissance platoon for an entire year, during which it actively took part in the reprisal actions. He and his men participated in the raid on the village of Nahlin, Operation Cigarette to capture Egyptian prisoners in April 1954, Operation Azun, the Kissufim Outpost operation in the Gaza Strip, operations to capture Jordanian soldiers to exchange for Israeli soldier Yitzhak Jibli, and raids on Beit Ur al-Tahta and Beit Likiya, to name only a few. In addition, there were many reconnaissance patrols across the border, which served as a continuation of what had been Unit 101's routine.

Both battalion commander Sharon and his deputy Davidi lionized Har-Zion and counted on his contribution to the reconnaissance platoon helping to achieve the objective of transforming the paratroopers' battalion into a fighting unit. In late December 1954, Har-Zion was hit by a devastating blow when his sister, Shoshana Har-Zion, and her friend Oded Vegmeister were murdered by Bedouins of the Rashaida tribe. Shoshana had attempted to duplicate one of her brother's hikes. He had walked from Jerusalem to Ein Gedi with his classmate Uri Oppenheimer. Uri and Meir had completed the journey unharmed, probably thanks to Meir's keen senses, which was why they were among the first members to join Unit 101; however, Shoshana and Oded were not as lucky. It wasn't until February 15 that Israeli Bedouins found the two bodies near Arugot Stream, on the Jordanian side. Har-Zion temporarily retired from military service and recruited former Unit 101 friends, all from the same class and from various kibbutzim – all civilians by then – for a private reprisal operation. The action concluded with the murder of four Rashaida tribe members in the area where Shoshana and Oded had been slain. However, they left one old Bedouin alive to tell the tribe of what had happened.[38]

Meir's private reprisal action naturally caused a great deal of controversy and considerable criticism. Ben-Gurion were worried and Chief of General Staff Dayan was furious. Although Har-Zion was able to avoid prosecution, he was "sentenced" to several months of "exile," herding livestock in Kibbutz Ein Harod while the furor cooled down.

Throughout the period of his absence, the reconnaissance platoon was skillfully managed by Shimon (Katcha) Kahaner, a childhood friend of Meir and fellow Unit 101 veteran. Meanwhile, Company A finished its squad commanders' course and most of its men, along with the reconnaissance platoon, were entrusted to Second Lieutenant Uzi Trachtenberg, who served as the company's acting commander, along with the two platoon commanders, First Lieutenant Tuvia Shapira and First Lieutenant Ovad Ladginsky. Meir Har-Zion returned to the battalion five months later and took back control of Company A, with Uzi as the company's deputy commander. A third platoon was quickly added, and the company was made into the paratrooper commandos. The teams' patrols across the border continued, and most included officers from other platoons of the battalions. Reprisal actions, in response to attacks carried out with the knowledge or even initiative of enemy governments, were executed on larger scales and became even more complex.

There were a few unpleasant moments in the battalion, which is understandable and quite natural, but Davidi was able to maintain a relaxed atmosphere. There were long days spent waiting for the authorizations which Sharon found frustrating. All that waiting was necessary considering the short response time between approval and action. While Arik pounded the corridors between the various offices, Davidi knew how to guide the

---

38 See Chapter 32 for a full account of these events.

commanders to properly utilize that uncertain waiting time. One of Davidi's diverse abilities was skill at chess. He would sometimes arrange a simultaneous game between himself and those who dared challenge him; these games took place in the officers and NCOs mess or the barracks. Davidi mostly won the games, but this afforded those who were challenging him, as well as the kibitzers following their every move, an opportunity to de-stress and provided some temporary peace of mind while waiting for the next action.

As mentioned above, the reconnaissance patrols were Sharon's way of evaluating the quality of his officers and NCOs. He begun the patrols in Unit 101 and, following the incorporation of the unit into Battalion 890, he emphasized them even more. Unlike the reprisal actions, which had to be authorized by high command, the battalion commander found he could decide for himself on cross-border patrols.

The story of Sergeant (later Brigadier General [Ret.]) Tzuri Sagi, the platoon commander, shows exactly how that system worked:

> During a period of patrols, there was one story which completely changed my perception of the importance of reconnaissance patrols. They were more of a test than an intelligence gathering mission. At first, I didn't understand what intelligence need was served by yet another visit to the bridges; everyone knew them and you could see them in every photo.
>
> Bardanov was a very good friend of mine. I was a sergeant, responsible for the company, and Bardanov was a corporal, but we were friends. Bardanov went on patrol with someone else and they made a mistake, messed it up and came back without completing their mission. Bardanov was afraid and told me, "I don't know what's going to happen, Arik will throw me out…" I told him, "Arik won't throw you out, nothing's going to happen to you, you're going [on patrol] with me tomorrow."
>
> The mission we got was to leave from Kissufim, go through the

outposts in the valley called Wadi Salka, and get to the road and train bridges that cross the valley right next to Dir al-Balah. We were to patrol there and then head west into the sandy area that would later become Gush Katif. We then had to go back through Khan Yunis and exit at Nirim. It was a kind of loop during which we had to check two bridges on a creek called Wadi Shatar.

We left Kissufim, made it to the border and crossed through the outposts. It was early evening and we saw an Arab man riding a donkey toward us, with an English rifle on his shoulder. We thought, if he doesn't recognize us as Jews, he would get to live. Otherwise, this could mess up the entire patrol. He came over, said, "*Markhaba*" [Welcome] and we responded, "*Markhabtein*" [Welcome] and kept walking. Then we gained confidence and thought, "Yay! They don't think we're Jewish." We went through the valley into the camp (either Bedouin or refugee), all the kids were running after us, the old people were chasing them away and the dogs were barking. For sure, no one thought we were Jewish, otherwise they would have probably run for their lives. That made us even more confident. We reached the railway bridge in the east, and decided to go on the road bridge, disguised as Arabs; we would look around and that would be the whole patrol, what more could we ask for?

We walked along the road between a few Arab women leading donkeys loaded with grass. As we got onto the road, to the left was a two-story house with a Bren gun in a sandbagged position. Between the road and the train was a conical tent with a kerosene lantern in it, and the bridge was patrolled by a guard. The Arab on the railway bridge shouted to us: "*Andak!*" (Stop!). We stopped. Yirmi was from Jerusalem so he knew Arabic. We were left alone with the Arab ladies with the grass on the bridge. The Arab man shouted, "*Ta'alu jai,*" which means "Come here." Yirmi answered him, "*Ta'al anti*," which means "You come here," then a sergeant came out of the tent and angrily shouted at us, "We told you to come here, so come here!" We went over. Yirmi went toward the guard and the tent. I fired a volley of three rounds and got the sergeant into the tent, and jumped in. There were seven soldiers there, they leaped for their weapons, but I was probably quicker than them and started shooting them all down. The tent fell down and the lantern set it on fire. What scared me more than the Arab men was having to change my magazine, if at a critical moment I'd have to change it I'd be in trouble… somehow it all worked out and we both headed west – since there were two more bridges to reconnoiter. We weren't afraid of the Arabs as much as we were afraid of Arik. What would he say? How were we doing compared to the rest? We ran west, to the sea of sand and then south, toward Wadi Shatar. We decided that this time we would do it quietly. We crawled for over an hour only to find empty bridges.

When we performed that action, the machine gun above our heads in the two-story building was firing at us but it couldn't depress any lower, so all its tracer bullets went into the Dir al-Balah train station. The train station fired back at them and all the outposts in the area started firing at each other, it was a whole mess. However, we were afraid to encounter an ambush when we left, so we walked slowly and carefully toward Nirim and caught a ride with a tractor from the kibbutz.

We went to Kastina, to Southern Command. The head of the Command was there and so were Ariel Sharon and Meir Har-Zion. They both debriefed us. Arik said, "Go back to the platoon" and that was all the confirmation we needed for completing the mission successfully.

As part of the battalion's ongoing activity, there were patrols made on a team level, like the ones operating in Unit 101, whether for routine purposes or ability tests. One day, company commander Meir Har-Zion, along with his deputy Uzi Trachtenberg and three other officers from Company A, left for a reconnaissance of the Husayma camps, twenty kilometers inside enemy territory. The operation, which included entering the camp and gathering a stack of papers from one of the offices, was a success.

Sharon decided to repeat this reconnaissance with Captain Yaakov Stern's team. Levi Hofesh describes the failure of that patrol toward the Husayma camps:

> We set out on patrol aiming to reach the Husayma camps, about twenty kilometers from the border. There was no intention of attacking it, only going in, looking around and coming back.
>
> On the route, not far from the Egyptian camp, we encountered an ambush that did not notice us at first. We were walking on the lower level and they were walking on the upper level. I told Yankele: "Look what's happening above us." A moment later I told him: "Yankele, we'll move ahead slowly, and I hope we won't be discovered," since we were ordered to reach the camp. Suddenly they opened fire on us from that outpost. Since we were lower, we didn't get hurt, but there was heavy fire. Yankele, the company commander, ordered us to retreat. We went back to Israeli territory without completing the mission. Arik summoned Yankele the following day to ask what had happened, and he told him the entire story. Then Arik told him: "Okay, you ran into an ambush, but why didn't you keep going?" And Yankele replied, "It was my impression that the gunfire was so heavy that there was no point in continuing." By the way, this was correct in terms of the general perception. But Arik immediately told him, "Take your things and go home."

A while later, I talked to Arik about it – after he had calmed down, of course – and he accepted the criticism I had about Yankele's removal. But he also said, "I was at a point we could not let anything go. For me, completing the mission is above everything else."

Sharon determined that the mission had failed and the company commander, who did not get another chance to prove himself, was forced to leave the battalion.

Levi Hofesh tells of another typical patrol by a team of officers under Arik's watchful eye:

> We left to reconnoiter a police station, probably Es-Safi, walking for fifteen kilometers each way. The team consisted of: Supapo leading the way, Motta Gur, myself and two others. We walked for miles and couldn't get there! Supapo had made a mistake in navigation... it was supposed to be thirty kilometers in total, and we had to come back before daylight. We got back to the base and Arik called us over. He started debriefing Motta, then Supapo, and then he turned to me and asked, "Levi, what happened?" I said we simply didn't make it to the target. Then Arik said, "Guys, tomorrow you go again, this time Levi Hofesh will lead." We did it and reached the exact location of the police station. I will never forget this patrol, we walked thirty kilometers in one night, took a break for one night and then walked another fifteen kilometers in each direction the following night. Supapo couldn't stop complaining, and Motta also had a hard time walking that much. The second time we arrived at the exact location there, like I said. We sat around, observed for a while and then went into the police compound. There was not much to see there, but it was important to get in. That was Arik's style; if you didn't complete the mission, you would try again the next day!

Eventually, it became clear that for the incorporation of Unit 101 into Battalion 890 to succeed, and subsequently to transform it into a fighting unit, three men were required.

Meir Har-Zion perfected the navigating and dedication to completing missions, both by arriving at the destinations as well as combat.

Sharon initiated missions and had them authorized, and planned them wonderfully. All actions, even the biggest and most complicated ones, were conceptualized within a single timeline: arrive, attack, go back. Sharon was constantly checking the combat level of the commanders in order for the battalion to have a quality command cadre that would fit the expectations he had for it.

Davidi and Sharon made a unique combination. They didn't always see eye to eye, but at the end of the day they appreciated and complemented each other.

Only the combination of these three pillars, Ariel Sharon, Aharon Davidi and Meir Har-Zion, led to success. Who knows what would have happened in the absence of any of them.

30. THE REPRISAL ACTIONS AND THEIR PART IN THE DEVELOPMENT OF THE ARAB-ISRAEL CONFLICT

The Arab-Israel conflict started long before the establishment of the Israeli state. The Arab Revolt, 1936–1939, was aimed at both Britain, which had received the Mandate to govern Palestine from the League of Nations after World War I, and the Jewish population, which grew larger as more Jewish immigrants arrived, mainly from Europe. The leadership of the *Yishuv* (literally the "Settlement," i.e., the organized Jewish population that was striving to establish a Jewish state) struggled with Britain on the political level, but largely avoided military conflict with the local Arabs.

Following the UN General Assembly's decision on November 29, 1947 to end the Mandate by partitioning the territory into a Jewish state alongside an Arab one, the attacks and harassment of Jews by the local Arabs increased, but those never amounted to an actual war. On May 14, 1948, the People's Assembly declared the independence of the Israeli state. With the immediate invasion into the territory of the newly established state by the surrounding Arab countries, the Arab-Jewish conflict took on an inter-state dimension and became the War of 1948 (War of Independence). The war was now also being waged against neighboring Arab armies, including units from the Iraqi army – which didn't have a physical border with the State of Israel – as well as local Arabs, and ended in a decisive if costly Israeli victory. The most notable outcome of that war was a series of armistice agreements, achieved via UN mediation, signed separately by each of the Arab countries.

The perception vis-à-vis security that developed in Israel following the war was based on three assumptions:

1. The State of Israel was under constant existential threat.
2. A practical assessment that believed there was no danger of total war in the coming years.
3. The need to uphold the armistice agreements in a way that would serve the country's interests.

At the level of the existential threat, there was an assessment that the Arab countries did not, and would not soon, accept the existence of the State of Israel. The various proposals for negotiated territorial changes and the returning of refugees into Israeli territory were perceived by Israel as an effort to destroy the State in a way other than war. As for Israel's strategic situation, there were various assessments about the dangers of yet another war. At that time, the predominant opinion in Israel was, as mentioned, that war was a long way away and therefore efforts could be made to reorganize the IDF. As for the armistice commissions, these were the scenes of daily confrontation with mutual complaints about not following the agreements meant to regulate the relationships of Israel with its neighbors along the armistice lines. Variant interpretations of the wording of these agreements caused severe disputes between the sides, which were beyond the capacity of the UN personnel, facilitating the discussions, to resolve.

Infiltration was and remains one of the most difficult problems facing Israel in terms of relations with its neighbors, and especially with Egypt and Jordan. Each of the armistice agreements contained provisions and regulations requiring the armed forces to prohibit civilians from crossing the armistice lines.

The infiltration phenomenon was complex and multifaceted, and included the infiltration of people who had moved to Jordanian-controlled territory or fled to the Gaza Strip during the battles of the War of Independence, leaving homes and farmland in post-war Israeli territory. These refugees were placed in temporary camps and expected to return to their homes at the end of the war. However, Israel refused to accept refugees from Jordan and the Gaza Strip, and a significant portion of the infiltration was motivated by "economic" reasons. This segment of infiltrations has diminished over the years, but intrusions for the purposes of theft and robbery had remained constant. Intelligence officials, as well as religious-political elements in Jordan and the Gaza Strip, began recruiting frustrated refugees, who were suffering from economic hardship, to participate in intelligence gathering and sabotage operations. Israel tended to see all the incursions into its territory in the broad context of the Arab-Israeli conflict, which led the IDF to react to infiltrators with gunfire. The casualties caused thereby led, in turn, to an increase in the number of revenge attacks perpetrated by the Arabs.

The Border with Jordan

The incidents listed below consist mainly of attacks performed on Israeli civilians by infiltrators from Jordan in 1953:

During the second half of January 1953, the relationship between Israel and Jordan took a turn for the worse, and border clashes between the two countries resumed. The Jordanian prime minister made things even worse by announcing that the agreement to prevent infiltration was cancelled and that the Jordanians had renounced the entire armistice agreement. The day after his declaration, a battle took place near the Jordanian village of Falame. Jordanian soldiers attacked an Israeli unit in the Hebron mountains. Another major clash against infiltrators coming in from Jordan occurred in the Sharon area.

The infiltrations multiplied, especially the armed ones aimed at sabotage and murder. Israeli forces responded to intrusions with retaliatory actions, but they failed to effectively deter further repetitions. The British government officially warned the Jordanian government and demanded that armistice agreement violations must be stopped. However, on April 21, the day after Israeli Independence Day, there was a severe clash with Jordanian forces in Jerusalem when Legionnaires, stationed on the walls of the Old City, opened fire on Israeli positions.

The wave of murders on the frontiers was also on the rise. Jordanian infiltration squads raided houses in villages, placed explosives and even threw hand grenades and opened fire into houses. One of the residents of Kfar Hess, in the Sharon area, was murdered. The house of another settler at Moshav Mishmar Ayalon was also attacked. Three moshavim in the Ben Shemen area were attacked during the night. In the course of this attack, one woman was murdered and other women and children were injured. Two Jews were murdered in Jerusalem by Legion soldiers firing on them from their positions on the wall. Two Jewish guards were murdered in the Judean mountains. IDF guards in the Hebron area were attacked. In the Galilee area, a car was attacked by infiltrators. The car was transporting Jewish boys on a trip through the Galilee, and one of the boys was killed in the attack. The Israeli forces launched a counterstrike and tensions reached a peak.

To forestall a greater military escalation, the great powers applied pressure on the Hashemite Kingdom, and in June 1953, Jordan renewed the agreement to prevent infiltrations. But the attacks on the frontier settlements did not end. Night after night, armed infiltrators operated in Israeli territory; it was clear that they were being centrally directed. On June 7, 1953, a young man was killed and three others were injured in a series of shooting attacks on residential neighborhoods in southern Jerusalem. On June 9, 1953, infiltrators attacked a moshav near Lod, firing every which way and throwing hand grenades, and they succeeded in killing one of its residents. That same night, a group of infiltrators attacked a house in Hadera; this happened one day after an agreement was signed between Israel and Jordan, mediated by the UN. In that agreement, Jordan had guaranteed to prevent infiltrators from entering Israel via its territory. On June 10, 1953, infiltrators from Jordan demolished a house at Moshav Mishmar Ayalon. On June 11, 1953, infiltrators attacked a young couple at their Kfar Hess home and shot them dead.

On September 2, 1953, several infiltrators entered Israel from Jordan, reached the Katamon neighborhood at the heart of Jerusalem and threw hand grenades indiscriminately. Miraculously no one was hurt.

On October 13, 1953, Jordanian infiltrators from a *fedayeen* unit threw a hand grenade into a house in the Yehud settlement, near Petah Tikva, murdering a mother and her two children in their sleep. This act, which followed a series of murderous attacks, evoked even more reaction in the Israeli population than those that preceded it, both for its cruelty as well as its location, close to the most populated center of Israel. On October 15, 1953, an Israeli force raided the village of Qibiya in reaction to the shocking murders and blew up dozens of populated houses.

The Qibiya action, as previously described, was a turning point. Its scale – injuring many civilians, among them women and children – led to a change in policy. In future, attacks would be aimed at military objectives. Jordan noticed the change and, on the one hand, attempted to limit the scale of the infiltrations, while at the same time making arrangements to deal with any large-scale IDF reprisal actions. The task of guarding Arab localities was entrusted to the National Guard, which received advanced weapons and training. The Legion, a trained and efficient army, made preparations to face the IDF. The alert level of the Legion units only increased, which could be seen in their responses to the Azun, Hussan and above all Qalqilya actions, in which the Israeli commandos given the roadblock mission were surrounded and in serious danger until they were rescued by half-tracks.

The Border with Egypt and the Gaza Strip

The border between Israel and Egypt was not peaceful either, and there were many armed incidents there, both from the Gaza Strip as well as the Nitzana demilitarized zone. The IDF's takeover of the Negev all the way to Eilat during the War of 1948, and the disruption of land continuity between the Sinai and Jordan, had brought about the creation of two additional groups of infiltrators: Bedouins and smugglers. The Bedouins, who had spent hundreds of years herding in the area undisturbed, had a hard time adjusting to the limitations Israel placed on their movement in the Negev. The Gaza Strip's situation was complicated. Although Egypt administered the area, they refrained from annexing it. Egyptian intelligence representatives in the Strip were free to train and operate civilians from the Strip, especially refugees who knew the area well, for espionage missions in Israeli territory. From there, it was a slippery slope to "spicing" intelligence actions with murderous attacks. Israel's actions to prevent infiltration from that area – such as Unit 101's action at the al-Bureij refugee camp – were not especially effective.

The terror acts out of the Gaza Strip, did not cease and the infiltrations and murders continued unabated. Tensions increased following the trial of eleven Egyptian Jews accused of belonging to an espionage and sabotage organization in Egypt. Two of the defendants were sentenced to death and executed by hanging on January 31, 1955. Egypt stepped up its infiltration, sabotage and murder operations. On February 23, 1955, an armed cell infiltrated a government facility near Rishon LeZiyon and stole important official documents. On February 25, 1955, a Jewish cyclist was murdered by an Egyptian squad on the Rehovot–al-Qubayba road. While making its way back to base in the Gaza Strip, the squad encountered an Israeli guard, who killed one of the terrorists. When the body was searched, reports on Israeli vehicle movement on the southern roads were found. The reaction was the "Black Arrow" action, in which an Israeli force raided an Egyptian base near Gaza on February 28. Thirty-eight Egyptian officers and soldiers were killed in that raid, and dozens were injured, with the IDF loosing eight men in the battle.

The reprisal action led to rioting and chaos in the Gaza Strip; thousands of protesters burned down the UNRWA's food and clothing warehouse near Rafah. The Egyptian authorities clamped a curfew on Gaza and demanded an emergency meeting of the UN's Security Council. Following that incident, Egyptian threats and the bloody border incidents continued unabated. Eventually, the great powers decided to condemn Israel for the raid and simultaneously called on both Israel and Egypt to cooperate with the head of the UN's Observer Headquarters to implement his plans to reduce tensions at the border. The demands of the Egyptians and their supporters to sanction Israel were not accepted.

The provocations continued, with an Egyptian landmine laying action resulting in the deaths of two IDF soldiers and the injury of four more. The firing from Egyptian outposts on Israeli positions also continued. On March 24, 1955, infiltrators threw hand grenades and opened fire on a crowd at a wedding in the agricultural community of Moshav Patish in the Negev. A young woman was killed and eighteen people were injured in the attack.

Egyptian aggression increased and in April 1955, Egyptian artillery bombarded Kibbutz Nahal Oz, near Gaza. IDF guards traveling on the "patrol route" along the armistice line were also attacked. Two soldiers were killed in the attack and the rest were injured. Following that attack, Israel issued a stern warning to the Security Council and the major powers, that it would have to respond forcefully to Egypt's aggression. The Security Council postponed discussion of the sixteen complaints Israel had submitted until after receiving a report from the head of the UN observers. In the meanwhile, two more IDF soldiers were killed on the "patrol route" with several others injured. The IDF guard kept absorbing fire from Egyptian outposts.

On May 17, 1955, Egyptian mines laid in the Kissufim section of the western Negev, adjacent to the Gaza Strip border, led to the deaths of three IDF officers and the severe injury of two more. The following day, an IDF unit attacked an Egyptian outpost opposite that section.

On May 30, Egyptian bombardment on an IDF unit and the settlements of Nirim and Ein HaShlosha resulted in the deaths of two Jewish men and severe injury of four more. The IDF responded with heavy artillery fire.

On August 29, 1955, an attack took place on Beit Oved. A Palestinian *fedayeen* squad fired small arms into a group of Israeli workers. Four were killed and ten were injured.

While the head of UN Observers was in Cairo to discuss the agreement regarding aggression and prevention of bloodshed across the armistice line, the Egyptians attacked an IDF guard position near Miflasim in the Negev. The Israeli unit countered by occupying the Egyptian outpost from which the attack was launched. Three Egyptian soldiers were killed and eight were injured.

The Egyptians bombarded Nahal Oz and there was gunfire and explosions along the entire border with the Gaza Strip. Egyptian soldiers managed to perform five actions within a single day, which appeared to be a well-coordinated military operation. They seized two hills inside Israeli territory, killed a member of the Yad Mordechai kibbutz, attacked vehicles on the roads along the border and fired on the Ashkelon area. The Egyptians laid mines along the road near Be'eri and an IDF vehicle was hit; three soldiers were killed, and others were injured. For these provocations, the IDF responded with a ferocious artillery attack.

On August 30, 1955, Egyptian commando units performed acts of murder and sabotage deep within Israeli territory. The units penetrated all the way to Kfar Menachem and the orchards of Nes Ziyona. They killed six Jewish civilians, attacked an IDF vehicle and attempted to sabotage equipment of the broadcasting authority. Three Israeli soldiers were killed at the border, and Kibbutz Erez was bombarded.

The night before September 1, 1955, an Israeli convoy infiltrated about six kilometers into the Gaza Strip, raided the Egyptian base at Khan Yunis and used explosives to demolish the main building of the *fedayeen*'s central command – "the Suicide Corps" – that operated under the instruction of Egyptian military officers and was commanded by a top Egyptian intelligence officer. This bold and aggressive reprisal action resulted in the killing of sixty Egyptian officers and soldiers, and injuring dozens more. The Israeli unit suffered one dead and eight lightly injured.

The Egyptians attacked in the south, in a surprise raid on an Israeli police station at Be'erotayim, near Auja al-Hafir. An Israeli policeman was killed, three more were injured and two policemen were taken hostage. At first light on October 29, 1955, Israel reacted with an IDF reprisal action on an Egyptian military base at Kuntilla, in the Sinai desert.

It is important to remember the strategic context of the relationships between Israel and Egypt. The barring of Israeli ships from the Suez Canal, the process of the British leaving Egypt and the Canal Zone, as well as Egypt's agreements with Jordan – all of these were for Israel several times more serious than the threat posed by infiltration.

The Border with Syria

The situation on the Israel-Syria border was completely different. At the end of the War of 1948, Syrian forces had taken territories west of the international border that had separated Syria from Mandatory Palestine. The armistice agreement between Israel and Syria, signed following long and tedious negotiations, led to the withdrawal of Syrian forces from these territories and designated them as demilitarized zones. The question of sovereignty over the demilitarized zones remained open for discussion between the sides, and was set to take place in "a separate framework." The armistice lines in the Syrian sector did not separate farmers from their lands as it did on the Jordanian and Egyptian borders. Though tens of thousands of Palestinian refugees had fled to Syria, they found refuge there and were integrated, both socially and economically, which also explains the lack of infiltrations at that border.

The question of sovereignty in the demilitarized zones occupied the Israeli-Syrian armistice agreement committee and remained on the agenda of both UN and the Western powers.

A dispute with Syria did arise from the project of draining the Hula Lake, which began in January of 1951, leading to a military conflict between the two countries. Part of the digging and draining works took place east and southeast of the lake, which, since July 20, 1949, had been classed under the armistice agreement between the two countries as a "demilitarized zone." The conflict erupted when bulldozers started operating south of Hula Lake, on land inside the demilitarized zone that was owned by Syrian Arabs. The Syrians demanded that, before excavating, Israel must first settle the issue of compensation for use of these lands, and filed a complaint with the Israeli-Syrian Armistice Commission. The matter was handed over to Major General William Riley,[39] head of the United Nations Truce Supervision Organization (UNTSO), and, at the beginning of March, he announced that Israel should stop its work in the demilitarized zone until the issue of compensation for Arab lands had been resolved. Israel rejected Riley's ruling and did not acknowledge the Syrians' right to file complaints to the Armistice Commission on matters that were essentially civilian, or the committee's right to discuss such complaints.

Israel continued to work in the western demilitarized zone, but not on Arab-owned lands. On March 13, digging works also began in the eastern area of the Jordan River, and Northern Command was tasked with securing the operations in what was known as "Operation Drainage." On March 15 there was a shooting incident at the location, when local Arab men – apparently Syrian soldiers in civilian clothes – fired on an Israeli tractor and hit it. The following day, Israel agreed to stop work on all sections for ten days, to allow the conflict to be resolved. When no resolution was reached, Israel renewed the work on March 25. The Syrians responded by opening fire, causing injuries on the Israeli side. Attempts to resolve the issue through talks between the two countries' Deputy Chiefs of Staff were unsuccessful, and Israel toughened its stance.

On March 30, a decision was made by political and military elements to continue working in the area despite the exchange of fire, and even perform actions within the demilitarized zone that would show Israel's sovereignty in the area. Among other things, it was decided that the IDF would transfer residents from two Arab villages in the demilitarized zone to the Sha'ab village in the Galilee, and provide the local residents with Israeli ID cards. At the same time, at the beginning of April, Israeli representatives took part in the Armistice Commission's discussions on finding an arrangement, even as the IDF's Operations Branch ordered a state of alert for both land and air forces

---

39 A veteran of the US Marine Corps, he held this post from September 1948 to June 1953.

all along that sector. The military alert took into account the limitations on introducing military forces into the demilitarized zone and was based on holding reserve forces on the edge of it while relying on the air force. On April 4, just a few days after the order was issued, the IDF sent a "police" patrol to the demilitarized zone in al-Hamma, to demonstrate Israel's sovereignty over the territory, which was technically Israeli but was actually controlled by the Syrians. In response, the Syrians attacked the patrol and seven Israelis were killed. The following day, the Israeli government decided on a reprisal action, and that very same day the air force bombed the police station at al-Hamma and several Syrian outposts in the area. That was the first time since the end of the War of Independence that the Israeli Air Force was called on to attack military targets.

Following the tension and bloody clashes, the Western powers stepped in and brought the subject up for discussion at the UN's Security Council. The United States demanded Israel and Syria immediately stop the conflict. Abba Eban, the Israeli delegate at the Security Council meeting, had to apologize for the air force bombing at al-Hamma.

The world's stance against Israel encouraged Syria and, as a result, a major Syrian provocation took place in the area north of the Sea of Galilee. At the beginning of May 1951, Syrian forces infiltrated Israeli territory and settled in Tel al-Mutila, north of the Sea of Galilee. An Israeli guard patrol that encountered the force suffered four casualties. Reinforcements were called in and a continuous and brutal battle broke on the hill and near it. Both sides resorted to cannon and mortar fire, and the Syrian forces attacked the Israelis repeatedly, in an attempt to repel them. The front shifted back and forth until, after three days of fighting, the Syrians were finally pushed back east across the Jordan River. Thus, the Syrian attempt to secure important positions west of the Jordan River, on the Israeli side of the demilitarized zone, was foiled. The Security Council, which had been discussing whether Israeli was entitled to perform drainage works at Hula Lake in the demilitarized zone, ordered Israel to cease work there from May 19.

The Sea of Galilee's eastern coast had been defined in the 1948 Ceasefire

Agreements as the southern demilitarized zone, with three-thirds of the area Israeli-owned and the remaining third Arab-owned. Shortly after signing the agreement, and before the Syrians evacuated the southern demilitarized zone, Israeli representatives vigorously sought to purchase the Arab-owned lands at that area. Soon enough a new settlement was established, HaOn, and the already-existing Kibbutz Ma'agan was expanded. The people of Ein Gev simultaneously expanded their agricultural activity to the areas in the demilitarized zone, while occasionally being subjected to fire from Syrian forces. Israeli fishermen who would sometimes get close to the eastern coast of the Sea of Galilee were also fired upon.

31. THE IMPACT OF THE REPRISAL ACTIONS ON ISRAEL'S INTERNATIONAL STATUS AND POLITICAL STRATEGY

At the end of the War of 1948, Israel, with the help of UN mediation, signed armistice agreements with its neighbors. Though the agreements did not lead to negotiations for peace treaties between the former combatants, Armistice Commissions, led by UN representatives, were established to deal with complaints regarding violations of the agreements, and Israel viewed the armistice mechanism as an appropriate framework for managing its relations with the other countries. The commissions soon had their agendas filled with complaints from both sides. Israel entrusted the responsibility for working with the committees to the defense establishment, assuming that most of the topics to be discussed would be security related.

From the outset, it was clear that Israel and the Arab states shared no agreement, or common interpretation to certain clauses in the accords. At first, a major topic the commissions had to address was the war on infiltrations — and its related issues — on the Egyptian and Jordanian borders. The demilitarized zones at the Syrian border and the Nitzana area, near the Egyptian border, were focal points for countless conflicts and complaints. Later, as military reactions to the infiltrations and attacks grew, the commissions had to address those issues as well.

The Border Police, established in the summer of 1953 as part of the Israeli Police, was entrusted with guarding the border and the safety of the civilians on the frontier. The responsibility for cross-border actions, which were supposed to prevent infiltrations and attacks, remained in the hands of the IDF.

Israel attempted to manage a combined policy, in which military and political actions were taken in parallel. The local commanders' agreements, signed as part of the armistice agreements, was supposed to promote understanding between the sides. These agreements included an obligation by all parties not to allow the border to be crossed, as well as a prohibition of opening fire on infiltrators. The political policy was mainly conducted via contact between the local commanders, but Israel – not convinced that the commanders' agreement would bring about restraint in infiltrations – asked to change their format to allow occasional military action.

The US State Department, led by Dean Acheson, severely criticized the asymmetry between the infiltrations and Israel's reactions. The State Department clearly stated Israeli military incursions into Jordan or other neighboring countries (Egypt and Syria) should not be allowed. They claimed that Israel should consider the difficult and unpleasant outcomes that such an activity could bring upon them.

At the beginning of January 1953, Israel had found a pretext to cancel the commanders' agreement with Jordan. An Israeli representative at the Armistice Commission claimed that Jordan was holding Israeli soldiers captive who had accidentally crossed the border near Latrun. Accordingly, the Israeli representative at the committee announced that the agreement was cancelled. The Jordanians, for their part, announced that they were the ones who had cancelled the agreement. The IDF's high command wanted to perform a reprisal action the moment the agreement was cancelled, without tying it to a murderous attack by the Jordanians.

Prime Minister David Ben-Gurion supported the action but since a summit was taking place between British Prime Minister Winston Churchill and the new American president, Dwight D. Eisenhower, Ben-Gurion felt the timing was not right and decided to postpone the action by a few days. The aforementioned Givati Brigade's action against the village of Falame, with its two unsuccessful attempts, was a resounding failure. Three other reprisal actions, this time by Paratrooper Battalion 890 against the villages of Rantis, Hussan and Idhna – before the forming of Unit 101 – were not considered great successes either.

Minister of Foreign Affairs Moshe Sharett raised the claims made in prior government meetings to the American ambassador to Israel, Paul Davis. Sharett made it clear to the ambassador that both the IDF and the Ministry of Foreign Affairs were dissatisfied by the way the Jordanian Legion had been dealing with infiltrations from their territory. In an uncharacteristically assertive and sharp way, Sharett insisted that, as long as Jordan did not act to prevent the infiltrations, Israel would maintain its self-defense policy, meaning reprisal actions. The Israeli government's argument did not soften American criticism against it, and Secretary of State John Foster Dulles accepted the position of the head of the Armistice Commission, who believed that the Israeli initiative stemmed from a concern as to the Western powers' intent to provide Western weapons (mostly via the US and Britain) to Israel's neighbors. Israel itself had invested significant effort, led by the Ministry of Foreign Affairs, to acquire new and advanced weapons systems from those same countries. It should be noted that Britain had a unique relationship with the Kingdom of Jordan and the Legion's command – which was made up of British officers – during the War of 1948 as well as many years afterwards. Israel was aware of the US strategic interest in strengthening its foothold in the Middle East against Soviet efforts to do the same, thus adding another political and strategic consideration to the internal Israeli factors militating for performing reprisal actions every time there was a murderous attack in its territory.

The deadly attack in which a mother and two of her children were murdered in Yehud raised tensions along the Jordanian border. IDF and Border Police units were put on alert, expecting possible escalation and an incursion by the Jordanian army into Israeli territory. A warning about the matter was conveyed to representatives of the three Western powers in Israel, but the representatives were very skeptical. The three Western powers feared that Israel was attempting to lay the groundwork for a military initiative on all three borders.

On the Syrian border a crisis arose over Israeli attempts to dig a canal in the area of the Benot Yaakov Bridge. On the Jordanian border, the Qibiya action was seen as an unusual threat due to its large scale and the high number of civilian casualties. On the Egyptian border, there were skirmishes in the al-Auja demilitarized zone, in addition to the attack on the al-Bureij refugee camp. The representatives of the superpowers believed that Israel's goal was to prevent, at any cost, whatever it considered to be strategic threats.

Israel's relationship with Egypt was more complicated than its one with Jordan. The infiltrations were mainly economically motivated; Egypt had avoided the annexation of the Gaza Strip and its policy was also to avoid any severe conflicts with Israel. The activity of the Armistice Commission in the area was, therefore, practical. That was not the case when it came to maritime freedom for Israeli ships in the Suez Canal, as Egypt prevented their passage despite the British still holding a key position there.

At the end of February 1954, a series of incidents occurred on the Gaza Strip border, including fire from outposts on IDF patrols and ambushes inside Israeli territories. In discussions in the Armistice Commission, Egypt claimed that these were the actions of Palestinian refugees and hard to control. Israel, for its part, addressed the three Western powers – via the Ministry of Foreign Affairs and its staff – to demand that they intervene and calm the incidents along the border.

At the end of April 1954, the shooting incidents from the Strip resumed and IDF intelligence traced several sabotage operations within Israeli territory to squads sent by Egyptian intelligence. Defense Minister Lavon eventually received authorization from the Prime Minister and Minister of Foreign Affairs Sharett to perform a reprisal action against an Egyptian outpost in the Dir al-Balah area, across the border from Kibbutz Kissufim. The action was carried out by a paratrooper company that occupied the outpost, killed several Egyptian soldiers, and blew up the fortifications before leaving the area. Egypt declined to respond, preferring to avoid an escalation that might have disrupted the critical stages of the Anglo-Egyptian agreement to evacuate British forces from the Suez Canal. This agreement was part of a larger trend that had started at the end of World War II, in which

Britain and the US attempted to incorporate Middle Eastern countries into a pro-Western regional pact. Iraq was the main axis for the Western powers, but Nasser, who objected to Iraq's leading role in the agreements, managed to form a military pact between Syria and Egypt, and later on also with Saudi Arabia and Jordan. By doing so, Nasser preserved Egypt's premier position in the Arab world.

Israel viewed these processes taking place in the Middle East, especially in Egypt, as dangerous. It feared that the pacts, both that made with Baghdad and the parallel alliance lead by Egypt, would bring a flow of Western weapons into the Arab countries. Israel likewise viewed the exit of British forces from Suez as a severe strategic threat, leaving no buffer between Israel and Egypt. The failed attempt to sabotage Western targets in Egypt by young Jewish men – operated by Israeli intelligence – known as "the Affair," or the "Lavon Affair," only gave Nasser cause to harden his stance against Israel.

The hangings of the members of the Jewish cell, Moshe Marzouk and Shmuel Azar, intensified the rift in contacts between Egypt and Israel. However, an even more significant event was the February 28, 1955 attack on the Egyptian forces' headquarters in the Gaza Strip. The operation was ordered by Chief of General Staff Moshe Dayan and authorized by Defense Minister David Ben-Gurion (who had just returned from a "vacation" at Sde Boker), as well as Prime Minister Moshe Sharett, in reaction to a murder performed by Egyptian intelligence agents near Rehovot, the culmination of several accumulated attacks. It was also – and perhaps mainly – related to larger developments in the Middle East, such as the signing of the Baghdad Pact and Israel's inability to convince the US to formally guarantee its security. The Gaza action, focusing on military facilities and soldiers rather than the refugees in the Strip, was a harsh blow for the prestige of Egyptian President Nasser. The Security Council condemned Israel for the action and Britain and the US supported the condemnation decision in the hopes of solidifying the status of the UN Observers on all fronts. The Security Council's decision following the Gaza action was to demand that General Burns – the head of the UNTSO – act in order to find an arrangement between the sides. Israel could not afford to initiate any large-scale operations like the Gaza action as long as Burns complied with the Security Council directive. Nasser, on the other hand, was preoccupied with two tasks: restoring Egypt's prestige from the damage it had suffered as a result of the action, and the agreement between Iraq and Turkey, which hindered his ambitions to lead the Muslim world.

However, Ben-Gurion did not change his mind about the necessity of retaliatory actions. Sharett, on the other hand, made many efforts to convince the US Secretary of State – in light of the formation of the Baghdad Pact – that the US must commit to protect Israel and its borders and provide it with military assistance. Secretary of State Dulles promised he would consider Israel's request. Israel was kept in the dark regarding contacts between the US State Department and the British Foreign Office aimed at regulating the relationships between Israel and its neighbors.

Over the years, various US presidents have occasionally come up with ideas for political arrangements that would later include all the countries in the region. (As these lines are being written, President Trump's "Deal of the Century" between Israel and Palestine is on the table.) The Anglo-American program nicknamed "Alpha," was supposed to bring about an arrangement that would include, among other things, border changes, the end to the Arab economic boycott of Israel, and the opening of the Suez Canal to Israeli shipping. During 1955, the "Alpha" program was the key component of the US's political activity to resolve the conflict in the area, but eventually, despite Burns's efforts, the incidents along the border only grew at the initiative of the Egyptian army, and the ambitious political initiative evaporated.

The Gaza action (operation "Black Arrow"), as well as the preceding Kissufim outpost action (operation "Eye for an Eye") marked a change in the character of the reprisal actions. No longer were the actions targeted against civilians and bandits; they were now to be strictly military actions against the Egyptian, Jordanian and Syrian armies to impose accountability on the governments that tolerated and sometimes encouraged the infiltrations. Though international criticism of the reprisal actions diminished, the human price Israel paid for the new approach constantly increased.

32. MEIR HAR-ZION'S PERSONAL REPRISAL ACTION

Shortly after Meir Har-Zion arrived in Unit 101, Major Ariel Sharon, the unit's commander, recognized his outstanding capabilities and appointed him commander of one of the squads in the unit. Sharon, who relied on Har-Zion, assigned operations to him and his squad that were perceived as complex, such as operation "Silk Gloves" in Hebron; and Har-Zion unofficially became the third most important person in the unit after the commander, Ariel Sharon, and his deputy Shlomo Baum. In January 1954, when Unit 101 was merged into Paratrooper Battalion 890, Har-Zion was appointed commander of the battalion's reconnaissance platoon. Har-Zion took part in many actions, which gave him the reputation of a fierce warrior, gifted scout and an unusually skilled commander. His men were willing to follow him through hell if need be, without thinking twice.

In late December 1954, Shoshana Har-Zion and her friend Oded Vegmeister left for a hike in the Judean desert, during which they crossed the border with Jordan. The two left from Kibbutz Ramat Rachel on their way to Ein Gedi, following a route that had been successfully taken by her brother Meir and his friend Uri (Ofir) Oppenheimer, who would go on to serve with him when Unit 101 would be formed. A week later, when the two did not return at the planned time, an extensive search was begun. About six weeks later, on February 15, 1955, Israeli Bedouins found the two bodies near the Nahal Arugot channel, inside Jordan. It turned out the two had been murdered by Bedouins from the Rashaida tribe. Har-Zion decided to relieve himself from his military service in Battalion 890 and go on his own personal reprisal action in order to exact revenge on his sister's killers.

On the night preceding March 5, Har-Zion and a few of his friends, also civilians, left for the reprisal action: Amiram Hirschfeld (from Kibbutz Degania B, Battalion 890 veteran), Ze'ev Slutzky and Yoram Nahari (both classmates of Har-Zion from Ein Harod, and Unit 101 veterans). Two other friends, Yishai Zimmerman and Eitan Bentov, nicknamed "Hanabat," who were probably with them, left the team as the action ended, and got away unpunished. The squad members raided a Bedouin encampment in the Judean desert, about nine kilometers east of the Israeli-Jordanian border, the area where the two were murdered. They captured four Bedouins and led them to the nearby wadi to execute them. About a kilometer and a half away from the wadi, Har-Zion and his squad encountered two more tents. While they attempted to enter them, two of the inhabitants ran away. One was shot dead and the other escaped. An old Bedouin who was in one of the tents was taken by Har-Zion and his friends. The Israelis tried to question the five captives, to no avail, and eventually murdered four of them. They left the fifth one, the old man, alive, so he could go back to his tribe and tell them why the others had been killed.

The Prime Minister and Minister of Foreign Affairs at the time, Moshe Sharett, characterized the revenge component as "an absolutely wrong provocation," as he defined it. That was why, though punishment and revenge were seemingly intertwined and could not always be separated, Dayan introduced the goals of the reprisal policy while making it clear that a reprisal operation was "not a revenge action. It is a punishment and deterrence action, signaling to the country in question that, if it does not take control of its inhabitants and prevent attacks on Israel – Israeli forces will wreak havoc on their land."

The way the public saw the reprisal actions, from their beginnings in 1955 all the way to the 1980s, reveals the changes in the moral standards of Israeli society. Throughout that period, there was public criticism toward the murder of the Bedouins, without assigning any responsibility for the murder of Shoshana Har-Zion and Oded Vegmeister. However, it is unclear whether the majority of the public still views Meir Har-Zion's personal reprisal action in the same critical light.

Israel's government ordered no reprisal action for the murder of Shoshana Har-Zion and her friend. Similarly, as there was no action taken after the murder of the Israelis who travelled to Petra.[40] The fact that the young victims in Petra had illegally entered a neighboring country's territory, and that their deaths were not caused by an infiltration squad, contributed to the considerations not to act against Jordan. However, such considerations brought no rest to Har-Zion. He told those close to him, "One thought plagued me all these days; you are constantly making sure murderers are punished, but your sister's murder goes unpunished?" This was Har-Zion's justification to ask his friends, the veterans of Unit 101, to join him on his private reprisal operation. At the end of the action, Har-Zion and his friends returned to the border and received a written message, thrown at them from a light aircraft, saying that they were to return to the Tel Nof base immediately.

It must be said that Har-Zion's private reprisal action was in line with the official military reprisal policy, especially in the paratrooper battalion to which he belonged, which always sought to retaliate for the murders of Jews. However, the element of vengeance in this private reprisal action, the lack of discipline and the breach of authority it expressed, as well as the fact that it was carried out for the murder of two travelers who went beyond

---

40 In the 1950s the ancient, abandoned city of Petra exerted a romantic (and even fatal) attraction on young Israelis. Many braved the dangerous and illegal journey into Jordanian territory to visit the site. In August 1952, five former Palmach members sought to reach the legendary spot. They penetrated about fifteen kilometers past the Israeli border into Jordan, near Bir Madkur, when a Jordanian soldier shot and killed them. Another seven Israelis were subsequently killed in four more attempts. In an attempt to reduce the obsession, Israeli government-controlled radio was prohibited from playing a popular song called "The Red Rock" that romanticized the quest.

Israeli borders in a place they should not have been, seemed wrong to Chief of General Staff Dayan, as well as the military's leadership. Dayan ordered the transfer of the four men to police custody, severely reprimanded them, and even informed them they were relieved of their position in the reserve paratrooper unit.

The IDF began a series of internal probes as early as the following day, March 5. The first investigation was held by the Central Command's Intelligence Division Officer, Lieutenant Colonel Shmuel Galinka, together with the head of Battalion 890 Lieutenant Colonel Ariel Sharon. Following Galinka's assessment that the participants in the raid had received weapons and assistance from the battalion, and that he was not sure whether other men, including those within the ranks of the battalion, knew about their intentions, Chief of General Staff Moshe Dayan ordered the head of Central Command, Major General Zvi Ayalon, to appoint a committee that would determine whether or not Battalion 890 aided in that personal revenge action – and if so, to bring the culprits to justice. None of that stopped Dayan from announcing the following day at the March 6 Foreign Affairs and Security Council meeting: "I have looked into the matter and it turns out it was not a military unit that executed this action, and the men who did it had no help from any military unit." Even though Dayan knew full well who had committed the murders, he preferred to cover for the paratroopers battalion and the army, and conceal the information he possessed. At the government meeting taking place that same day, Ben-Gurion – who had been made defense minister in the Sharett administration only a few weeks prior to the incident – also determined that the murder of the Bedouins was a private action and had nothing to do with the army, despite the very strong suspicion indicating that the opposite was true.

The following excerpts from Moshe Sharett's diaries faithfully detail the assessments and contemplations the prime minister had while dealing with Meir Har-Zion and his friends' private reprisal action:

Saturday, March 5, 1955

Our cup of troubles overflowed this Shabbat with the addition a new incident on our part, of the worst kind. The military says that last night, a "private" act of vengeance was carried out for the killing of the man and woman [Oded Vegmeister and Shoshana Har-Zion], who hiked in the region of Ein Gedi [in February]. According to this version, a group of men crossed the border, among them the woman's brother [Meir Har-Zion] (the woman was a daughter of Kibbutz Beit Alpha), attacked a group of Bedouins and killed five of them. The army knew that such an act was being planned and was about to prevent it; however, according to their intelligence, the act was scheduled for tonight and there was an assumption that it could still be prevented; alas, the men decided to move the action up and what happened, happened. The Jordanians have been publishing a completely different version all day! It was twenty soldiers who had committed the murder: hurt six Bedouins, murdered five, left one alive and told him it was in retaliation for the two that were murdered by the same tribe, so he would tell the others about it. In the evening and in light of the Jordanians' complaint, the IDF Spokesman announced that an investigation had been held, and it was proven that no IDF unit took part in this action and that the IDF was still investigating whether civilians were involved.

It is clear that this kind of action is the last thing we needed right now. This might serve as conclusive proof that we have decided to switch to an all-out bloody attack, on all fronts. The reprisal at Gaza, something at the Jordanian border today, tomorrow some incident in the Syrian demilitarized zone and so on. I told myself that I would demand a criminal trial against these men in tomorrow's cabinet meeting – otherwise we will be forever guilty in the eyes of the public, as we will also lose the right to demand that our neighboring countries punish murderers.

Sunday, March 6, 1955

The only topic on the meeting's agenda, other than the Gaza action, was the killing of the five Bedouins. BG [Ben-Gurion] gave a detailed report about it and did not spare us the details of the brutal murder – how our four young men captured Bedouin boys, how one by one, they led them to the wadi and murdered them with knives, one by one, how they tried to interrogate them before they died about the people who had murdered the man and woman, and couldn't understand their answers because they did not speak Arabic. The one leading the men was the brother of the murdered woman, [Meir] Har-Zion of Ein Harod. Ben-Gurion himself demanded that the four be tried – they had turned themselves in to the army and admitted without any reservation what they had done – and proposed that a committee of three minsters – the prime minister, justice minister and defense minister – set the procedure.

We had a meeting of the committee of ministers regarding the murderers of the Bedouins. Both BG and I saw the advantage of having them court-martialed, but it turned out there was doubt as to whether or not there is a legal basis for such a procedure. It is preferred that prolonged prison sentences, which the four are expected to get, be given by a military court since a sentence from civilian courts would be viewed as improper by the military.

In the evening, the minister of justice and the attorney general informed me that they found no legal possibility of sending the matter to a military court. I contacted BG and had him order the army to transfer the four to police custody so we could announce, as soon as this evening, that we have arrested four suspects and are investigating them.

By the way, it turned out that the same Har-Zion who initiated the act of vengeance and recruited three of his friends, all now reserve paratroopers – two of them friends of his from Ein Harod [Ze'ev Slutzky and Yoram Nahari] and one a friend of his from Degania B [Amiram Hirschfeld] – was himself discharged from the army after his sister was murdered, to stand by his parents in their time of grief. It is easy to imagine what will happen to the parents when their only remaining child[41] is sentenced to prison for avenging his sister. And all this unfolding tragedy is nothing but the fruits of a wild act of youth – a man and woman, of their own accord, on a trip in an enemy country, and this is after other precious victims have already fallen as a result of such adventures.

I have spent the entire evening transferring the four men from the army to police jurisdiction. The transfer was delayed since the chief of general staff was unavailable – probably attending some Purim party – and so word of the arrests has not been announced tonight, much to my chagrin.

Friday, March 11, 1955

[Police Commissioner] Yehezkel Sahar came to report on the matter of the four. As mentioned, they have refused to confess, or even give evidence. They only provided their identities – their names and places of residence. The commissioner turned to the chief of general staff and asked if the army was willing to aid in their investigation, meaning whether the police could send its investigators to military sources and find out what they know. The chief of general staff said he would consult the defense minister, and then replied in his name that he did not allow it. The commissioner came to me at a loss; it is obvious that the army

---

41 Sharett was misinformed; Meir had another sister.

is covering for these men. He has no means of investigating the matter without direct cooperation from the military, since the suspects are refusing to speak. Since there is no cooperation and no evidence or testimony can be collected from any other source, there will be no choice but to release the suspects and close the case. He asked for my advice. In his mind, this behavior from the army should not be tolerated, as it amounts to defying the authority of the legitimate government.

I was concerned. Did BG not see how he might get caught up in this? It was he himself who brought the matter to the government's attention, who relayed the essence of the military report and offered to hand the men over to be tried. The committee, formed at his suggestion, was only designated to settle the manner in which they were to be handed over to trial – whether military or civilian, and on what charges. He now practically authorizes the sabotaging of the police investigation and jeopardizes the government's decision to bring the suspects to justice.

…I had time for a quick chat with Isser [Harel, head of both Israel's internal and external intelligence services] as he was about to go abroad on personal business. According to his understanding, there is almost no one in the country who will convict these men of murdering the Bedouins. Public opinion is definitely on their side. Handing them over to the police to be interrogated seems like going through the motions for outsiders, and not as an educational step from the inside.

Musik [Gidron, a relative of Sharett's, who would later become head of IDF Human Resources] came to tell me that the entire revenge action was conducted with the active aid of Arik [Sharon], the commander of the paratroopers' battalion. He equipped the four with weapons, food and other equipment, drove them a long way in the battalion vehicle, and sent squads along their route to guarantee their safe return. It is unclear if Moshe Dayan also knew about the operation in advance, but I understood that he did not rule it out. Furthermore, the men are silent now due to Arik's explicit order – once again, unclear if this is coming from the chief of general staff as well. It is true that there is incitement against me for publishing the names. Arik rages and shouts that it is as if I left them [the four accused assailants] exposed to revenge murder, and if they were to fight in the army once more, and fall into enemy hands, they would surely be executed.

Arik and his friends are now using this claim of endangering the men to justify covering for a crime. Their reasoning that "if they should fall into enemy hands, they would surely be executed" drives me mad. Is it possible that the army will ever again seek the assistance of these men, who committed a crime against their country, and did so using military weapons no less?

Thursday, March 24, 1955

I have received a letter from Police Minister Shitrit regarding the four: since the army is refusing to cooperate, it is inevitable that we will have to set them free, and this will essentially end the entire matter. I called Rosen and found that he is still hoping to achieve a positive solution. I was not convinced. This demonstration of incompetence by the legal authority when confronting the military – there is no telling what its malignant outcomes might be.

When I returned home for lunch, I found Dudik [David Golomb, son of Eliyahu Golomb], Mira [Dudik's wife] and Navoth [Yehuda Sharett's son] dining with the family. I found myself in distress before this dear young man, a sergeant in the paratroopers' battalion, who I know aided the four in committing the atrocious crime – indeed by an order he received from his commanders. Within minutes Navoth attempted to glean something from me regarding the fate of the four men, but I was reluctant to reply.

…A frantic spirit is raging inside Moshe Dayan's head and he cannot bring himself to sit still – he must always come up with a new crisis. Musik [Gidron] returned and confirmed that Arik [Sharon] had arranged help for the four men and, once they were arrested, ordered them not to speak, and it was he who summoned that hotshot Shmuel Tamir [the lawyer from the Herut party] to be their attorney.

The chief of general staff was adamant that he would keep the avengers away from the paratroopers, but it wasn't long before they returned and served in the battalion's reserves. Meir spent a few months at Ein Harod and made do with leading his herd to pasture instead of leading men to battle. As the cooling-off period ended, he rejoined the army and took command of Company A, who would later become the first paratroop commandoes.

33. ARIK SAYS FAREWELL

On April 25, 1957, at a conference for brigade officers, both active duty and reserve, Ariel Sharon bid farewell to Paratrooper Brigade 202. It was a unique and not particularly happy occasion for the departing brigade commander. Just as the Suez Crisis (Sinai War) came to a close, the senior officers had rebelled against Sharon, complaining about his actions in the Qalqilya operation and especially his conduct in the Battle of Mitla during the war. The high command felt that these serious claims, especially regarding the large number of casualties at Qalqilya and Mitla, showed that Sharon's behavior had crossed a line. Major General Haim Laskov, deputy chief of general staff and the chief of general staff designate, headed a team to look into the Battle of Mitla and drew grave conclusions regarding Sharon's conduct. Laskov found that Sharon had disciplinary issues and failed to comply with some of orders of the High Command. Laskov also noted some "inaccurate reports" made by Sharon about the Battle of Mitla. These actions led to Sharon's removal from command positions in the IDF for several years.

Sharon's farewell speech, as a commander not knowing if or when he would return to prominence, candidly summarized his success story, which began with the establishment of Unit 101 and went on to reshape Paratrooper Battalion 890, which would later become Brigade 202. The brigade officers, both active and reserve, listened avidly to the brigade commander for over two hours. Ben-Gurion, to whom the speech was directed more than to the officers, also listened to Sharon's account of his own successes and failures on his long and winding journey.

Ben-Gurion, who had protected the valued officer from angry generals throughout the past four years, accepted Sharon's invitation and was the guest of honor at the farewell. A considerable part of Sharon's words were surely meant for Ben-Gurion, who had served as prime minister and defense minister for most of those four years. This is some of what the commander of Brigade 202 had to say at his farewell speech:

> Honorable Prime Minister,
>
> You are at a conference of officers of Brigade 202, both active and reserve. This conference is meant to sum up the operational achievements of the paratroopers unit over the last three years and to present the development of our capability and operational thinking, and its impact on us and other IDF units.
>
> With your permission, I will start with a synopsis.
>
> I have to admit, I am excited to summarize these chapters of combat to you. It is a volume of dozens of chapters of operational actions, some of which are hard, complicated and brutal. Many of them are bloody; that is what the paratroopers have gone through. We started as a small unit with just a few dozen men and became a combat brigade. In these operations, we have lost some of our best fighters, both commanders and men. These operations often revealed unprecedented courage, talent and abilities. On the other hand, there have been many failures, mistakes and moments of weakness.
>
> It seems to me that at the basis of the Paratrooper Battalion's achievements is its willingness to openly evaluate its operations, without concealing mistakes or over-glorifying its successes, as well as our constant will to learn from our experiences. Surely, anyone who assiduously followed the operations we executed

would see constant development in our fighting methods, unit organization and combatant education, the fruit of experience acquired in previous actions.

This evaluation will not be of casualties, weapons seized or the number of actions carried out. Obviously, these points will come up here and there. This will mostly be an evaluation of the development of operational thinking at its various stages. We cannot, however, overlook the extent of our casualties, for the sake of demonstrating the weight of the tasks we were given.

In the last three years, we have lost 105 dead in various combat actions. This number includes casualties from other units who fought under our command in the various actions. In addition we suffered 360 wounded. Among the dead are about 25 officers, and among those are 7–8 company commanders. Among the wounded were company commanders, deputy battalion commanders and battalion commanders. It seems all of those sitting before me had experience in that field.

My review will deal with the period starting with the establishment of Unit 101, in August 1953, all the way to the Suez Crisis, without impugning the reputations of those who came before us, who did their lion's share of developing parachuting in the IDF eight years ago, and were pioneers of their own field.

Before us are a few maps and sketches, most of them mainly for presentation and review, and they do not represent the entire scope of activities we performed or all their various locations. On the right is the patrol map, where we can see arrows coming out of almost every location from our borders to almost any location across them that we could reach. We see the map of the main actions we have performed, marked with flames. On the right, a map of the Sinai Peninsula with the same places our men fought during the Suez War, from An-Nekhel, Mitla and Rus-al-Nard all the way to Sharm el-Sheik.

I would like to take you back to 1953, when the murderous Arab actions increased. The infiltrations shifted, almost completely, from infiltrations for the sake of theft to ones for the sake of murder. The atmosphere was fraught. Leaving your house in the frontier areas, and sometimes even in the inner regions, often involved mortal danger. There were even brutal murders committed inside settlements and homes on more than one occasion. I remembered this was a period in which there was a feeling of helplessness. The IDF performed several operations – Falame, Idna, Surif, Rantis and more. These actions did not resolve anything, nor did they change the situation. We had to advertise the fact that we had performed reprisal actions in our press; we had to make sure that the Arabs – who we retaliated against – knew that we had performed these actions. This was basically the case.

Even four years ago, the IDF was a good army. The people who established this unit were IDF people. However, the IDF faced one of its most severe problems back then – fighting during peacetime. Fighting during wartime engulfs everyone in the excitement of war and combat. Fighting in peacetime, when you know everyone on the home front is peacefully living their lives, needs to have its own atmosphere. It seems to me that we developed, in the last few years, this "profession" called "creating a wartime atmosphere." I do not know how this has affected you, but I myself have lived with this feeling for almost four years, and still do today. If not today, then tomorrow, the day after tomorrow, or in a month, we will fight. When I look back on how many of you served additional tours and how many of you are still serving under us – I believe you have also been affected by that. I will honestly say that this mantra has not only been chanted for the sake of extending military service – though it has been suspected of such – but it was a feeling that accompanied members of the unit's command for many years, and still continues to do so today. The IDF will surely have to fight, and if it does, we will be the ones that will tasked, and will shoulder, this difficult part of fighting.

Unit 101, established in August 1953 with the aim to break through the stalemate resulting from previous IDF actions, was not, in fact, militarily superior to any other unit. The difference was that it contained a small number of commanders who were determined to fundamentally change the way they fought and to do what they thought needed to be done. I have to openly say that this is what influenced all future development. When I was given the role, I wasn't the expert and you the rookies. Some of you were actual rookies at that time, but I didn't come there as the military expert. Throughout that period, we worked, fought and learned this doctrine together.

We started out with small actions, living under the shadow of "the legend of the impregnable Arab village" – that the National Guard defended every wadi and trail with ambushes and therefore the chances of success were pretty slim. It all seemed dark, dangerous, hopeless. Back then, there was an entire "ideology" as to why we could not perform those actions.

Some of you, perhaps, remember our beginnings – I see some among the reservists here today. Those who remember "encouragement" patrols we had in Abu-Laheya, near Ma'ale HaHamisha, or the drill we performed at Khirbet Akur, where we spent the whole night looking for the place and we couldn't find it because it no longer existed. We attempted to develop a not-so-successful doctrine of avoiding movement on roads and side-roads, in order to evade the enemy that was supposedly "lurking" everywhere, waiting for our forces. When we retreated from that drill, I was left behind on the side of the mountain, by a group of oak trees, completely exhausted and despairing.

Or perhaps you remember the ambush we set near Beit Sira, on the way to Latrun, when we attempted to stop a car by placing a tire on the road, an operation that took as long to prepare as the Qalqilya and Hussan actions.

These initial actions brought about a complete mindset that conventional methods would not get us very far. If we were not willing to run more risks, and get to know the enemy and its territory sufficiently, and train vigorously – we would achieve nothing.

Following those initial actions, we had the opportunity to carry out a major operation – which actually led to a turning point, mostly due to the change in the IDF's attitude toward us, and the recognition of the unit as one that delivered. I am talking about the action that hasn't been talked about in recent years – the Qibiya action, which followed the murder of a woman and her two children in the village of Yehud. In fact, this operation gave us the push we needed. I am not sure what our superiors thought about us back then, but we went in with the decisiveness that we would turn that village into a mound of ruins. The ones who took part in the operation, going there, remember that we were quite a small force and we carried about 300 kilograms of explosives. Everyone except myself and Davidi, who I imagine didn't have any explosives on, were overloaded.

The force itself was comprised of two parts: a small part of our unit and Battalion 890's Company B with Davidi, which wasn't so cohesive yet – only two years in service but performed quite well. Our part, a more cohesive company, received the task of breaching the village. Davidi's part was assigned to occupy the position at the entrance to the village, on its northwestern side.

I don't want to go back and describe this action at length. When we started out, we didn't have much of a chance. I myself was warned by the head of the Operations Branch, right before leaving for the action, that we should settle for something smaller just in case it didn't go as planned. We set out determined – and those of you who remember the talks Davidi and I had with some of you in the Ben Shemen woods know that it was clear to us that the force was filled with resolution and will. I won't go into the details of this action as they are probably well known.

Qibiya fell, and with it fell – at least for us – the legend of the unconquerable Arab village.

When we came back from Qibiya, we were drunk on victory. Though externally we had a certain feeling that the IDF was on one side, and on the other side was Unit 101, and although it numbered only twenty-five men, the IDF could not progress without it. While this was a good feeling, it was unhealthy. If you looked at what happened honestly, you could see that the action only succeeded in Qibiya itself. The other two operations, Nilin and Shukba, were not carried out according to instructions. (I guess there must have been someone who "congratulated" them on these failures the next day, when the results of the operation in Qibiya itself became known.) We did [look at it honestly], and concluded although our knowledge of the enemy was greater and the terrain was clearer to us – we had already walked the wadis – we had yet to solve the issue of enemy ambushes. Our self-confidence had increased tremendously, but one thing was clear – we had only succeeded because of the large scale of the action.

When we started to investigate the matter, one thing stood out

– the need for talented commanders who could independently execute the tasks they were given. This vision for commanders continued to concern us, for months and even years to come.

An extremely important and real conclusion we reached from these actions was to hold our fire until the last minute. This conclusion has been with us to this very day. Those of you who remember, and those who were there, know that the fall of Qibiya was not a result of a physically breaking into the village. I do not think we killed a single Arab before Qibiya was taken. It was their spirit that broke. And that was the result of the advanced force holding fire until the last minute. The order was to not fire before the forces entered the target. We were discovered about an hour before we attacked. The Arabs were firing like crazy and we lay in hiding on the terraces. Once the order was given to advance, our men entered both the outpost and the village without firing a shot. We later saw that opening fire too early causes the attacking force to be discovered and encourages the enemy. When you [the enemy] are fired upon and fire back, it gives a sense of equality. On the other hand, the silence causes chaos; [they] hear a stone tumbling, [see] a flitting shadow – they know they are being attacked but they don't know how big the force is or where it's coming from.

We later reached another conclusion: in order for us to perform an action, we had to operate the forces in unconventional ways, meaning no straight lines; if need be, a force following another force. And to avoid "spraying" fire, rather aiming only at pre-determined, clear targets.

We were a bit apprehensive after Qibiya. There was a natural uneasiness of a unit sitting around. Such a unit doesn't have the option of maintaining operational readiness without performing an operation. In December we were called for a series of small actions, Operation "Silk Gloves," following the murder of two soldiers at Al-Dawayima. In these actions, which were the first multiple small-unit actions, we achieved two records, in this case by the same man, Meir Har-Zion. The Bereichot Shlomo action, in which we killed a Legion captain, though later it turned out he was a (military) doctor, and three or four days later, the raid on Hebron itself, the longest night raid the IDF ever performed to this day. Fifty kilometers in one night, using a Roman road that leads from the Valley of Ela to Hebron. We should remember that these actions took place during the snowy nights of December 1953. Other actions we performed during those two nights were less successful.

I am afraid to admit before the previous and current heads of IDF Human Resources that I promoted Meir in rank after every operation. From sergeant he was promoted to sergeant first class without going through the required period for advancement. I should admit that he wasn't the greatest sergeant first class…

In December or early January, the decision was made in the General Staff that there was no reason to have two elite units in the IDF, and Unit 101 was chosen to be dismantled and merged into Battalion 890. We could have an entire conference just to describe the merging of these two units. It saved both Unit 101 as well as Battalion 890. Despite the difficulties and vigorous objections we encountered in the beginning, on both sides, we managed to make them into "one flesh" in a relatively short time.

Following the Gaza action on February 28, 1955, performed by Battalion 890 under my command against the Egyptian military camp, Defense Minister David Ben-Gurion came to visit the battalion's wounded and congratulate its troops. In an extraordinary letter to the chief of general staff, following Operation "Black Arrow," Ben-Gurion wished to inform the unit and its men of the following:

At the cabinet meeting on Sunday, March 6, 1955, I gave details of the Gaza battle, and the cabinet has unanimously instructed me to express our feelings of appreciation and admiration to the unit that participated in the battle, its soldiers and commanders, and the entire Paratroopers Battalion, in light of the spirit of unique Jewish heroism they have shown in that battle, and abilities demonstrated in planning and execution by the Paratroopers Battalion.

Ben-Gurion adds: "I am certain this feeling of the cabinet is shared by the entire nation. The love of the Israeli people and its admiration is bestowed on the Paratroopers Battalion, which once again has proven to the entire world the supremacy of Jewish courage and has added a distinguished page to the book of the Israel Defense Force's victories."

In January 1954, it was clear that we had to transform, as quickly as possible, into a combat battalion. We demanded reconnaissance patrols and operations. Anyone who was at the Operations Branch at that time remembers that we would keep the phone lines busy for hours every day. We would ask, every morning, "Was anyone murdered?" Anyway, we saw the way to get the battalion into a fighting mode in the actions and reconnaissance patrols. We weren't given serious actions back then. We would do a series of operations called "Whiplash Operations," in which the IDF attempted to match the property theft of the Arabs from the Gaza Strip – without any great success, by the way. I do not know how many of you saw Davidi and I take apart pump engines and steal plows. These actions did not much resemble special commando operations. Before me sit some of those who did it themselves. But we were willing to accept any small mission and any "tiny tot" patrol in order to get the battalion operational.

In March of 1954, following the murder of a guard at Har-Tuv, we were ordered in the afternoon to attack the village of Nahlin that very night, the 25th. Those of you who remember the village know that it had two parts: the old, densely populated part and the new part. The goal was to kill only National Guardsmen, only five or six of them, but to avoid hurting any women or children and to avoid destroying any houses. In order to do so, we decided to occupy one part of the village by infiltrating it without opening fire. This is where we used the experience we'd had at Qibiya to attack only one part of the village. We each had a flashlight attached to our clothes. We broke into houses and when we found a National Guardsman, we killed him. I wouldn't want to perform that action again, but we did it. Our second decision was around Nahlin. This was the first time there were Legion reinforcements near Hussan. We decided to prepare a landmine ambush on the road from Hussan to Nahlin. This was our first landmine ambush. All in all, I do not think it was the best ambush and the land-mining wasn't the best either. We didn't know back then that it wasn't enough to just launch an ambush with a landmine, but that we also had to attack after it. The village was occupied, the road was blocked, and the Legion's reinforcements were hit and destroyed. Between twelve and fourteen Legionnaires were killed in this mission, and we learned quite a lot from it.

When we retreated, one of our units encountered an ambush. Back then, the IDF's biggest nightmare was ambushes. The surprised unit attacked the ambushers, and the latter ran away. In the beginning, we thought that in order to complete the mission – in case you wanted to reach further [across the border] – there was no other option than to travel through the wadis, rather than by roads and tracks. The solution came by accident, because of this unit that encountered the ambush. They were confused for a moment but then attacked and the ambush took off. We started thinking about how to deal with ambushes. It turned out that the ambushes were not as terrible as we thought. That was how, since we developed a method to deal with ambushes, we realized that we could walk on the roads, even though the enemy could be lying in wait.

A few days later, we carried out an operation to capture prisoners in the Gaza Strip, prisoners to trade to free our captured company clerk. This was called "Operation Cigarette" because we thought our man was kidnapped while asking for a cigarette. It later turned out that he didn't even smoke. After many efforts, we were also able to capture one of their company clerks. We had our first injury in those actions. We used a device called fougasse for the first time. The aim was to stop cars by use of a fireball. We mostly counted on the fear factor. It was obvious that we had to carry out ambushes that would allow us to attack from close range, and when you place a landmine, you don't have the option of striking from close range and attacking immediately after the explosion. The first fougasse was placed and I don't think it was set off at the best time, because it was the first time we'd tried it. We were lying behind an olive tree, then a car with an officer in it, a sergeant first class and a few other men with him, came along. We set the fougasse off too soon. However, the car did stop and with great effort we were able to take the clerk who remained in that jeep.

We then had almost three months without any action. We used that time to organize and train. The unit was lacking two major things: good men – those of you who remember the people in the battalion know what I'm talking about – and good men means men that would become commanders. We were also lacking good commanders that would lead the men into battle and raise future commanders. As a result of the efforts we put in, we started getting good commanders and men. That is when Supapo – may he rest in peace – Danny Matt, Motta and others arrived.

We then decided to act. The first conclusion was that we had to work on the principle of small units where the commander had better control. Those who know the conventional IDF frameworks knows that a platoon consists of about forty soldiers and a company is about 140 soldiers. We concluded that we couldn't make the best use of every soldier in such a unit, or control such a unit with a single commander. We reached a second conclusion: a unit commander cannot control a unit of more than twenty to thirty men at night. Such a small platoon would be able to do more with fewer casualties than a larger one, since it is quicker, smaller and easier to command. We then built our own platoon, containing twenty-five men, a squad of eight men and a company of ninety-three men.

The measure of a company, which is the basic unit, was viewed by us – and still is, to this day – not by the number of men but by its ability, in terms of command, to carry out an "independent mission." The strength of a battalion depends on the number of command teams in it. At the time, the trend was to hold onto as many sub-units as possible, meaning a maximum number of command teams that could act independently. I would like to expand a bit on this point. We believe that a company of fifty men is still considered a company or a company of sixty men is also a company. An existing, fifty-man company, could have forty men added to it at the last minute. But building a new company by gathering men from different units, this we could not do in a short period of time.

After that, we always had not three to four companies in the battalion, but five to six. We wouldn't disband companies but keep them until the men reached their maximum potential. If that same company commander could squeeze everything out of these men – then they fought well.

Another conclusion we reached then – we heard about it and it was known since the War of 1948 – was that soldiers in a cohesive social framework fight better than those who operate as individuals. The same was true for us; the reconnaissance platoon – which later become Company A – fought better than Companies B and D. And once those companies became more cohesive, they also fought better than before. We talked about this matter, mostly Davidi and I, but also with Meir [Har-Zion], because we wanted to find out what motivates people. We concluded that the main factor was self-respect. Love of country and national spirit have no real effect during battle. Maybe during preparation that may spur a unit onward in training, but when you lie next to one another [during battle], no one thinks about national spirit. I tried testing what they were thinking about in that moment – there was no Zionism. In many cases, they thought about how the person at their side will look at them. A soldier that is responsible to the social construct he is living in will do anything to excel, or at least not disgrace himself. In contrast, the socially disconnected soldier never has reason to be ashamed, so he is not part of a social construct. When the fighting ends, he lies alone in his room; such a soldier will never excel in combat.

Nowadays in Battalion 890, Company A is like Company D and B is like F. Those of you who remember Company A; it was unlike any other company, and B was nothing like D. Motta's Company D did not resemble any other company and Raful's Company E was something else altogether. Another conclusion we reached at the time was regarding the flexibility of operating different frameworks and weapons. The battalion's commander produced a document and those of you who read it found an important paragraph there stating, "The company is solely an organizational structure from which combat teams can be assembled, according to the mission." We started to turn our thoughts toward assembling forces and weapons according to each mission. Those who look back on the actions from that time can see that there were already daytime and nighttime weapons. We would replace tools before each action, exchange teams and set up new ones. In any event, the idea had begun to germinate, and it might have been one of the main causes of many of our achievements.

Another conclusion reached was that we should maintain an elite unit in order to spur on the rest of the units. We always had such an entity. In the beginning it was the reconnaissance platoon. As time went by, the other companies advanced to its level, but the reconnaissance platoon kept progressing.

At the end of June 1954, a Jew was murdered in Ra'anana. We were tasked with raiding the Legion base at Azun the following day. It was a company camp, northeast of Azun. It was a long way away and there were force limitations. It was obvious that to cover that distance and penetrate the camp, the active force had to be small. It was a small action, only six men, but it was a difficult one, commanded by deputy battalion commander Davidi. We reached a decision, still valid today, that the rank of the commander was not dependent on the size of the force but on the character of the mission. Sometimes a squad commander would command a battalion and sometimes a battalion commander would command a squad. The commander's rank and status isn't determined by the size of the unit, but the nature of the operation and the tasks that need to be accomplished. The Azun action involved encountering several ambushes and, as you may recall, that was the first and only case in which we left a wounded man behind, who was then captured, and the story of his captivity is known to us all.

Two weeks later, on July 9, a vehicle carrying Druze soldiers hit a landmine near Kissufim. We were tasked with attacking the enemy outpost the following day. This plan was known as "Eye for an Eye." This was the first operation, following the war [of 1948], in which an IDF unit attacked a fortified and dug-in position. We faced several issues while considering the plan. It was necessary to take care of a more-or-less fortified position – later we faced more fortified positions – which were better attacked from within. There was the issue of the destination, planning and having to learn about it based on aerial photographs. We set a general combat plan along clear axes. There we suffered our first death and several wounded men.

After this operation we came to a few conclusions regarding fighting against fortified objectives, which in fact began in this operation and were summarized a few months later. We had a discussion and decided on our new method for fighting fortified objectives, which became the entire IDF's method in the last year. Everyone is well aware of this doctrine by now, so I won't repeat it.

One of the significant conclusions of that action came as the result of a mistake by one of our forces in finding the communication trench we had to fight alongside. They had the wrong trench and as a result, some of the objectives were not captured in the first stage. This was the northern part of the outpost and we suffered several casualties. While the force did regroup quickly, we reached a conclusion that it is vital to thoroughly study the target and plan each and every detail of the assault with aerial photographs, and construct the force accordingly. In addition to the planning, studying and construction of the force, the entire force must practice based on those aerial photos and schematics before setting out, so they will have, at least, a minimal orientation.

In the action at Khirbet Sika on August 30, 1954, we mainly wanted to take prisoners. Though we didn't manage to do so, it was good practice for the battalion. In the Beit Likiya action on September 2, 1954, the mission was accomplished but it was full of failures due to inadequate discipline. That is the reason we held a commanders' meeting on discipline, which improved as a result, as shown in the Gaza action.

This leads us to the Gaza action on February 28, 1955. I would be accurate if I said that our true operations actually started there. 1954 had been important for us to unify the battalion, to draw important initial conclusions, to appoint commanders and recruiting good men. 1955 found us strong, with a five-company battalion, a reconnaissance platoon and excellent commanders. There were about 200 men from kibbutzim, high school graduates and other good material. For the first time in the history of the paratroopers, we really had good men. We had a significant squad commanders' course at the battalion, experience in rapid battle protocols and a lot of self-confidence.

When we set out to plan the Gaza action, we were faced with a fortified camp, and our conclusion on how to conquer it was that it was crucial to isolate the battle zone by dealing with the adjacent objectives. There were three objectives: the Egyptian forces' headquarter base in Gaza, the train station, and a camp on the east side [of the road]. It was obvious to us that we had to deal with all three objectives. It wasn't yet obvious to us that we had to do it simultaneously. We saw there was a heightened risk of ambush. On the way to Gaza we deployed our anti-ambush technique, which has been accepted and taught to the entire IDF this year. We are no longer intimidated by ambushes. We operated a forward unit, which would be the main unit, commanded by one of our fearless commanders [Uzi Trachtenberg Eilam] who had proved himself exceptional. He counterattacked the ambush, overcame it in a matter of seconds and the force kept advancing.

We had foreseen the possibility of [enemy] reinforcements, mainly from south of the city of Gaza, from Khan Yunis. Our conclusion was to place a massive blocking force six kilometers south of the city. We planned to pass between the Egyptian positions and decided to leave a force behind to secure the retreat.

The action itself was one of the most brutal and aggressive ones we've ever performed. At some points during the action, its success was in very serious doubt. The objective had not been studied sufficiently, an adjacent objective was attacked instead, and the enemy had time to regroup.

The success of the action sprung from our men's decision to achieve close-quarters combat with the enemy. From that moment on, they resumed the attack – following the initial mistake about the identity of the target – with an attempt to breach the camp's eastern gate. The company commander was killed and the gate was not breached. The action was not only questionable because it wasn't completed, but also due to the loss of many men. The moment Uzi [Trachtenberg-Eilam] broke in with his men from the north – following the failure at the eastern gate – and started penetrating the positions, from that moment the balance of power shifted. The moment our men breached the positions and engaged in close combat, the enemy stopped resisting and started fleeing.

That is one of the main conclusions that would have a deep impact on all our actions that followed; the enemy broke at the point when we actually charged. Firing on the enemy from a few meters away doesn't faze them when they are in prepared positions, alert, while we are tired from walking for many kilometers. This breaking point, even now, is almost always psychological. I do not recall any action in which we physically broke the enemy, not at Gaza, not Khan Yunis, not Kuntilla, not Sabcha nor Kinneret. We didn't suffer many casualties while charging the objective. Our men really charged it. It was the same at Gaza, Kuntilla, Sabcha and Kinneret – everywhere we fought. The annihilation [of the enemy force] was a result of this (psychological) breaking point and it was proven throughout all the actions. In this action we carried out an excellent ambush of the enemy's reinforcements. This was also where we settled on the requisite quality of a blocking force.

I think we proved a level of discipline there, and only those who saw that retreat at the Gaza action with their own eyes, the evacuation of casualties, could appreciate it. Anyone who saw that convoy packed with our dead and wounded, with almost every man having some sort of injury. There were no casualties or wounded left behind, not a single weapon either. As for discipline, there were ups and downs. The Gaza action was a good example proving what could be done with a disciplined unit in the field. Whoever saw Company D when they got the order that every four of them had to carry a wounded or dead man, and how they got to it with or without a stretcher, quietly and without saying a word. They took the men, under fire, and kept moving. Those of you who saw it in the later stages, when we encountered ambushes, when we crossed the last ridge, when we reached the wadi and then ran in the open field – I couldn't believe we took them all. We counted the men and it turned out we did evacuate all of them.

The Gaza operation led us to yet another conclusion: knowing who the commanders would be. Until then we operated in the old-fashioned way – the military has ranks, seniority, promises [of positions] and more. In fact, that's what you do to build a command level. But there is also talent, which you cannot dismiss. After the Gaza action we had a few conversations on what a commander should be, who should be the commanders of the platoons, the commanders of our companies. These are the people who actually conduct the fighting. We reached the conclusion that we had to choose commanders not so they could plan – that was for the battalion commander – and not to keep the unit on standby. Achieving the operational goals results from the personal influence of the commander who charges forward with the men following him. These platoon and company commanders who are personally managing the charge of their men should be the best fighters of their units. We reached a conclusion about this, but to this day we have yet to receive approval of the Staff Administration, that the appointment of commanders – and I want to stress this, *in combatant units* – should not depend on seniority. It shouldn't depend on ranks or solving personnel issues, or on promises made to this or that officer. Those who command should be those best fitted to do so. I had talks with you about this, who will be the commanders in each unit? We managed to break the accepted norm two or three years ago. It happened more than once that a lower ranked soldier commanded a superior officer. It is not the accepted approach; it wasn't with us either, and I know people who would get bitter about it, but we did it and I think it worked. Today we face the same problem, because over time the commanders progressed, and the best platoon commanders became the best company commanders; those who were good company commanders became battalion commanders. We no longer see a need for that action, which is non-military and creates objections, but we did it. I remember there were talks here in the [officers'] club and another thorough one at Tel Yeruham, as part of the first battalion training: Who would be the commanders of this unit? I have to say it worked well.

We've reached the Khan Yunis action, "Operation Elkayam," August 31, 1955, where we first used half-tracks. Using those, Motta's Company D penetrated through a highly populated area and from there all the way to the Khan Yunis police station, which was blown up like the police stations we would blow up a year later. When we started planning the Khan Yunis action, we recognized that the police station was inside a densely populated area, meaning that we could not achieve total surprise. We would reach it only through six to seven kilometers of a highly populated area. We knew there was a substantial force inside the police station, two units, and the structure was fortified. We decided to solve this using half-tracks and reaching the destination at maximum speed. The aim was to attack the force [within the police station] and surprise them before they got a chance to regroup. We had conducted quite a few raids in the past, but had never performed a sudden penetration at night, traveling in vehicles all the way to the target.

We reached the conclusion that in order to bring down the police station, there was no need to occupy the entire building. It would be enough to pin down [those in] the building and clear the location where the explosives go. We feared some forces would intervene, so we placed roadblocks to the north and south. In light of our experience in Gaza (action), we opened a route to secure the retreat. The retreat route was secured by Raful's company. We held a large reserve outside the battle zone. There was a company force by the border, ready to go, to aid either the roadblock or breaching forces.

That is where we used a light aircraft for the first time, to set up contact with our roadblocks, whom we had lost communication with. From that action on, we always had a communication aircraft with us, and we used it to solve the onerous communication problem. This was the first action we performed using the fortified objectives doctrine, in mid-1955.

On October 22, 1955, we performed an action at the Syrian border and captured several Syrian soldiers. At the end of 1955, we entered a heightened stage of activity in which we performed three operations: Kuntilla, aiming at capturing soldiers; Sabcha, destroying a battalion; and Kinneret, destroying the Syrian positions along the Sea of Galilee and capturing prisoners. These were record-setting activities, each on its own right, and they were all complete successes.

We drew several conclusions based on these actions. The Kuntilla action came against the backdrop of the abduction of our police officers two days earlier. When we assessed the Kuntilla objective, which comprised three fortified and elevated stone structures, one next to the other, we reached several conclusions. The task of taking prisoners is a hard one, requiring a lot of discipline and restraint. It's easy to storm in and kill, but it's difficult to storm in, take someone captive and lead him away by the hand.

The enemy had the opportunity to lend assistance from one objective to the other. In order to prevent them from coming to each other's aid, Battalion 890 developed the concept of simultaneous assaults on all the objectives. We worked under enormous time pressure. We got the order on Thursday morning and had to execute it that night. There was an entire day's ride to the border. While in previous actions we had set out combat protocols, here we had no time and had to skip it. In the Kuntilla operation, most of the forces knew about the objective only when they were right next to it. That is not a good way to do things, but you can be flexible regarding combat protocols when there is no choice, and significantly shorten them.

In addition to the time pressure, there was also the issue of distance. I do not know how you walked to Kuntilla; to me it was probably the greatest effort I ever had to make. Not so much going there but coming back. Not only hefty people like me were struggling, but even those eighteen-year-olds who were light on their feet. When I thought about it later, I reached the conclusion that although we were in good physical shape, it was still not good enough.

We carried out the operation and achieved things we didn't think we could. We captured twenty-eight prisoners, killed twelve Egyptians and left there packed with weapons in amounts we had never seized before. I would say there was some relief when we displayed that same ability [as previously]. I did not quite believe that our people could raid, storm in with the Egyptians in front of us, and pull the trigger. There were a few cases in which we stumbled upon an ambush about 200 meters from our target, and the soldier ran and physically grabbed the [Egyptian] machine gunner without firing a shot. There was even such an incident with Meir [Har-Zion]. There were later cases in which troops stormed positions without opening fire and upheld the "hold your fire" order.

We lost two dead here, who possibly would have died anyway, but these were clearly the result of that strict discipline the men had shown in penetrating those posts in order to take prisoners without killing them.

The second action was Sabcha, in which we stormed a fortified regimental position. Well, maybe it wasn't so fortified, but it was definitely well defended. It was a few days after the Kuntilla action, and we were a little more experienced. We decided to attack all the objectives simultaneously, including the headquarters and the supporting fire position. The aim was to prevent them from offering a defense as a unified body and reduce them to fighting as individuals or one position at a time. The facility was fortified at the front, which led us to think that we should penetrate it from the back. We left Be'er Sheva in a huge convoy, through Tel Yeruham and Sde Boker. We reached Har Azuz [Jabel Aziz in Arabic] at dusk, descended the mountain and infiltrated into the heart of Sabcha. We attacked from the inside out. We feared the enemy's artillery during that action, so we placed a block on the road leading to Qusaima. The roadblock did stop the artillery from arriving but was not enough. All in all, the action was a bigger success than we had hoped for, as well as quicker than we thought it would be.

The Kinneret action was carried out on December 11, 1955. We faced a number of problems there that we had not encountered before. We were about to attack an enemy protected both by fortifications and natural obstacles. We made several assessments of the matter and eventually went ahead with the operation.

Our main conclusion, which we knew already, had to do with deciding on the number of units to be employed, their structure, weapons, and commanders. We had to match the commanders and units to the mission before going into it – and those would vary from operation to operation. There were many times in which we did that, but it really stood out in [operation] Kinneret. We faced some serious issues there. The Kursi target was one of the hardest ones due to the size of the enemy force within it and the number of positions it had. It was almost impossible to reach it without being seen. The necessity of inserting such a large force on the one hand, and the need to reach it without being seen, on the other, made it a difficult task. We sent Meir's [Har-Zion] Company A there, since its commanders were, by nature, capable of crawling for two hours before reaching the target. Backing them up was Gulliver's Company D.

We selected the commanders according to the nature of each action. Just as it was important to assemble the weapons, how many bazookas, submachine guns and squads according to the operation – so it was vital to take the commanders' human material under consideration and the nature of the executing unit. Today, there is a big difference in the nature of the various units.

From these questions we drew a number of conclusions. The first was the issue of speed of execution and speed of penetration into the heart of the enemy. It is vital, as mentioned, to bring the enemy to one-on-one or position-on-position combat. We should prevent them from defending as a cohesive position or an entire outpost. This can only be achieved by rapid and vigorous penetration, without wasting time, without any rigid frameworks or organized war. I would like to explain this point:

If you remember, in the Sabcha action we had a company from the Nahal platoon commanders' course under us, equipped with human material that surpassed ours, and their mission was to conquer the outpost behind the Sabcha. That unit suffered more casualties than any of our other units because how tightly they clung to conventional fighting. The men went in straight and organized lines; they were ordered to straighten the line. In the meantime, the enemy regrouped, and this company suffered seven dead and a considerable number of wounded. It had more casualties than Company B, which wasn't the best and was the least organized company. In my opinion, Company B stood out by not fighting conventionally; one force ran in front of another. There was no organized formation, they didn't try and maintain the aesthetics of combat. I would like to remind you what the Egyptian officer said in a talk we had with the captives after the action. The Egyptian officer who was captured at Sabcha excused his failure by saying, "The Israelis are fighting in an unorganized way!" The Egyptian understood that it would not always be possible to follow a preset defense plan.

To wage such an "unorganized war" it is vital to allow the units freedom of action. You need to let each platoon commander act independently. If the platoon commander had an objective and the platoon commander to his left did not complete his objective, this should not stop the former and he should forge on. It is important to educate commanders that if they have a certain mission and the platoon commander in front of them has not reached his objective – let's say the forward one – it shouldn't prevent the first commander from reaching the rear of the objective, even if the front one has yet to fall. This is what I mean by unorganized war.

You should try and attack a maximum of objectives simultaneously. Rely less on reserves because they don't always get a chance to go into action. We never used the reserves. You should count more on deep penetration and less on the reserves that are lagging behind.

In the matter of the ratio of forces, it is possible that on a strategic level, when a battalion operates a few companies, it should have a 2:1 or 3:1 ratio between attacker and defender, as is the accepted wisdom. It is probably over the top but it seems that on a strategic fighting level, we shouldn't take into account the ratio as much as we should the objective we are about to conquer.

When we attacked the enemy at Khan Yunis at a 2:1 ratio, we were not deterred, even though we didn't have the element of surprise. If we had wanted to work by the book, we would have had to bring in a force of six companies of half-tracks. But if you've seen how much space the eleven half-tracks took, you could only imagine what would have happened if we had put in more.

When you plan an action, you shouldn't build it according to a balance of forces but according to the nature of the terrain. The terrain is important, not only to the attacker, but also the defender.

We went to the Kursi outpost with one company against another. We charged the main outpost with a force of twenty men facing about fifty men. I believe that had we taken 200 men, as we were supposed to, we would have had many more casualties. Excess men means excess casualties.

When we start planning an action, we should construct it, first and foremost, by taking into consideration the terrain, both for us and the enemy. You certainly also have to take the [number of] enemy into account. If there is a battalion at Khan Yunis, you can't make do with a company.

These were the main conclusions, and now we come to 1956. This was the year we became Unit 202. Before us were a relatively quiet six months of training. The unit's manpower, which had now reached brigade strength, was [further] reinforced. The Nahal's Battalion 88 was placed under our command, and we formed a reserve battalion as well.

In the summer we entered a period of activity. On September 11, 1956 we operated at Ar-Rahawa, on September 13, 1956 at Gharandal, on October 3, 1956 at Hussan and on October 11, 1956 at Qalqilya.

Following these actions, we entered the Sinai War (Suez Crisis) on October 29, 1956.

I want to say that, when we got to these operations, among them tough ones like Qalqilya and Hussan, and the Suez Crisis, they had already become our daily bread and butter. When we approached these actions, we had already reached solid conclusions, we weren't surprised anymore. Ar-Rahawa and Gharandal were relatively small actions, mostly fulfilling the desire of some of the troops for action. After a long period of quiet, the men were demanding to fight. We also forsook our principles of balance of forces in those two actions, just to let some commanders fight, because that was important at that time. I remember Ovad (Ladginsky), who later died in Sinai, saying that the whole of the rest of his military service hinged on whether Raful would let him take down the machine-gunner at Gharandal or not. Perhaps for fear of losing Ovad as a company commander, Raful later attacked the tower and hunted down that Jordanian gunner.

In the Hussan and Qalqilya actions we once again drew our conclusions. These reinforced the ones we had already reached according to what went wrong at Hussan, while we were conquering the outpost. We had abandoned the standard method of taking a fortified objective. In the Hussan operation, the method was not implemented, and we suffered a number of losses which were, in my opinion, unnecessary. In terms of adapting the method, we realized this is the right way was to deal with all objectives simultaneously. At Qalqilya, we did not deal with all the objectives simultaneously, and it hurt us a little.

Another thing we did was roadblocks. The roadblock at Qalqilya was an improvement. We started with one and moved up to a double and triple roadblock. It turned out that even a triple blockade wasn't enough.

I want to say a few words about two entities, which it happens I will talk about together – one is the enemy and the other is the IDF. I don't intend to equate one to the other!

I will start with the enemy – we had the chance to see the enemy and their ability to resist in the dozens of operations we carried out. I haven't even touched on all the actions; we carried out over forty-five different operations in the last four years. We had the chance to size them up and realized that their standard in combat is extremely low. It took us almost more time to conquer Kissufim outpost than Sabcha, because they fired back at us and fought at Kissufim. They also fought at Gaza, and to give credit where it's due, in some places they even fought back pretty well. At Khan Yunis they didn't fight as much, and even less than that at the Sabcha. When it comes to the Sinai War (Suez Crisis), I don't want to diminish our role and say that the Arabs did not fight, but all in all, we all know that, except for a few specific places, there were no fierce battles. The Egyptian standards in the Suez Crisis continued their decline.

As for the Syrians, we only performed one action there, but it also felt like the Syrians declined. The Jordanians, who bragged so much after the Qalqilya action when Battalion 88 suffered twenty-three casualties, my personal estimation was that their [the Jordanians] fighting did not excel.

From here I draw a personal conclusion, there is no option of destroying 40 million Arabs, nor is it my desire to do so. But it seems plausible and necessary to take the will to fight out of the representatives of these 40 million people. And this can be done. I believe that if we succeed, as we have for the last few years, in holding enemy units at a constant military disadvantage, their resilience will decrease. It's my hope there won't be any more wars, but my preferences will not be the thing to eventually decide it. It is obvious that it is better to fight the Egyptians after the Suez Crisis, as it was better to fight in the Sinai following the operations we performed there; just as it was better to fight the Syrians following Kinneret and the Jordanians following Qalqilya.

As for the IDF – we are part of it and see ourselves completely as part of its structure. It is not the same gang of bandits it was back in 1953. I believe we have managed to understand that the paratroopers are not the entire IDF. The paratroopers cannot fight all of the country's wars and there is a great and good army – but it seems we were able to aid the IDF, if even a little, by setting combat standards. Nowadays, when a unit goes on an operation, it has a certain standard to match that has already been reached, just as the reconnaissance platoon is the one to elevate Battalion 890. It seems to me that the paratroopers have the same effect on the IDF. Furthermore, as a result of the wars we've had, we've been able to make our small contributions into those conflicts.

In my opinion, the strength of this unit, as well as the IDF's force, depends on the relationship between the paratroopers and the entire IDF. We have done more in this field in the last few years than all the previous ones combined.

I would like to sum up and say, these things were not accomplished in one day. These things were accomplished over many years. I would like to say that our progress was slow and deliberate. But I think that when we dealt with [operational] objectives we did so quickly.

I have done my part here. The Prime Minster has agreed to say a few words.

Ben-Gurion's statement at the 202 Brigade Commanders' Convention, May 25, 1957:

> Friends, as for the unit itself, I cannot add a single word to what Arik has said. I wouldn't be able to say to you the things he has told you, which I have found informative.
>
> He established this unit, trained it, led it into actions, and perhaps the most important thing of all – he served as a personal, living example for it.
>
> I may not have understood Arik well, and I may have been wrong, but I have never seen eye to eye with his great thirst for operations.

Thus, Ben-Gurion concluded his short statement on that special occasion.

34. CONCLUSIONS AND TRANSITIONS IN FORMING IDF'S POWER

The security-oriented mindset in Israel started long before the state was established. It began during the transition from an essentially passive defense to "beyond the fence" actions that the unique British officer, Orde Charles Wingate, instilled in us. We adopted the principles of Wingate's doctrine and learned how important it is to seize the initiative. We learned to use the dark of night to perform actions that employed the element of surprise as a key component of combat. Wingate's spirit pulsed through the Palmach and – once the War of 1948 had concluded – this same spirit came to our aid and prepared us to deal with the infiltrations and attacks along the borders. Ariel Sharon adopted Wingate's principles, as well as the Palmach's, when he formed Unit 101 with the raid as its main tool.

Israel's reprisal policy included three main principles, set by the security-oriented mindset already found in the pre-state Jewish community as far back as the 1930s and '40s. This mindset spoke of punishing the attackers, deterring them and their neighbors from performing similar acts in the future, and taking revenge on them or their neighbors. Punishment was perceived by most of the Israeli public as a deterrent. The policy was based on the assessment that a rational consideration of profit and loss motivated both sides. According to such principles, one side would avoid action for fear that the other side's action would bring greater damage upon them than the benefits their action was intended to achieve. In contrast, "revenge" meant a response that was more emotional than rational.

There is no doubt that the reprisal actions were meant to lift national morale and offer a sense of security, especially to those living on the frontier. An institutional reprisal policy was also meant to prevent independent acts of retaliation, so as to prevent the country from facing any embarrassing surprises by people showing private initiative. Ben-Gurion feared that the people would not be able to bear the existing state of security forever. Sharett too was afraid that if the state did not perform reprisal actions, the people would. Perhaps this was why Ben-Gurion announced, at the end of 1953, that IDF reprisal operations did in fact restrain the frontier residents, and were preventing them from performing private actions.

The reprisal policy was meant not only to reassure the Israeli public, but also to comply with the demands of the military, which between 1954 and 1956 pressured the government to approve such actions. The main pressure came from Ariel Sharon and Battalion 890, who, having absorbed Unit 101, had also adopted its principles of combat – seizing the initiative and precise navigation. Failing to carry out reprisal actions was considered destructive to the military's operational training and the morale of its units who eagerly awaited action. One can also assume that the reprisal policy was meant to preserve the political status of the ruling Mapai party (a left-wing socialist party) as its leadership feared that avoiding reprisal actions would cause them to lose votes to the right-wing Herut party – and possibly also to the leftist Ahdut HaAvoda party, which demanded a more hawkish reprisal policy.

And indeed, from the end of 1953, following the establishment of Unit 101 and its success, the Israeli reprisal policy gained momentum and received the support of the public, against the backdrop of a sad and helpless atmosphere in the frontier settlements. As mentioned, it aided in raising the national morale and encouraged the residents. The reprisal policy fit one of the main narratives of the Israeli national culture: the narrative of the "new Hebrew man" (self-reliant and self-confident) who sought to form an antithesis to the vulnerable "exile Jew" (dependent on the protection of others, that historically was seldom to be relied upon). As a result, Israeli public opinion was dominated by the hawkish approach. Although the dovish approach was limited to small social groups, their voices were heard in the cabinet, parliament and some parts of the press. There was often criticism of the reprisal policy among intellectuals, though this criticism was rare among the general public. One piece of evidence for the preference of the public for a hawkish approach is the outcome of the national elections that took place in July 1955, in which the power of Ahdut HaAvoda and Herut, both of which favored reprisal policies, increased, while the strength of Mapai – led by Prime Minister Sharett – diminished.

From 1953 to 1956, there were hundreds of terrorist attacks. The paratroopers continued to carry out reprisal operations, but these years also saw other elements contributing to the actions. Examples include the participation of armored vehicles in the Khan Yunis action and tank fire on the Qalqilya police station, as well as the half-track convoy to extract the commandos. Adding the Nahal Paratroop Battalion, troops from the Givati Brigade, and further incorporating the Golani Brigade in the operations, helped spread the warrior spirit throughout the entire IDF.

Was Moshe Dayan the first to realize the true state of the IDF? Was he the first one who strove to improve its abilities? It is hard to answer these questions with a definitive "yes." One could try to answer by comparing Dayan to his predecessors. The two former Chiefs of General Staff, Yigal Yadin and Mordechai Maklef (who, between them covered the years 1949 to 1953), mostly focused on establishing and organizing the army. During their time, nearly the entire army was occupied with those goals. Presumably, the military's inadequate abilities did not escape Maklef's notice, even though – at his own request – he only served for one year. Despite his efforts, he did not have enough time to propel the IDF toward improving its capabilities, especially those of the reserves. The proposal to establish Unit 101 was drafted during his time in office. It was first brought before him by the head of the Jerusalem Brigade, Colonel Michael Shacham. Maklef agreed to form the unit and even gave it its mission. It was a groundbreaking decision which was only fulfilled during Dayan's term as chief of general staff. In Maklef's defense, during his short term as chief of general staff he initiated the direction of high-school graduates toward the field combat units. This was a vital and significant move in order to improve the quality of the combat troops. However, in the case of the IDF, the entire army's ability could not have been improved before its structure was established and settled.

Dayan's tenure as chief of general staff, which lasted a little over four years, was characterized by a long process of improving the IDF's fighting ability as well as stepping up reprisal actions. At the time Dayan was due to be appointed for the role, the IDF was already a large army that had established its organizational infrastructure. Technical, professional processes began to form at a reasonable pace within it, and training for both regular as well as reserve units became an annual event. However, there was one key component missing: the fighting spirit. The declining security along the armistice lines required a much more resolute army that strove for contact; yet the combat units were having a hard time meeting the trials of combat. Ben-Gurion was, in many ways, preoccupied and troubled by the fear that, should the security situation continue to deteriorate and a war broke out, the army would not be able to deal with the enemy. This is a crucial difference to the situation of the fighters at the beginning of the War of 1948. Their willingness to fight overcame both their shortcomings as soldiers and the organizational inadequacies of the fighting force. Dayan understood, better than his predecessors, that the change had to start from the bottom, and occur simultaneously with change in strategic and operational thinking among the high command.

A phenomenon similar to Unit 101 and its legacy can be seen in other armies. There were militaries who allowed the formation of special units, limited in size, characterized by operational approaches that would be considered subversive and unacceptable by regular forces. These types of units were given a freedom of thought and action which were often extraordinary, in the hopes that the changes set by this special group would later seep into the entire army. As we know, this phenomenon was practiced by the British army during World War II.

In addition to merging Unit 101 with the paratroopers, Dayan also incorporated the Nahal shortly thereafter. In the long run, this merger was far more significant than the previous one. Brigade 202, formed in 1956, contained Battalion 890 as well as the Nahal's advanced training unit – the latter being upgraded to become Paratroop Battalion 88 and Reserves Battalion 771. The service in the Nahal paratroop unit was different from that of a regular battalion. It was possible to serve only six months in regular service and then move on to the paratroopers' reserves. This meant that for every two and half years of service by a regular paratrooper, there were five Nahal soldiers trained as paratroopers. Therefore, most of the paratrooper reserve troops in the 1950s and '60s were Nahal soldiers who were graduates of the youth movements, who were considered the best "material" there was.

It is important to state that the change in combat readiness was initially only accepted in the Infantry Corps; however, the Sinai War brought on a serious upgrade in the role performed by the Armored Corps as well. The Six-Day War proved that the entire IDF had transformed into a combat-ready army, willing and capable of taking the initiative.

35. EPILOGUE AND LOOKING FORWARD

There is no doubt that Unit 101 played a key role in improving the IDF's fighting ability. The phenomenon that the unit and its legacy embody is not unique to the Israeli military and can be seen in other armies as well. Other nations' militaries have similarly formed special units, restricted in size and characterized by operational methods that would be seen as unorthodox and unacceptable in regular units. These kinds of forces were given extraordinary freedom of thought and action, in the hopes that the changes they had initiated would seep into the entire army.

This phenomenon was practiced, for instance, by the British army during World War II, and the outstanding example of such a unit brings us full circle to Orde Wingate and his Chindits in Burma. The name was suggested by a Burmese officer and is a mispronunciation of the word "Chinthay," a lion-like creature from Burmese mythology. The force Wingate commanded employed techniques far more advanced than those employed by the British army at the time. Special operation units were also part of the American army's fighting in Afghanistan and the Second Gulf War. Such units have a completely different character than their regular counterparts. They are characterized by a "heretical" approach in the operational fields and present creative thinking and new conceptions of action.

Every army needs a "subversive" entity within it to advance its abilities. Over time, wise General Staffs will institutionalize those "subversive" methods and make them templates for methods of operation in other parts of the military or even in the entire army. Ben-Gurion and Dayan did exactly that, a phenomenon that did not really repeat itself in the following years.

Dayan's lead in this direction affected all branches of the military. We cannot determine with certainty that even those units from the armored corps, air force or navy that did not take part in the reprisal actions drew the fighting ability they displayed during the Suez Crisis from the paratroopers' extraordinary example. Although it is obvious that the infantry's way of fighting is different from that of other parts of the armed forces, the influence of the new fighting spirit on the entire military was positive and noteworthy.

To what extent did Dayan's change influence the reserve units that only served occasionally? A close inspection shows that the changes did, in fact, take root. The reason: the reserve units that were normally designated only for training were also called up for reinforcing security, some of them even physically supporting the operational actions. Furthermore, the commanders of the reserve units were, in many cases, regular officers and therefore kept their troops "in the picture." Yet another influence was the press. The reprisal actions received enormous exposure at that time, especially in print media.

No one in the country could remain unaware of the ongoing developments in fighting methods, the series of raids dubbed "reprisal actions." From these actions a unique spirit emanated, one that influenced the public – both directly and indirectly – even if it did not significantly improve the overall ability of the reserves. Indeed, even at the time, the maneuvers (that had expanded into brigade exercises) continued to take place routinely, without any sign of a major increase in the operational abilities of the reserve units.

The contribution of Unit 101 – and later on Battalion 890, led by Ariel Sharon – to the fighting spirit of the IDF is beyond question. The correlation between the use of the raid and the increased competence of the IDF as a whole is beyond dispute. Meir Har-Zion contributed the importance of navigation to the target and setting mission completion as a top priority. Ariel Sharon was the one who insisted on getting more and more authorizations for raids. He was also the one to push toward increasingly extensive actions while Chief of General Staff Dayan supported him every step of the way.

One of the most important questions arising from the raids Sharon planned and executed so successfully in the 1950s involves his continued adherence to the principle of raiding. As a division commander during the Six-Day War, Sharon conquered the Abu Agila outposts in the Sinai Peninsula through a sort of extended raid, using the "Pow, and it's over"[42] method. The Yom Kippur War demonstrated Sharon's refusal to jeopardize his crossing of the Suez Canal – which in his opinion would be the single action that would determine the outcome of the war. He once again correctly perceived the problem but insisted on solving it with a simplistic move and in the style that had become his trademark – the raid. And what about the first Lebanon War, when he served as defense minister? Unfortunately for him, this was not a situation that could have been solved in one fell swoop, in the style of the raid.

It is obvious that a single raid, or even a series of raids, by the IDF is not enough to change, or even shape, the fate of a protracted campaign. Any limited war does not have the ability to shape a geostrategic political architecture in the Middle East. Then Chief of Staff Ehud Barak believed that a raid to assassinate Saddam Hussein in a targeted bombing would shape the architecture of Iraq and the region. The move failed during preparations, perhaps luckily so (following the commando disaster that occurred during

---

42 The original Hebrew phrase, coined by the Israeli humorist Ephraim Kishon. "*Zebang v'garmarnu*" could be literally translated as, "BOOM, and we are done," and implies one quick and crushing blow leaving the opponent no hope of recovery.

drills meant to prepare them for the action).[43] U.S. President George W. Bush, who was probably not as wise as his father, charged forward like a young bull to wage a limited war to change the regime in Iraq. The outcomes of the Second Gulf War, which President Bush had hastily initiated, and the rise of Iran as a significant strategic force following of the fall of Saddam Hussein's regime, show that the wisdom of the old bull was still needed.

Should we, in Israel today, adopt a strategic view and not settle for a series of raids that fit the situation back in 1953–1956? It seems that the answer to this question is "yes." In a complex situation on multiple fronts – Hamas in Gaza, Iranian influence and aid to Hezbollah in Lebanon, and Iran's presence in Syria, as well as the Palestinian Authority in Judea and Samaria – we cannot rely only on raid operations. It also seems that we should not draw analogies between today's situation and Wingate's raids, which were right for 1936–1939, or the impressive achievements of Unit 101 and Battalion 890's actions in the 1950s. The way to deal with non-state terror organizations is not through "a single blow" – even if it is a rather strong one. The revolutionary thinking of yesterday must not become the inflexible doctrine of today. Rather, creative thinking, like that of Wingate; the courage to step outside the accepted framework, like that of Unit 101 and Paratrooper Battalion 890; and striving to learn lessons and teach the IDF and the defense establishment – these are the three components that point the way forward.

---

43 Operation Bramble Bush was a 1992 plan by Israel to kill the Iraqi dictator during a public procession, in retaliation for Iraqi Scud missile attacks on Israeli civilians during the First Gulf War. On November 5, 1992, a rehearsal for the operation at the infantry training base near Kibbutz Tze'elim in the Negev Desert went awry when five members of the elite Sayeret Matkal special forces unit were accidently killed by their comrades when live rounds were used in the rehearsal. The accident is known in Israel as the Tze'elim Bet Disaster.

APPENDIX A: (PARTIAL) LIST OF ATTACKS, 1953–1956

May 25, 1953: An infiltration squad raided houses in Kfar Beit Nehemia, planted explosives, threw hand grenades and opened fire into the houses. A woman was killed, her husband and two children were wounded.

June 10, 1953: Infiltrators penetrated Moshav Mishmar Ayalon and murdered a young woman, nineteen years old.

June 11, 1953: A settler from Kfar Hess, in the Sharon region, was murdered.

June 19, 1953: Two Jewish guards were murdered at Beit Nekofa in the Judean Mountains.

May 30, 1953: In the Galilee, a car transporting boys on a trip was attacked by infiltrators. One boy was killed.

June 6, 1953: Two Jews were murdered in Jerusalem by the Jordanian Legion, who fired on them from their positions on the wall.

June 7, 1953: A young man was killed and three were injured in a shooting attack on a residential area in the south of Jerusalem.

June 9, 1953: Infiltrators attacked a moshav near Lod, throwing hand grenades and firing indiscriminately. One resident was killed.

June 11, 1953: Infiltrators attacked a young couple in their Kfar Hess home and shot them dead.

July 9, 1953: Two IDF soldiers were killed while guarding Moshav Even Sapir near Jerusalem.

September 2, 1953: Terrorists infiltrated from Jordan. They reached the Katamon neighborhood in the heart of Jerusalem and threw hand grenades indiscriminately. Miraculously no one was hurt.

September 9, 1953: Two young men, on their way to Moshav Achiezer, were murdered near Lod.

October 13, 1953: A mother and two of her children were murdered in their sleep when Jordanian *fedayeen* infiltrators threw a hand grenade into a house in Yehud, near Petah Tikva.

March 17, 1954: There was a brutal and murderous attack on an Egged bus in Ma'ale Akrabim, which deeply shocked the Israeli public. Infiltrators ambushed the bus, traveling from Tel Aviv to Eilat, and opened fire from close range. They boarded the bus and shot each one of its passengers. Eleven men, women and children were murdered, two were badly injured, and only three passengers, whom the attackers believed to be dead, were unharmed.

March 25, 1954: In a shooting incident at the Gaza Strip Border, a soldier was taken hostage.

March 27, 1954: A group of infiltrators murdered a Jewish guard at Moshav Kislon, in the Jerusalem Corridor.

June 19, 1954: Jordanians murdered three Jews at Mevo Beitar.

July 1, 1954: In Jerusalem, the Jordanian Legion opened fire on Israeli passersby. The shooting lasted for three days and resulted in the deaths of four Israelis and the wounding of many others.

September 2, 1954: The Jordanians opened fire on Shal'abim from the east, and two soldiers were killed.

January 2, 1955: Bedouins killed two travelers in the Judean Desert – Shoshana Har-Zion and Oded Vegmeister.

January 18, 1955: Two tractor operators from Mevo Beitar were murdered near Moshav Agur.

February 23, 1955: An armed squad penetrated a government facility near Rishon LeZiyon and extracted important official documents.

February 25, 1955: A Jewish cyclist was murdered by an Egyptian squad on the Rehovot–al-Kubiba road.

February 12, 1955: Members of the Arab Legion gunned down two IDF soldiers near Beit Guvrin.

March 24, 1955: Infiltrators threw hand grenades and opened fire on a crowd at a wedding in the agricultural community of Patish, Negev. A young woman was killed, and eighteen others were injured in the attack.

April 1955: Egyptian artillery bombarded Kibbutz Nahal Oz, near Gaza. The IDF guard unit traveling the "patrol route" along the armistice line was attacked. Two soldiers were killed and the rest of the unit were injured.

May 17, 1955: An Egyptian mine in the Kissufim section of the western Negev – bordering the Gaza Strip – killed three IDF officers and wounded two others.

May 30, 1955: An Egyptian bombardment of an IDF unit and the settlements of Nirim and Ein HaShlosha resulted in the deaths of two kibbutz members and severely wounded four others.

August 29, 1955: At Moshav Beit Oved, a Palestinian *fedayeen* squad attacked a group of Israeli workers with knives and guns, killing four and wounding ten.

August 30, 1955: Egyptian commando units carried out murder and sabotage actions deep inside Israeli territory. The units made it all the way to Kfar Menachem and the orchards of Nes Ziona, and killed six Jews.

Infiltrators performed four coordinated sabotage actions near Tirat Zvi. At Moshav Alma in the Upper Galilee the infiltrators blew up several homes. In a shooting on an Egged bus near Meiron, on the way from Haifa to Safed, two passengers were killed and ten were wounded.

October 18, 1955: IDF soldier Yaakov Minkowsky was kidnapped by Syrian soldiers.

October 29, (1955): Syrian forces launched a surprise raid on an Israeli police station in Be'erotayim, near Auja al-Hafir. An Israeli policeman was killed, three were injured and two policemen were taken captive.

March 12, 1956: An Israeli policeman was killed when Jordanian troops opened fire on the village of Barta'a, east of Karkur, and armed gangs attacked vehicles on the Wadi Ara road.

April 3, 1956: An Israeli soldier was shot dead in an Egyptian ambush near Kibbutz Nirim.

April 7, 1956: A *fedayeen* squad infiltrated Israeli territory all the way to the Tel Aviv–Be'er Sheva road, and murdered Gad Samuel and Michael Kafri of Givat Haim.

April 7, 1956: *Fedayeen* sapper units raided all across the south and the Negev, attacking settlements, water facilities and vehicles, killing four.

April 7, 1956: An Ashkelon resident was killed when infiltrators threw hand grenades into her home.

April 11, 1956: A squad of Arabs infiltrated Moshav Shafir, near Ramla – a Chabad village. The squad opened fire on a synagogue full of children. Five children and a teacher were killed on the spot and five more were injured. Later on, the same squad attacked a house in Moshav Achiezer and two buses on the Ramla road; six passengers were injured.

April 23, 1956: Jordanian terrorists infiltrated Israel, murdering four Tahal water company employees on the 122nd kilometer of the road to Eilat.

April 29, 1956: Egyptian soldiers gave covering fire for infiltrators who viciously murdered Roy Rotenberg of Nahal Oz, who was harvesting in the fields. Roy was twenty-one years old when he died.

Jordanian aggression continued in Israeli territory throughout August of that year. Nine Jews were murdered and fifteen injured. In addition five UN observers were also wounded.

August 16, 1956: A bus on its way to Eilat was attacked by twenty Jordanians of the "Jordanian Desert Commandos." This encounter occurred north of Be'er Menucha. A female passenger was killed, as well as three IDF soldiers who were in the vehicle accompanying the bus, and nine other passengers were wounded.

August 29, 1956: Two IDF soldiers were killed by a mine in the Nitzana sector.

September 10, 1956: Six IDF soldiers were killed by a Jordanian ambush in the Al-Dawayima village sector, near Beit Guvrin.

September 13, 1956: An infiltration squad penetrated the Ein Ofarim drilling station in the Arava valley, north of Hatzeva. Three Druze guards were murdered.

September 23, 1956: About one hundred Jerusalem residents were attacked at Ramat Rachel, as they arrived to view the archeological digs in the area. Surprise machine gun fire from a nearby Jordanian position killed four and injured many more.

September 24, 1956: A tractor operator from Kibbutz Maoz Haim and a woman in Kfar Aminadav who was harvesting olives were murdered by infiltrators.

October 4, 1956: Ten *fedayeen* attackers gunned down five Jews in an ambush on the Sodom–Dimona–Be'er Sheva road.

October 9, 1956: Two Jewish workers were murdered in the orchards of Even Yehuda.

October 20, 1956: Three IDF soldiers were killed when their vehicle hit a landmine in the Nitzana demilitarized zone.

APPENDIX B:
"THE REPRISAL ACTIONS — THE WAY WE WERE AND THE ACTIONS WE PERFORMED"

A retrospective by Prime Minister Ariel Sharon, March 20, 2003[44]

For over two years we have been in the midst of a war on murderous, continuous terror,[45] one of the toughest we have ever known, nurtured by the Palestinian Authority and its leader.[46] Naturally, the most effective approach to fighting terrorism is a central issue on our national agenda and the subject of public and political debate. Since the 9/11 attacks, terror has also become a central international challenge to the continued existence of democratic society and the free world. As a result, there is a greater understanding of the steps taken, past and present, by Israel. (…) There are some who criticize the IDF's reprisal policy of the 1950s, using it as an example of the failure of fighting terrorism by military means, of facilitating the Soviets' increased influence in the Middle East and as an excuse or explanation for the political stalemate.

---

44 Transcript of a speech delivered at Sapir College in Sderot, on the inauguration of the "Black Arrow" website for the heritage of the paratroopers' reprisal actions.

45 The so-called "Second (or Al-Aqsa) Intifada" which lasted from late September 2000 to approximately 2005. It was marked by widespread terror attacks against Israeli civilians including suicide bombings.

46 Yasser Arafat (1929–2004).

I'll admit that sometimes, when I read what is written about the reprisal actions I led as commander of paratroopers Unit 101, I find that there is an enormous difference between what we experienced back then, fifty years ago, and what the so-called "new historians" nowadays describe. It is not every day that a prime minister has the opportunity to speak about what he did as a battalion and brigade commander during his service, what the units he commanded did – which were at the center of events at the time – and to tell the story, not as someone who read about it, but as someone who did it.

At the outset, I would like to stress one key point: in order to understand and correctly evaluate the reprisal action period, you must judge it according to the tools and options we had on hand at that time. It would be a mistake to judge what we did then according to the tools, abilities and experiences we have now.

Therefore, I'd like to take you back in time to the first years after the War of 1948. The Jewish state had just been born in struggle and war; we had just come out of the trenches of the War of 1948, where the Jewish settlement lost over 6,000 of its sons and daughters. The Jewish settlement in Israel was still small, numbering about 600,000.

Much of the population lived in transit camps – some of you might not even know what transit camps were, luckily for you.[47] Some of them were new immigrants in the frontier settlements. Israel, which was taking in massive waves of immigration, was powerless in the face of the harsh terror attacks. The attacks came mostly from Judea and Samaria, which remained under Jordanian rule following the War of 1948. At first it was under Jordanian and Iraqi rule, then the Iraqis withdrew, and the entire territory

---

47 The *Ma'abarot* (transit camps) were temporary communities established for the wave of new immigrants who arrived after the founding of the state. They were inhabited by Jewish refugees mainly from the Middle East and North Africa, as well as Holocaust survivors from Europe. Conditions were poor and unemployment high. The disproportionate number of Middle Eastern and North African Jews in the camps would leave a long lasting legacy of perceived discrimination.

remained under Jordanian rule. The Gaza Strip remained under Egyptian rule after the end of the war.

The IDF, as the people's army, lacked a military tradition, and was in the midst of massive reorganization after the war. Most of its attention was directed toward establishing larger military formations. The reserves had just been established. Add to these factors the difficulty of operating units during peacetime, as well as the retirement of many of the outstanding young officers following the War of 1948. The government of the only democratic country in the Middle East was taking its first steps.

The foundation of the reprisal action policy was the recognition by David Ben-Gurion, his fellow leaders, and IDF commanders, that the Jewish state was founded, first and foremost, in order to give the Jewish people back the right and ability that had been withheld from them for 2,000 years – the right enjoyed by every nation and people – to defend themselves by their own efforts. This right and its realization have brought us so far, with all these great achievements and with all the hardship and pain, to the twenty-first century, with its risks but also with the great opportunities that the future holds for us.

The leaders of the Jewish settlement, with Prime Minister David Ben-Gurion at their head, realized that Israel faced a long and ongoing struggle, rooted in the unwillingness of the Arab countries and their leaders to accept and come to terms with the innate right of the Jewish people to an independent state in our historic homeland. That is why this is a long and uncompromising war, which might not stop even after we achieve formal peace treaties with our neighboring countries. Our belief in this right, and the necessity of building a country and society while constantly struggling, brought about a need to create an ongoing sense of deterrence in our enemies. I will now read part of a quote by Dayan, which encapsulates the perception of those days. Some of you may have already heard it today, but it seems to me to be a decisive element in that policy, so I will repeat it once again. Moshe Dayan, then chief of general staff, best described and defined the deterrence component of that time's reprisal actions (in his lecture "Reprisal Actions as a Means to Ensure Peace," July 1955). He said, and I quote:

> We cannot secure every water pipeline from being blown up, or every tree from being uprooted. We cannot prevent the murder of all those at work in the orchards or every family in their sleep. But we do have the power to set a high price for our blood, a price too steep for the Arab community, the Arab armies and the Arab governments to pay.

He also writes:

> The meaning of the reprisal actions is that Israel sees the infiltrations (the infiltrations – that's what they called terrorism back then) as an intolerable act of aggression, and it instructs its forces to cross the border and harm the land of the Arabs. The harm is not vengeance; it is punishment and deterrence.

Arab terror is a long established method of waging war on the State of Israel. This is not how it is commonly perceived by other countries, but, in light of the development of extremist Islamic terror, I believe they are also changing their approach. There was a perception, which was prevalent among us as well, including among people I knew and valued and appreciated. What was the perception? That Arab terrorism is a tactical problem, not an existential problem. But Arab terror was and remains an existential-strategic challenge for us.

You could see its roots in the attacks on the Jewish settlements and settlers at the end of the nineteenth century. You could see it, of course, in the riots against Jews in 1920–1921, in those of 1929, in the bloodshed and riots of 1936–1939. While all of you are young here, and do not remember, 1933 was also a hard year. Large terror waves would not usually break out all at once. They would always evolve, in a slow and complex manner, from many individual acts of sabotage and murder leading up to the events of the years I've mentioned.

Palestinian terror, which was renewed after the UN resolution of November 1947,[48] expanded with the arrival of an "Arab Liberation Army" and later on, the invasion by Arab countries of Israel in May 1948.

If we try to look for a starting point for this war, we have to go back to the start of the new Jewish settlement in the country, over a hundred years ago. This war had many faces, it has had ups and downs, but it has always existed.

I once tried to search for what defines the starting point for the terror activities. There is a monument on Mount Herzl for those civilians who died in terror attacks… There are names on that stone wall, and when I looked, I found that the first action recognized as a terror attack was from 1864; that's the first name on that wall. If we say it was over 120 years ago, we would certainly not be exaggerating.

The IDF and security forces are preparing for this war, and the task they face now is the same as it was back then – to find a proper response that will lead to the elimination of terrorism.

The reprisal actions, then as now, were executed outside times of full-scale war, and were therefore constrained by strict political considerations. It was necessary to get (them) done exactly as the orders stated, and to not fail. Peacetime actions must make every effort to reduce casualties among our men, as much as possible. Sacrifices must be minimized in any action or war, and that is the IDF's way, but during peacetime it is an even more sensitive matter.

Given the unique conditions in which the State of Israel exists, it was necessary for the reprisal actions to be performed as an immediate response to the enemy's actions, and more than once – as an extension of enemy actions. The situation demanded a constant state of alert, the willingness to act in every sector, against every enemy, within mere hours. Only a unit that understood and felt the motivation of both the highest military and political ranks could have maintained such a level of alert. I had the privilege

---

48 UN General Assembly Resolution 181, November 29, 1947, called for the partition of British Mandate Palestine into independent Jewish and Arab states. It was accepted by the Jewish representatives and rejected by the Arabs.

of commanding such units over the years.

When things began to worsen in 1952 and the beginning of 1953, there was an attempt to organize civilian volunteers. These were men who had fought and excelled in the War of 1948 and were known to several commanders. This did not help either. In order to succeed, they had to have a lot of experience, knowledge, organized training and perseverance. This could not be the responsibility of a group of volunteers, even if they were of high quality and willing. The regular IDF units were also unsuccessful in many of their actions. The border consisted of hundreds of kilometers of mostly mountainous natural terrain with obstacles, all of which stood in the way of any kind of military operation, not just counter-terror actions. We were unable to protect it.

And so, after a string of failures, a decision was made to establish a special unit, Unit 101, that would successfully perform operations across the border.

The initiative for the unit came from below; the proposal was made to the Chief of General Staff – then Mordechai Maklef – and Defense Minister Ben-Gurion by Colonel Michael Shacham, who was then commander of the Jerusalem District. I was a student in Jerusalem at the time and a reserve battalion commander in the Jerusalem Brigade.

Against this background, the Prime Minister and Defense Minister David Ben-Gurion decided to approve the creation of the unit. I, who had been appointed the unit's commander, believed that we could operate differently and change things completely.

I set up Unit 101 in August 1953. Immediately afterwards, its men started carrying out missions. The unit acted in complete secrecy back then, and within a short time, proved there was no task it could not perform.

There were a series of actions, but I will only mention two of them; the ones that stand out the most were Qibiya and Hebron… These actions changed the IDF's operational concepts and caused it to regain confidence in its power.

These actions had an immediate effect on the enemy. The Lod area – where there was a lot of enemy activity and we suffered many casualties

– became quiet for many years. We achieved a similar result in Jerusalem.

In January 1954 Moshe Dayan, who had just been appointed chief of general staff, assigned me the responsibility of merging Unit 101 with Paratroopers Battalion 890. He understood the sweeping impact the small unit would have on the paratroopers – and later on, the entire IDF.

The small unit, which started out with only twenty men, became a great paratroop battalion and, within a short time, a combat paratroop brigade, capable of carrying out any mission. Indeed, the missions we were tasked with were numerous and critical. I would like to mention that most of the targets we attacked were suggested to the General Staff by us, because we knew the area and the targets across the border so well since we carried out endless patrols there. In 1954–1956 the paratroopers carried the full burden of reprisal actions almost alone. They performed dozens of operations, among them in al-Khader, Gush Etzion, Nahlin, Azun, the Egyptian outposts near Dir al-Balah, and the Beit Likiya raids; the raids on Gaza, the Rafah outposts, Khan Yunis, Kuntilla, the Sabcha outpost; the Syrian outposts across the Sea of Galilee, Hussan, Gharandal. Ar-Rahawa, and the Qalqilya raids. And I have listed here only some of the actions.

The IDF gathered a lot of experience and confidence, and the political echelon also grew confident in the army's abilities. There is no doubt that many decisions were influenced by these achievements.

Simply performing the missions was not enough for the paratroopers. The paratroopers under my command back then had a say in setting the goals and the pace of operations. You could say that the ideology of the reprisal actions was largely formed within the paratroopers.

The way we chose to fight terror back in the 1950s can be a model for unconventional thinking. We applied unconventional thinking to organizing the units for this kind of warfare as well as in planning and executing special operations, and also in training the Battalion 890 commanders who would become future Chiefs of General Staff: Motta Gur,[49] Raful[50] who was one of ours, a company commander, Moshe Levi[51] (Moishe and a half), Dan Shomron,[52] were all company commanders with us, as well as Amnon Shahak,[53] though he was drafted a few years later. I think this spirit and method of building up commanders still exists today.

To try and give you an idea of security conditions in the nascent Jewish state, I will present you with some data.

From 1949 to the end of 1952, Arab terror and sabotage actions were of a disorganized nature. In the beginning, there were mostly infiltrations by Palestinians aimed at robbery and theft. Later on, there were increasingly more murders, until 1953–1954, when the random sabotage and terror actions became an all-out terror war.

1952 set a record regarding hostile activities on the borders. In that year, there were about 3,000 infiltrations, including all types of actions.

I should mention that the hostile activity damaged both settlements on the borders as well as ones in the center of the country. Those facing these attacks were mostly civilians, the majority of whom were new immigrants.

There was great tension in the border settlements, and daily life was severely disrupted. As I mentioned, the attacks were not limited to border communities, and many murders occurred in the interior and urban centers.

Among the notable cases of 1953 – I will review a few just so you can understand what went on there – were the murders of soldiers on the main road from Tel Mond to Kfar Hess, and the murders of two civilians in Jerusalem's Qiryat Moshe neighborhood.

In May, a murder in Moshav Azriel in the Sharon, a murder in Jerusalem's Givat Shaul neighborhood, a murder of two guards in Moshav Ktura in the

---

49 Mordechai "Motta" Gur, 1930–1995. Chief of General Staff, 1976–1978.

50 Rafael "Raful" Eitan, 1929–2004. Chief of General Staff, 1978–1983.

51 Moshe Levi, 1936–2008. Chief of General Staff, 1983–1987.

52 Dan Shomron, 1937–2008. Chief of General Staff, 1987–1991.

53 Amnon Lipkin-Shahak, 1944–2012. Chief of General Staff, 1995–1998.

Jerusalem Corridor, as well as a murder in Moshav Nebalat.

In June, a murder in Jerusalem's Katamon neighborhood, a murder in the Sataf military camp near Unit 101's headquarters.

The murders were accompanied with acts of savagery, which made them even more horrifying. [The terrorists] would often cut off the victims' heads, which obviously left a very powerful impression on the residents, many of whom had only recently come to the new country.

In August, the murders of three people from Beit Guvrin, the murders of two people near Moshav Achiezer, an attempt to murder a guard in Jerusalem's Bayit VeGan neighborhood.

In October, a murder in Kibbutz Neve Ilan; and in the same month, the murder of a mother and two of her children in Yehud.

In addition to these cases, which ended in death and address only part of the Jordanian sector, there were many other murders around the country. Later on, the murder of the five children in a Tel Aviv suburb, not far from Kfar Chabad.

It was clear to us that we could not accept Palestinian terror acts as an integral part of living in Israel. We never agreed to "live with the terror." We felt confident in our strength, but also felt the siege around us. We should also remember the context of the period: the poverty of the "period of austerity" and the transit camps, to which the immigrants from the Arab countries and the refugees from the European Holocaust were directed. Prime Minister and Defense Minister David Ben-Gurion and the General Staff had an immediate dilemma: how to prevent the murder of Jews, or at least minimize it, until they uprooted the infiltration phenomenon from the Egyptian-ruled Gaza Strip and Jordanian-ruled Judea and Samaria. And in parallel, they also had to deal with the difficult security issues within divided Jerusalem. This was all happening as they continued to take on more immigrants, and strove to prevent the financial, social and political development of the young country from being disrupted.

The dilemma that faced what we now call the "political echelon" and "defense establishment" was how to create a reprisal mechanism that, as Moshe

Dayan described it, would exact a price for every Jewish person murdered or tree uprooted.

The reprisal actions did not start in 1953; they had started a few years earlier, but most of them were unsuccessful. Those that were successful were small-scale and did nothing to change the situation.

In the War of 1948, the IDF had defeated the armies of seven countries. However, in the post-war era, the same army was now helpless in the face of the situation that had arisen. The same IDF that, in its infancy, had withstood all the Arab armies that invaded Israel during the War of 1948, was not competent at dealing with this type of war, and often suffered disgraceful failures in the actions across the border.

David Ben-Gurion, who served as both prime minister and defense minister for most of that period, wanted to be sure that the reprisal actions were the right policy, especially since the robbery and theft infiltrations became *fedayeen* murder actions directed by Egyptian intelligence from the Gaza Strip.

He wanted to be sure he had someone who could execute such a policy, and that each operation would succeed, since a failure might only encourage the other side. For this reason, then Chief of General Staff Moshe Dayan had to be convinced of the force's ability to perform. In order for him to be convinced of that, we – first in the 101 and later on in the paratroopers – had to prove that everything we undertook we also successfully executed, whether it was in Jordan, the Gaza Strip or along the Syrian border.

The confidence and ability to execute operations came from the bottom up. Our role as warriors was to paw the ground, ready for battle. The political echelon is usually the one that needs to be restrained, to take into account every consideration, political or otherwise. But from below, we always have to paw the ground – and we did!

The decision-making system was always "interactive," with a strong connection between the political echelon – Prime Minister and Defense Minister David Ben-Gurion – the military establishment – Chief of General Staff Moshe Dayan – and the actual troops in the field.

We were unified by the same principle, that "Jewish Blood Cannot Be Shed for Free" and our duty is to exercise the greatest right entrusted to us, that of self-defense. We, as soldiers of Unit 101 and the paratroopers, saw our role as always having operational briefs ready to go, and executing them as soon as the order was given by the political rank, or cancel them if need be, which also happened. This level of preparedness obviously made it necessary to have designated routes for movement. Of course, I cannot compare the army of today to the one we had then – today's military really achieves extraordinary accomplishments, it is well equipped, sophisticated in all areas – but back then, a unit like ours would have received an order in the morning, or suggested an operation in the morning, and had to execute it that very evening, even the most complicated ones. And our successes were not by chance. We knew the area, we constantly patrolled it, we prepared briefs and operations. Getting to know the terrain was of the utmost importance.

The achievements of the paratroopers did not come easily. Much effort was put into planning and developing new combat tactics, educating the commanders[54] and men, familiarizing them with the country and its borders, constantly learning lessons and attempting to figure out what motivated the soldiers to fight. We were mostly occupied with educating commanders and developing them; we were all very young. I remember my conversations with the commanders; I told them that a commander has two tasks: first and foremost, to complete the mission, that's why they had been selected for that role. However, there was another task that was just as important – making new commanders. How do you make a commander, cultivate them? When I previously mentioned the list of battalion and company commanders from the paratroopers that became Chiefs of General Staff, other than their own talent and courage, that was the outcome [of our cultivation].

There was much work invested in educating them to report accurately, grueling training and many patrols across the border. The accomplishments

---

54 In the IDF the term "commander" is often used to describe anyone in a command position, whether NCO or officer.

of the paratroopers came with a heavy toll in blood. Combat doctrines are not written in books and then practiced; combat doctrines are studied on the battlefield – and at great cost. During those years, it was mostly the paratroopers who paid the price.

The paratroopers, who acted alone for years, influenced the entire IDF and swept the whole army along with them. The paratroopers of Battalion 890 quickly caught up with the achievements of Unit 101, and the rest of the military units matched their achievements later on. Meanwhile, [the paratroops] did not stand still, but continued to lead and form the vanguard of the IDF.

That new confidence and spirit that blew through the IDF was well expressed by Chief of General Staff Moshe Dayan [in a review of the ongoing security situation, July 3, 1955, as an introduction to his book *Avnei Derech* (Milestones), 1982], and I quote:

"The success of the paratroopers' operations, first Unit 101 and later Battalion 890, restored to all IDF units the belief in their own strength, and their operational capability increased. It had been proven that daring actions could be performed both in small forces as well as large ones, deep within enemy territory as well as against regular army units."

As part of imbuing the paratroopers' spirit into the IDF, Dayan obligated IDF officers to undergo a parachuting course, and he, as chief of general staff, brought all the senior command staff of the IDF to the parachuting school. I also had the privilege of pinning his parachute wings on him.

The IDF is an excellent army, each of its branches – air force, armored corps, and infantry – are magnificent. In all of them you can find something of the spirit of the paratroopers. When looking at the IDF's achievements today, we can't help but notice the mark the paratroopers left from the days of the reprisal actions. I doubt whether any other unit had as much impact on the entire IDF, and for so long. I want you to know that it wasn't easy. It's not as if we came with different and new approaches to combat and the military warmly embraced them; that wasn't the case. Everything had to be fought for. This army is usually a body that operates in organized frameworks, according to the doctrines taught in military academies. We came with new methods, new perceptions. As I said, it wasn't easy, it took us years until we were able to get our proposals adopted by other IDF units. It mostly happened because our officers went on to be commanders in other brigades in the IDF. Motta, for instance, who became the Golani Brigade's commander, brought with him the methods we had developed there. So it was for other units, once our commanders grew and were transferred to other posts. We were also largely able to overcome the objections that our methods faced.

When talking about "adherence to the mission" nowadays, which is one of the IDF's fundamental principles, we can't help being reminded of actions such as the Hebron raid on that snowy night in 1953, the raid on the Azun Legion base in 1954 or the raid on Kuntilla in the Sinai in 1955, actions that embodied determination and adherence to mission at its highest levels.

As an example of adhering to mission, I am particularly reminded of the Hebron operation from December 1953. I suggest reading Meir Har-Zion's book, *Pirkei Yoman,* where he describes many of the actions as someone who took part, executed and was severely injured in them. The IDF certainly lost one of its best commanders [when he retired].

While still a part of Unit 101, in retaliation for the murder of Israeli soldiers at Beit Guvrin, Meir Har-Zion, who was one of the most courageous and daring commanders the IDF ever had, led a four-man squad on a rigorous forty-two kilometer trek to Hebron on foot, on a snowy night, for a reprisal action.

I remember telling Meir back then (we called him "Har"): "We have carte blanche at Mount Hebron." Before me stood a twenty-year-old guy, it was a snowy night and a forty-two kilometer hike to the destination was before him; back in the old IDF, we couldn't have even dreamt about helicopters and night-vision goggles. That journey required navigating at night, according to a map and the stars, all the way to the destination, just so we could quickly respond to the murder. Meir made up his mind and determined that it could be done.

I don't think there were many people who would have been happy to make that trek in a single night. But he was not alone; there was Katcha, who still volunteers in the reserves to this day, and two others. During the grueling journey to the destination in deep snow and freezing cold, his comrades suggested changing the mission and carrying it out in the nearby Khalkhul village instead. Despite the fatigue and physical difficulty, Meir insisted on Hebron, and this is how he describes it in his journal: "There is no way we are going to Khalkhul. We are executing the operation. We're doing so despite all the temptations and intoxicating emotions. We're doing it and that's that, without figuring out to ourselves why, wherefore or how." And the mission was indeed completed as planned.

Another action I remember well was the one in July 1954, a raid by the battalion under my command [Battalion 890] on an Egyptian outpost between Kissufim and Dir al-Balah. This action was a milestone in implementing special fighting techniques against fortified targets, which we later applied while operating large forces and armored formations in the Six-Day War, and possibly this technique is still used today. Perhaps this method should be changed already, but it's probably impossible to bring forward an alternative yet.

The outpost was conquered, the Egyptians suffered nine dead, a few injured and two of them were taken captive. Our forces suffered one killed and five injured.

In his journal, Meir Har-Zion gives a vivid description of the sense of power and confidence in fulfilling the mission – a sense that permeated not only the soldiers in the field but also spread up to the ranks commanding us.

But beyond the vital operational aspects, it is important for me to say something on a personal note; this action had a personal meaning for me. In this action, during which I led the forces as Battalion 890 commander, I was wounded in my hip. It was July 11, 1954. The injury was in the same place and similar to the one I'd suffered in the Battle of Latrun during the War of 1948. The physical pain of the injury was the same, sharp, but back then at Latrun I was a young platoon commander, an injured soldier abandoned in the field after a hard battle and a military defeat – while in the Kissufim action, named after the outpost, despite the pain there was a sense of security. [This time it was] an injury after a victory, when you are among friends and a unit that is confident and full of fighting spirit, and above all, have the certainty and confidence that you will not be left behind. Knowing that the camaraderie of my fellow brothers in arms would withstand any test it faced was what gave us, from the most senior commander down to the last private, the tenacity and confidence to get any mission done, during that time as well as in the wars that followed.

One of the principles we cultivated was the aspiration and willingness to make contact, to engage in face-to-face combat with the enemy. This IDF quality was nurtured in the paratroopers. At first, we would do it artificially, handing out weapons with a bullet in the chamber and the safety off, just to save that short time in order to be able to fire immediately upon coming to close quarters with the enemy. This quality was expressed in the conquest of the Egyptian outpost at Kissufim in 1954, in the attack on the Egyptian Forces' headquarters in Gaza in 1955, in Operation "Black Arrow" and the paratrooper raids on the Syrian outposts east of the Sea of Galilee that year. In Operation "Olive Leaves," a response to continuous Syrian fire on Jewish fishermen in the Sea of Galilee and a Syrian attempt to take over the eastern part, you could see how this fighting method evolved and was actually implemented.

In the Six-Day War, some of the most fortified enemy formations in the Sinai were conquered by the 38th Division under my command, at Um-Kataf and Abu Agela, by attacking from the rear, the flank and the front all at the same time, by dropping in forces using helicopters, and by combined operations of armored, infantry, paratroop and air forces. I want to tell you that when the operation was over, I kept thinking about it. My experience as the paratroopers' commander during the reprisal actions deeply affected the plan. You can also find the 1950s lessons of the paratroopers in the action of the 143rd "Crossing" Division which I commanded during the Yom Kippur War.

This combined operations approach was developed in the paratroopers, and you can see its beginnings in the motorized raid on Khan Yunis in 1955, the operation where Motta was injured; in conquering the Egyptian positions at the Sabcha, brought down by a surprise attack from the rear; in the attack on the Syrian outposts at the Sea of Galilee, which combined forces moving on foot, forces that landed by sea and forces that crossed the Jordan. You can add the Qalqilya action to those, which was performed just before the Suez Crisis (Sinai War) in which paratroopers, armored and artillery forces were combined. The actions were very complex. The thing I always strove to apply was the principle that the complexity of the action would always be at senior command level, and at the levels below there would be simplicity of operation. This approach did, in fact, prove itself both in small unit and large-scale operations.

The combat technique we use to this very day also began with the paratroopers – fighting within fortified targets, ambushes and raids. These were all developed and became the common property of the entire IDF. Standards of combat, of command, of missions that can be performed, which are the domain of every unit in the IDF today, all were set by the paratroopers.

Above all else, the daring that characterizes and sets the IDF apart from all other armies grew in the paratroopers and became the norm and a permanent asset. In addition to military achievements, the paratrooper units set moral values that influenced the image of the army. The commander's position on the battlefield, his personal example, treating the wounded, securing the release of a captured comrade – all these formed and nurtured a brotherhood of warriors that was unparalleled.

I would like to stop for a minute to address the matter of [our men being taken] prisoners. In our unit, there was a special kind of sensitivity when it came to prisoners of war; we once held a meeting about it, and I said that we had a prisoner held by the enemy and the entire country shuddered. And then, if I recall correctly, Motta stood up and said: "I think you might be mistaken. [The shuddering] happened, but mostly in our unit." It was something hard to describe, and we took a lot of prisoners [for exchange].

We brought forty-three from the raid across the Sea of Galilee, forty from the Sabcha action, twenty-nine from the Shatila raid – all to exchange with our prisoners of war along the way.

Dayan then coined the term: he said we needed a "Bank of Prisoners." That is why, at each of the fronts, there was no way of knowing who would eventually be one of those prisoners we would take. And so it sometimes happened that the prisoners we took were people who were very important to the Syrians, Egyptians or Jordanians. By the way, we were unable to obtain the release of our prisoners without taking enemy captives. I would like to tell you how we planned and operated then, just so you can see things as we saw them.

Back then, the "[Lavon] Affair" prisoners were in an Egyptian prison, and I still cannot understand why they were not released until later in 1956. I think it requires a thorough investigation. We had many Egyptian prisoners – the Egyptian general that commanded the Gaza Strip was our captive. I only give this as an example, so you know that the whole prisoner issue was weighing heavily on the unit. It was there like a cloud over our heads. I'm not saying that now [the army] forgets about prisoners or neglects them, but the amount of attention and attempt to [capture enemy] prisoners was beyond anything you could possibly imagine.

I was happy to see that Yitzhak Jibli came to the ceremony today, with all the strength he had left in him. When he was captured, it created a serious problem because his father was sick in the hospital and when I went to see him, he said to me, "Promise me one thing, I want to see him before I die." We did everything we could. We had a series of "Gil" operations, "Release Jibli Yitzhak,"[55] that was the operations' name. We took prisoners wherever we could, and in one of the actions we were able to capture an officer and some soldiers – and those were enough to obtain his release. I have to say that I still have tears in my eyes, to this very day, when I think back on how

---

55 The Hebrew initials of the phrase spell "Gil."

we welcomed him in Jerusalem, at the Mandelbaum Gate.[56] I told him that his father had passed away shortly before we obtained his release. There was also the case of Uri Ilan of Gan Shmuel, who was from a group of paratroopers and Golani commandos. They were captured during an intelligence operation in Syria. This issue, of securing the release of our prisoners, was something that gave no rest, and I talk about it because of this sensitivity and feeling that people felt on this subject.

The dozens of operations we performed, aside from being milestones in the IDF's own advance, represent high points in standards of planning and execution that any army would boast about.

The IDF's reprisal actions prior to the Sinai War, about seventy of them, reduced Arab terror attacks and turned them from disorganized but wide-ranging actions to more limited operations. On the other hand, the attacks became more organized and were now directed by the Arab governments. This is also the reason why our targets became more governmental: that is, objectives that when hit damaged the government, those responsible for the terror. When the governments in the Arab countries felt that our reactions endangered them, they stopped the terrorist activity against us.

Those who carried the burden of the reprisal actions, almost all on their own, were not as bloodthirsty as they were often described by the "new historians."[57] These were great young men, graduates of the youth movements, who came from kibbutzim and moshavim of all political streams, as well as city boys, youth who were imbued with extraordinary faith and courage. If I had to define these warriors in one sentence, I would say: "These were the ones who cared." And perhaps I would also add a personal aspect from that

---

56 A crossing point for diplomats and foreigners between Jordanian- and Israeli-controlled Jerusalem. It became a symbol of the divided status of the city.

57 A loosely defined group of Israeli historians who, since the late 1980s, have challenged traditional versions of Israeli history. They are generally critical of Israeli policies and actions from 1947 onwards and what they see as a hagiographic depiction of Israel's foundation. They have been, in turn, criticized for sloppy and agenda-driven research.

period: in light of the results we gained on the battlefield, we knew to keep secrets for many years as part of our defense system, we did not give out any operational details, we did not give any interviews or offer commentary.[58] The names of the soldiers were only unfortunately published when they fell in combat, and many of those good men did fall.

In retrospect, the reprisal actions did provide the deterrence and consequently the security that was necessary for the further development of the young state.

Moshe Dayan summarized the reprisal action period with words that are still relevant for us today, by saying [in his lecture "Reprisal Actions as a Means to Ensure Peace"], "We do not initiate battles during times of peace! The goal of the battles along the border and beyond was to ensure peace. Peace is a condition to fulfilling the character and calling of the State of Israel. Without peace at the borders, the lone worker on the tractor could not plow, the shepherd could not lead his flock, the new immigrant could not put down roots as a farmer in the frontier communities."

Our doctrine, that there is no operation we cannot execute, guided Israel as early as the 1950s. And later on too, the raid on the Beirut Airport in 1968, "Operation Spring of Youth" in 1973, and "Operation Entebbe" in 1976. By the way, there were always paratroopers in these forces, just as they were part of the operations to rescue Ethiopian Jews through the Sudan in the beginning of the 1980s, driving out Palestinian terrorists from Beirut in August 1982, assassinating the master-terrorist Abu Jihad in Tunisia in the late 1980s, and other daring operations. The same approach guides the IDF's way to this day, in its difficult and complex struggle with Palestinian terror. The means have changed and the experience adds up; technological sophistication, intelligence – all these went through extensive changes. But the spirit, belief and sticking to the mission, and their effect on the enemy, remain as they were, while the spirit of the paratroopers has remained the

---

58 Sharon was alluding to an alleged lack of discretion on the part of some in the military, coupled with an increased desire by the media to present more detailed reports of military successes and failures.

pillar of fire going before the camp to this day.

We paid a heavy and painful price. The families of those who fell, despite all our sincere participation in their grief and pain, have no consolation. Many of the commanders and soldiers whose names are engraved on the paratrooper's monuments, paid, with their own flesh, the price of our victories in Israel's wars. Many others carry the scars of those actions and that time in their bodies and souls, to this day.

In a historical view, we should evaluate these reprisal actions not only by the military objectives we achieved, but also according to what we were able to build here in the last fifty years.

Our reprisal actions were the hand that held the sword, the trusted, professional, sophisticated hand that made sure to maintain moral values. All so our other hand could take in the new immigration, build industry, agriculture, educational and scientific institutions – and also search tirelessly for the paths of peace.

Thanks to the fact that we were able to find the right answers for our security issues, we were also able to achieve periods of relative calm, periods which allowed us to reach thus far and look forward, in the hope of a thriving Jewish and democratic state that lives in security and peace.

The road has not been an easy one and I know we still face challenges higher up the mountain. But as I look back and see the glorious Zionist endeavor we have established here, that is the real reward of all the reprisal actions of the past.

APPENDIX C:
AN ARTICLE BY UZI EILAM IN HAARETZ FOLLOWING THE PASSING OF MEIR HAR-ZION

The paratrooper who became a legend in his own lifetime, Meir Har-Zion, passed away last Friday. Many great men have eulogized him and commended him for being a daring warrior and a role model of bravery for generations of soldiers. However, beyond his courage and the daring he displayed in crossing the border in countless reconnaissance patrols, and in taking part in most of the reprisal actions of the 1950s, Har-Zion made a unique contribution to the IDF's combat doctrine. The change brought about by Har-Zion touches on the essence of the commanders' behavior in battle, meaning the position and role of the commander on the way to the target and later on during the fighting itself.

The recognition of the crucial importance of land navigation by all commanders of all ranks was inspired by Har-Zion. His ability in this area led to the establishment of the commander's place as a guide, and as one who is at the head of the force.

Even as a teen, Har-Zion was a man of nature and the environment; hikes and land navigation became a part of him. His passion to explore the country gave him no rest and even led to his capture, along with his sister, by the Syrians in the summer of 1951, when he was only seventeen. Har-Zion never spoke of the terrible experience of Syrian captivity, but its outcomes manifested in his approach to the enemy. Har-Zion was not one for concessions and compromises. In the reprisal actions, he insisted on getting the mission done in its entirety and making sure that none of the enemies survived. The harsh experience of prison did not deter him from crossing over to Jordan. While in the Nahal, he went on a hike from Jerusalem to Ein Gedi with a fellow classmate from Ein Harod, Uri Oppenheimer. This tour was unauthorized and unknown to his commanders, but it became well known and caught the attention of Major Ariel Sharon.

The mission Sharon was tasked with was forming a special reconnaissance unit that would be able to patrol and even attack beyond the border. Then Prime Minister David Ben-Gurion and Chief of General Staff Moshe Dayan were worried about the loss of fighting spirit in the IDF in the wake of the War of 1948, and sought to establish a unit that would set an example and bring about a change. Sharon, who had previously served as Northern Command's intelligence officer, understood the importance of familiarity with the field and the ability to safely navigate to the target; Har-Zion and Oppenheimer were among the first to be drafted to Unit 101.

In the time before the establishment of the State of Israel and during the War of 1948, navigation was relegated to specialist scouts whose expertise was limited to this skill. Commanders would follow the scouts, who were supposed to know the way, and generally saw no need to navigate themselves. The place of battalion commanders, sometimes even company commanders, during battle, was in the rear. This fact led to problems in comprehending the course of the battle and the need to rely on reports from subordinates. Considering the limited communication combat units had at their disposal back then, the commanders obviously had difficulty correctly assessing the situation and giving appropriate orders.

The 890 Paratroopers Battalion, to which Unit 101 was to be attached, learned lessons from notable failures of IDF units in the early 1950s. One of those was a reprisal action by a battalion-sized force of the Givati Brigade on the village of Falame, northeast of Kibbutz Eyal. Among the reasons for the failure in the first attempt to attack the village were navigation errors. An action by the Golani Brigade's Battalion 13, commanded by Rehavam Ze'evi, was also analyzed. This was the occupation of Tel al-Mutila, which the Syrians had taken in May of 1951, giving them control of the Tiberias–Metula road. The grueling and long battle, which claimed the lives of forty-one soldiers and injured seventy, was studied and reviewed by the paratroopers, while emphasizing the place of commanders in battle.

It is to Sharon's credit that he placed such importance on the issue of navigation when establishing Unit 101. While navigation is obviously a natural ingredient of a reconnaissance unit, Sharon's emphasis laid the groundwork for its integration into the commander's "toolbox." Har-Zion's outstanding contribution was the unique operational concept of meticulous preparation, adjusted for each patrol, and, above all, the principle of placing responsibility for navigating and leading the men to the destination on the commanders. Quietly and without saying much, Har-Zion set an example regarding the position of the commander en route to battle and on the battlefield itself.

In the early years of Battalion 890's operation – the only battalion of paratroopers at the time – the officers were put to the test, and those who were unable to navigate lost their roles as commanders. The reprisal action period was a good opportunity for commanders to learn the navigation doctrine in an orderly fashion from the Har-Zion "academy." Memorizing the lay of the land in which they had to move, using topographic maps and knowing each crossroad and every hillside and wadi crossing, were necessary conditions for successful navigation.

Thus, by sending officers to command real reconnaissance operations, Battalion 890's Headquarters – Sharon and Aharon Davidi – was given the opportunity to evaluate the commanders' true standard. The ultimate test had to do with the commanders' ability to reach the targets where they would have to fight. Some of the lessons learned during that activity bore on the ability to bring the forces to the exact location where combat would begin. As we learned in the "Black Arrow" action, in the Gaza Strip in 1955, mistakes in the final stage of navigation could result in a heavy cost in blood.

Courage and a steadfast heart in combat, the ability to function under fire and to maintain the force's combat momentum, are all important, but the personal example of commanders in the IDF is what contributes to the education of generations of commanders that follow. The transition from the perspective of the War of 1948 and the beginning of the 1950s, according to which the scouts led the force, to the legacy of Meir Har-Zion in which the role of the commander is to lead, is itself a strategic transformation. Even today, in the age of advanced communications and plasma screens, the place of the commander is at the head, where he is better able to understand the battle, and it is only right that the doctrine left to us by Har-Zion will continue to guide us in the future as well.

SOURCES

The following works are in the Hebrew language:

Arie Avneri. *The Reprisal Actions.* Three volumes. "Madim" Library, 1969.

Mordechai Bar-Or. *When the Army Changed Its Uniforms.* Yad Ben-Zvi Publishing, 2017.

Prof. Yoav Belber. *Palestinian Time.* Kineret Zmora Bital Publishing, August 2018.

Dr. Ofra Graicer. *Two Steps Ahead of Everyone.* IDF, Ma'arachot Publishing and Modan Publishing, 2015.

Dr. Arie Gilay. "Paratroopers in the First Decade" website.

Dr. Brig. Gen. (Ret.) Dovik Tamari. *The Armed Nation.* Modan Publishing and IDF, Ma'arachot Publishing, 2012.

Dr. Gilad (Gili) Haskin. "Orde Wingate," a comprehensive online article: https://www.gilihaskin.com

Dr. David Tal. *Israel's Perception of Routine Security.* Ben-Gurion University Publishing, 1998.

Prof. Benny Morris. *Israel's Border Wars, 1949–1956.* Am Oved Publishing, 1996.

Tom Segev. *A Country at All Cost, Ben-Gurion's Biography.* Keter Publishing, 2018.

ACKNOWLEDGMENTS

Many books and important articles have been written on the security issues during the first years of the State of Israel. When examining the wide scope of events reviewed, one can ask what is left to say and what else could be explored in the military, security and political affairs that led us through the 1950s. I have chosen to focus on the description and analysis of the background to the reprisal operations of 1953–1956, while detailing a number of typical reprisal actions. There was a breakthrough in those years, from an army that failed to protect its settlements – mostly those on the frontier – to a self-confident fighting army.

I saw fit to start with the contribution of Orde Charles Wingate, the remarkable British officer who formed the Night Squads. I would like to thank Dr. Ofra Graicer for her eye-opening book about Wingate, *Two Steps Ahead of Everyone*. Yitzhak Sadeh independently came up with the idea of "going outside the fence" at the same time that Wingate did, in the 1930s, and the unit he formed was called the "Nodedet."

Forming Unit 101, as decided by Chief of General Staff Maklef following a recommendation by Colonel Michael Shacham, was the pivotal moment in recreating the IDF's fighting spirit. I am thankful to my fellow soldiers who agreed, willingly and surprisingly openly, to share with us their insiders' view of those five and half months during which the unit operated, before its annexation to Battalion 890.

I would like to thank the soldiers of Unit 101: Shmuel Nisim – Hafalach,

Shmuelik Merchav, Uri Ofir, Yishai Zimmerman, Shimon Kahaner – Katcha, Guy Kochva and Ze'ev Solel for unfolding the story of Unit 101 before us. The decision by Chief of Staff Moshe Dayan to annex Unit 101 to Paratroopers Battalion 890 and place Arik Sharon, who formed the 101, as its commander, was also a pivotal and crucial step in forging the IDF's combat spirit. Thank you to Elisha Shelem, Tzuri Sagi, Levi Hofesh, Aharon Eshel – Errol and Dovik Tamari, who answered the call and gave us insight into that wondrous process of constructing the fighting IDF.

I owe a special thank you to Arik Sharon, Battalion 890 commander and Brigade 202 commander, to Aharon Davidi and to Meir Har-Zion, who starred in this book. Arik Sharon took me from the commandos when I was injured, so I could be his intelligence officer for over a year. Davidi supported me and mentored me in my first stages as Company A's interim commander, and of course, Meir Har-Zion, whom I have served under as deputy commander of Company A, which later became the Paratroopers Brigade's first commando unit.

I would like to thank Dr. David Tal for opening my eyes with his doctoral paper, which became a book, on the perception of contemporary security in Israel, and Tom Segev, who with his biography of Ben-Gurion helped me understand Ben-Gurion's positions regarding the reprisal actions and constructing the fighting IDF. Thank you to Brig. Gen. (Ret.) Dovik Tamari for the selection of fascinating articles on tactical and strategic thinking. I would like to thank my friend Rami Tal for his wise suggestions and invaluable encouragement to dare to write this book. Thank you to my friend Yoram Schweitzer, fellow of Israel's Institute for National Security Studies, for his wise advice and encouragement to write. I have also received vital encouragement and inspiration from my friend Yoram Petrushka, who read chapters from the book while I was writing it and pushed me to complete the mission. A special thanks to Gal Perl, researcher at the Institute for National Security Studies, for his eye-opening comparison between the IDF then and now and the place of the raid today.

The IDF archives opened its doors to me with written materials and photographs involving the period covered in this book. I would like to wholeheartedly thank the archive's administration, Ilana Alon, Avi Tzadok, Yifat Arnon, Efrat Raz-Nagad and Orna Zohar, for their professional support and the wind in my sails that helped me clear all the obstacles lurking beneath the archive's documents.

I am grateful to Dovi Eichenwald, Director and Head Editor at Yediot Books Publishing, for the encouragement he provided me, from the initial stage of deciding to publish this book, all the way to its printing. I would like to thank Yediot Books, especially the editor Benny Mizrachi, for his in-depth and insightful edits. My heartfelt thanks also to Kuti Tepper, the book's producer, an old friend and a real pro.

Last, and closest to my heart, my dear family – my wife Neomi and my children Osnat, Nimrod and Noa – I am grateful for your support and the blessed quiet I was given in my small writing corner at home throughout the entire time. Special blessings to my daughter Osnat for recording, photocopying and printing all the interviews with my fellow soldiers. Osnat helped me gather the materials from the IDF archives and was involved in all the stages of writing the book, with her precise thinking and sage advice. Thank you, Osnat, and my entire family.

Printed in Great Britain
by Amazon